Sanskrit
and Development of World Thought

Sanskrit
and Development of World Thought

(Proceedings of "The International Seminar on the Contribution of Sanskrit to Development of World Thought")

Edited by
Vempaty Kutumba Sastry

Rashtriya Sanskrit Sansthan
Deemed University
Under M/o Human Resource Development
Govt. of India, New Delhi

D.K. PRINTWORLD
Publishers of Indian Traditions

Cataloging in Publication Data — DK
[Courtesy: D.K. Agencies (P) Ltd. <docinfo@dkagencies.com>]

International Seminar on The Contribution of Sanskrit to the Development of World Thought (2012 : Rashtriya Sanskrit Sansthan, Sringeri Campus)
Sanskrit and development of world thought: proceedings of "The International Seminar on the Contribution of Sanskrit to Development of World Thought" / edited by Vempaty Kutumba Sastry.
p. cm.
Includes bibliographical references.
ISBN 13: 9788124607442

1. Sanskrit language - History - Congresses. 2. Sanskrit literature - History and criticism - Congresses. 3. Thought and thinking - Congresses. I. Kuṭumbaśāstrī, Vempaṭi, 1950- II. Rashtriya Sanskrit sansthan. III. Title.

DDC 491.209 23

ISBN 13: 978-81-246-0744-2
First published in India, 2014

Published by:
Rashtriya sanskrit sansthan
56-57, Institutional Area, Janakpuri, New Delhi 110 058
Phones: (011) 2852 4993, 2852 1994, 2852 4995
e-mail: rsks@nda.vsnl.net.in
Website: www.sanskrit.nic.in

and

D.K. Printworld (P) Ltd.
Regd. Office: *Vedaśrī*, F-395, Sudarshan Park
(Metro Station: Ramesh Nagar), New Delhi 110 015-11
Phones: (011) 2545 3975; 2546 6019; *Fax*: (011) 2546 5926
e-mail: indology@dkprintworld.com
Website: www.dkprintworld.com

Printed by: D.K. Printworld (P) Ltd, New Delhi

Foreword

I FEEL immense pleasure in presenting this volume which highlights the contribution of Sanskrit in the development of world thought. This book is a collection of fourteen research papers of high value, by outstanding scholars of national and global repute in an international seminar organized at the Rajiv Gandhi Campus of Rashtriya Sanskrit Sansthan, Śṛṅgerī. The then Principal of the Campus, Prof. V. Kutumba Sastry, who is also the president of International Association for Sanskrit Studies and the present Vice-Chancellor of Somnath Sanskrit University, Gujarat, had convened the said seminar successfully. Being the editor, he has enriched this publication with an informative and scholarly preface. I had the opportunity to work under the principalship of Prof. Sastry during the days of the seminar. So I personally know his ability and the efforts, and pains taken by him in organizing the seminar.

I express my deep sense of gratitude to Prof. Sastry due to whose efforts Sansthan could bring the collection of articles to light in the present book form.

I take this opportunity to submit my *praṇāmas* to H.H. Sri Jagadguru Bharati Teertha Swamiji of Śṛṅgerī Math whose inspirations enabled us to achieve the fruitful conclusion of the seminar. I shall remember and thank the then Vice-Chancellor, Prof. Radhavallabh Tripathi without whose support the programme would not have become successful.

I thank all who have contributed to the present volume and other members whoever extended their support in various ways in organizing the seminar as well as in bringing out this publication. Thanks are due to Shri Susheel Kumar Mittal of D.K. Printworld also for his support as the co-publisher.

I hope this book will attract a wide range of readers.

20 January 2014
New Delhi

A.P. Sachidananda
Vice-Chancellor (I/C)
Rashtriya Sanskrit Sansthan
(Deemed University)

Preface

I AM glad and feel honoured to place the proceedings of the International Seminar on "The Contribution of Sanskrit to the Development of World Thought" held in the Śṛṅgerī Campus of Rashtriya Sanskrit Sansthan, Karnataka, India, in January 2012.

Sanskrit is the language of the first available text of not only of India but of entire human race. Decidedly, the earliest text available to human race today is *Ṛgveda* and its language is Sanskrit. As the text-writing tradition in Sanskrit continued till today, with ups and downs in different periods, there should have been considerable amount of thought content generated by it which can be considered as its contribution to the world thought. With this premise in mind we decided on the topic of the international seminar. It is also felt that international scholars working in various disciplines of Sanskrit can present the paper on the topic given from their respective discipline. Looking into the logistics of reaching a very remote place like Śṛṅgerī, a very small village in the hilly region of Western Ghāṭs, it was felt whether we shall be able to get good response from the scholars both quantitatively and qualitatively. But, we have experienced great amount of enthusiasm of international scholars especially regarding the topic and the place as well. We were able to get the presence of most eminent international scholars in the field of Sanskrit studies. I must say that we were fortunate enough to get world number one, two, three of international scholars present in Śṛṅgerī during the seminar. Just concluded 15th World Sanskrit

Conference, jointly organized by the International Association of Sanskrit Studies, Paris and the Rashtriya Sanskrit Sansthan, New Delhi had its share in causing these scholars reach India for the conference.

My sincere thanks are due to all those eminent international and national scholars who took pains to come to Śṛṅgerī and give us the benefit of their scholarship. My thanks are also due to Prof. Radhavallabh Tripathi, the then Vice-Chancellor, Rashtriya Sanskrit Sansthan, New Delhi for funding the seminar as well as delivering his learned keynote address.

Prof. George Cardona has been invited to deliver Shri Rajiv Gandhi Memorial International Lecture on this occasion on the theme of the seminar. My sincere and heartfelt thanks are due to him for taking pains to come to Śṛṅgerī despite his age and other engagements. Needless to say that his presentation and presence have enhanced the prestige and level of the seminar containing his findings of research of several decades. We shall ever remain grateful to him for his kind gesture.

A few words on the theme of the seminar may not be out of place here. As it is well known, the entire *Ṛgveda* is in the form of metrical composition. These metrical compositions do have mathematical precision. Though it has drawn less attention than Pāṇini's *Aṣṭādhyāyī*, Piṅgala's *Chandaśśāstra*, none the less, is scientific, mathematical and based on computational techniques. The twenty-six divisions of *chandas*, starting with one letter for a *pāda* to the size of twenty-six letters for a *pāda* culminated in presenting a mind-boggling number of varieties of metrical compositions. We see a number of such metrical compositions in the *Ṛgveda*. This fact suggests the height of mathematical acumen which has been gained by the *ṛṣi*s of the *Ṛgveda*.

Equally well known are the lofty ideas regarding nature,

life, environment, philosophy and human welfare. Seen from the point of view of antiquity the statements such as "*ā no bhadrāḥ kratavo yantu viśvataḥ*", "*śaṁ no astu dvipade śaṁ catuṣpade*", "*saṅgacchaddhvaṁ saṁvadadhvam*", "*madhuvātā ṛtāyatē madhu kṣaranti sindhavaḥ*", "*mādhvīrnassantvoṣadhīḥ*", "*devānāṁ sakhyamupasedimā vayam*", "*mātā me pṛthivī putrohaṁ pṛthivyāḥ*", "*madhu dyaurastu naḥ pitā*", "*mitrasya tvā cakṣuṣā sarvāṇi bhūtāni samīkṣe*", "*mā kaścid duḥkhamāpnuyāt*" and "*vayaṁ rāṣṭre jāgṛyāma*" present before us the evolution of human mind to the highest point ever reached by humanity. The huge volume of research output in the Vedic studies during the last two centuries stands in attestation of contribution of the Vedic texts to the development of world thought.

Even the concept of *devatā* in Sanskrit literature, which is usually understood as a matter of faith, is based on logical and scientific principles. Says *Bṛhaddevatā*:

> *nivāsāt karmaṇo rūpān maṅgalādvāca āśiṣaḥ* ।
> *yadṛcchayōpavasanāt tathāmuṣyāyaṇācca yat* ।।

Conceiving the presiding deity (*abhimāninī devatā*) in respect of natural objects and forces is not an insignificant event in the human history. The etymology of word *devatā* (*dyotanāt devaḥ*) reveals the mind of *ṛṣis*. Because of these and many more other underlying principles of concept of *devatā* the pantheistic approach of Hindu religion can be better appreciated. The idea of possibility of invoking and sending away of gods in any mundane object or on one's own self or idol is a unique and an interesting one in the Vedic tradition which is the basis for all the sacrificial rituals as well as patterns of worship in Indian culture. This was possible because of concept of *sarvātmabhāva* preached in the Vedic texts, directly or indirectly, which is a leap forward in elevating once own self. In fact, the idea of man becoming god is great with far-reaching effects (*mānuṣād daivyam upaimi*). All these Vedic efforts culminate in making man and world to occupy the centre stage.

The Śikṣā and Prātiśākhya texts also contributed quite a lot to the science of speech and standards of speech. First of all they came out with amazing theories of speech mechanism which are held scientific and perfect by the present-day scientists. Stating that *vivakṣā* kindles the bodily fire and holding the kindled bodily fire is responsible for generation of air which is very important for utterance and speech act is not only attested by present-day science but also gives us insight into the advanced stages of scientific evolution of those far off ages. As is well known they gave us the most scientific *varṇamālā* based on the starting and end points of striking of air against various places of vault of the oral and nasal cavities. Even though intonation and *svara* are natural phenomena and even though several other languages do have one or the other kind of intonation patterns, change of *svara* in the combination of group of words or in respect of *anuloma* and *viloma* recitational patterns is worth understanding along with the scientific background of such changes. Change of meaning of a word on the basis of change of intonation is a unique contribution which has larger bearing upon deciding the meaning of the text. Unfortunately, since Sanskrit could not retain intonation beyond Vedic period, the significance of intonation is understood less in degree.

Coming to the age of *darśanas*, theoretical and practical aspects of Yoga Darśana are the richest contributions to the world thought and humanity. The universal recognition received by *yoga* in the present age is based upon the practice of only a few aspects of *yoga*. There remains much to explore from theoretical aspects of Yoga Darśana. Pūrva-Mīmāṁsā gave 1,000 principles of textual interpretation which are well conceived and scientifically argued. I carry a feeling that much information is yet to be critically analysed about Pūrva-Mīmāṁsā. However, the area of *śābdabodha* studies, which is a significant contribution to the development of world thought, caught the attention of the super scientists working on natural language processing and machine translation throughout the world. The *śābdabodha* studies encompass three *darśanas*, viz. Vyākaraṇa, Nyāya and Pūrva-Mīmāṁsā. The logical and scientific nature of analysing of word level and sentential level meanings is being rated very high by the scientists. The concept of *ekavākyatā* of various levels is a unique contribution of Pūrva-Mīmāṁsā. This area comprising several monumental and cardinal texts such as the *Mahābhāṣya*, *Vākyapadīya*, *Bhāṭṭarahasya*, *Laghumañjūṣā*, *Vyutpattivāda* and *Śabdaśaktiprakāśikā* has several profoundest theories which are worth analysing and put to use in computational linguistics of current age.

Śāstras such as *Pāṇinīya Vyākaraṇa*, Āyurveda and Jyotiṣa are well studied in India and abroad. Scholars are presenting papers appreciating the thought contained in these Śāstras for the last several centuries. As is evident from the present volume, several such issues have been minutely examined and appreciated by the scholars.

Coming to the literature, the huge number of *śabdālaṅkāras* and *arthālaṅkāras* draws our attention towards endless varieties of *vakrokti* and immense potentiality of word-culture in Sanskrit. The so-called *adhamakāvya* or *adhamādhama* according to Jagannātha, namely, Citrakāvyas also deserve mention here as a unique contribution of Sanskrit language. Except in Sanskrit and Sanskrit-originated Indian languages there appears to be no possibility of making such Citrakāvyas in any other language in so many varied forms. While these types of Kāvyas are not generally rated as high they certainly stand in attestation of the richness and flexibility of Sanskrit verbal usage. They are, indeed, *adhama* or *adhamādhama* only from the point of *rasa*, but seen from the point of view of richness of language, flexibility and word-culture, they are *uttama* or *uttamottama*.

While it is not possible to go into details of the real merit of any single theory or concept at this juncture, Sanskrit has more in store to share than what has been so far shared. On account of great researches done in India and abroad only a small percentage of knowledge and wisdom of Sanskrit has been systematically analysed, brought out and appreciated. As several lakhs of manuscripts still remain in darkness, the knowledge contained in these books has not been known to us. Sanskrit belongs to the entire world and it offers valid insights into the intercultural and intercivilizational contacts and contributions.

I have intentionally and purposefully picked up very few peripheral and superfluous issues to say a few words on the unique contribution of Sanskrit to the development of world thought. Greater issues cannot sufficiently be discussed in the given space and they are thoroughly investigated and being investigated by great brains all over the world.

To sum up, I would say that enormous amount of advancement of thought over a period of three centuries world over in the fields of science, humanities, languages and linguistics did not disprove any single proposition put up by the Sanskrit writers thousands of years before not only in the fields of humanities, languages and language-based studies, but also in sciences and scientific studies.

Prof. Cardona, in his illuminating presentation, highlights on three major accomplishments of ancient Sanskrit grammarians: (1) the distinction made by them between phonetics and phonology, (2) their recognition of posited structures from which are derived utterances found in particular texts, and (3) their recognition of rules and possible relations among the posited structures that determine how the rules should apply.

Prof. Cardona writes:

> Pāṇini's greatness has been universally acknowledged. What pre-Pāṇinian thinkers and Pāṇini carried out in describing Sanskrit – both the current language (*bhāṣā*) of Pāṇini's time (*c.* 500 BCE) and the Vedic usage that preceded him – represents accomplishments in linguistic theory and methodology that merit being considered historically without precedent.

Prof. Radhavallabh Tripathi was kind enough to deliver the key-note address and to highlight the theme of the seminar in various fields of studies in the post-modern and post-colonial period. Drawing attention to the fact that interaction with K.J. Shah and Ramachandra Gandhi has resulted in carrying out fundamental changes in the philosophy of Wittgenstein, which are better known in the philosophical circles through the phrases "Earlier Wittgenstein" and "Later Wittgenstein", he proceeds to identify the roots of such changes as existing in the Vedic statement – *vāgeva viśvā bhuvanāni jajñe*. He finds the roots of many a writings of Ferdinand de Saussure in Indian theories of language. Drawing the attention of scholars to the parallelism between Sanskrit concept *sahṛdaya* and "readers' response" of Rolland Barth, he deals with how the theories of *rasa* and *dhvani* have helped Sussan Langer to evolve her theories of literary criticism. Citing Harold Coward's work, Prof. Tripathi opines that there is considerable influence of Bhartṛhari and Nāgārjuna on Derrida and of *Nāṭyaśāstra* on Brecht, Stanislavsky, Grotowsky, Peter Brook and others.

While conceding that it is natural for any nation to look back to its past and such looking back is necessary to build the present and future, Prof. Tripathi cautions against over glorification of one's own past to that extent that one turns a blind eye on others' past. Arguing well on this matter, he stands for openness and receptive attitude while discussing the matters of past. He emphasizes that saying this is our ideal and practice from time immemorial – "*janaṁ bibhratī bahudhā vivācasaṁ nānādharmāṇaṁ pr̥thivī yathaukasam*", "*yatra viśvaṁ bhavatyekanīḍam*".

John Brockington provides the readers with the *navanīta* of churning of *Rāmāyaṇa* through his researches along with those of his scholarly wife Mary Brockington for over good many decades in his paper, "The Rāmāyaṇa in World Literature". Restricting the scope of the paper to a few selected texts of South-East Asia and the impact of religion and sovereignty on the *Rāmāyaṇa* tradition, Brockington presents a birds' eye view of *Rāmāyaṇa* adaptations suitable to the times and context. So many changes are brought in by the Buddhists, Jains and Muslims in the adaptations of *Rāmāyaṇa*. Yet, the main plot-line and fundamental details of the original narration are retained by them only because of compelling and paramount nature of the original narrative. This is the contribution of Sanskrit to the world literature, that writers from alien cultures also could not resist the spread of the story-line of *Rāmāyaṇa*.

Brockington writes:

> . . . the story of Rāma is undoubtedly one of the most widely spread and popular not only within India, but throughout the rest of the Asia. Indeed, of all the epics composed in various parts of the world, it is the *Rāmāyaṇa* which has spread most widely, throughout India, Central Asia and South-East Asia, and been current over the longest time-span.

After detailed and authentic analysis, Brockington concludes saying, "the attraction of a good story, well told, cannot be overestimated".

> The impact of the knowledge of Sanskrit and its grammatical tradition on Western linguistics is well known and is dealt with in virtually all books on the history of linguistics (i.e. Morpurgo Davies 1992, Robins 1997).

Hans Henrich Hock begins his scholarly paper with the above words explicitly supporting the theme of the seminar.

Prof. Hock focuses his attention on an area of linguistics which is less covered in detail, namely, the influence of the Sanskrit phonetic tradition on Western phonetics. In an authentic way, he discusses and analyses the positive contributions of the Sanskrit tradition and the more problematic ones and establishes the fact of slow merging of the Sanskrit tradition and earlier Western approaches, a fact which is responsible for the present-day advancement of articulatory phonetics.

In his paper divided into five parts, Prof. Hock pin-pointedly shows the influence of Sanskrit on Western phonetics with examples. Dealing with the ancient works on Prātiśākhyas and Śikṣās, which are less studied even in India, he concludes his paper expressing that it is difficult to imagine what would have happened to linguistics in the absence of the knowledge of Sanskrit phonetic tradition.

Victoria Lysenko, in an interesting paper, discusses about methods and problems pertaining to translation of Sanskrit philosophical texts. She reviews various methods, such as literal translation, philological translation and philosophical interpretative translation, and finds limitation of one kind or other in each one of them. Basing her study on Russian Buddhologist and Indologist, Theodor Stcherbatsky and his illustrious disciple Otto Rosenberg, she puts the record straight quoting Stcherbatsky:

> With the help of local tradition, the rich content of the Sanskrit scholarly literature has become evident, and one has to replace the charge against Indians that they are incapable of exact thinking with the charge against European scholars that they are incapable to understand them.

After publication of Prof. Jacobi's translation of one of the best Indian works on the theory of poetry, no one will doubt that in the depth of analysis, in the power of thought and precision of expression, Indian scholars have no equals in ancient times. Finding that translation of technical terms poses greatest challenge to the translators, she prefers to use hermeneutical reflections in translation and various other methods depending upon the satuation in question, including using the Sanskrit terms as they are.

Prof. Pierre-Sylvain Filliozat, in his enlightening presentation, brings out the genius of Sanskrit mind and power of invention. Analysing the unique contributions of Sanskrit to the world thought on the basis of one single concept, namely, *lāghava*, he makes an in-depth survey into not only Vyākaraṇa tradition, but various types of *lāghavas* employed in various branches of studies in Sanskrit like Śulbasūtras, Pāṭīgaṇitas, Mathematics, Chandas and others. He also deals with the stand along distinction of Sanskrit, Sūtra literature and oral tradition and holds them responsible for striking the idea of *lāghava* as a matter of compulsion. He elaborates how *śabdalāghava* culminates in *arthalāghava*, economy of mental work in calculations, for reasoning and for argumentation. *Arthalāghava* is held higher in importance than *śabdalāghava*. In literature also *lāghava* has been accomplished through compound words. In a lucid and flowing style Filliozat delves deeper into the aspects of abilities of Sanskrit writers.

Dr Bettina Bäumer presents a comprehensive account of Sarvasarvātmakatāvāda from the Upaniṣadic period to the times of Abhinavagupta and beyond. Extending the research where Prof. Albrecht Wezler, who pioneered and contributed significantly to study this theory in a critical and historical manner left his studies, Bäumer presents the application and transformation of the theory in the hands of Abhinavagupta, where it has reached its culmination. Abhinavagupta made a grand synthesis of both the cosmological and theological implications of the theory without falling into the dangers of a naturalistic view or an ontological theistic view. Dr. Bäumer observes that Abhinavagupta did not develop this maxim in his philosophical works, but used it most extensively in his tāntric exegetical works as he treats this theory at par with Āgamic revelation, a given truth, which doesn't require argumentation.

Dr Bäumer concludes her elaborate presentation with an optimistic note saying that this theory has great significance and potentiality in the present scenario in bridging the gap between ancient Indian thought and the present-day situation as a measure of healing our present-day divisions in all spheres of human life.

Prof. T.S. Rukmani establishes the truth that the innate strength of a subject makes it take roots firmly and grow like wild fire even in an alien land despite opposition and deliberate attempt to thwart it. The interesting story of *yoga* in America proves it. Prof. Rukmani presents a historical account of how *yoga* entered into USA and how did it grow. She holds Swami Vivekananda was responsible for the introduction and initial growth of *yoga* and while colonial history of India provided the connectivity with the Western intellectuals in this regard, political circumstances in America and frustration and disappointment with Western way of living have resulted in its irreversible growth. She concludes, like all successful movements there comes a time when opposition and resentment build up and we see that happening now because of *yoga*'s huge success in the West. However, with the evidence of increasing well-being that *yoga* practitioners experience, *yoga* is bound to stay round the globe for a long time to come.

Dr Anindita Balslev, with her vast experience of development of thought both in the East and West and deep involvement in cross-cultural communications, analyses the present scenario in the field of philosophical and speculative thinking in a very bold and open way. Writing elaborately about the need of exploring the thought contents buried in the Sanskrit texts, she recommends three-tier effort in this regard. First, the concept, ideas and theories be studied and discussed in the medium of other languages. Second, more and more translation projects be undertaken. Third, original Sanskrit textual studies be made. She holds ignorance and lack of knowledge on the part of Western philosophical luminaries responsible for making incorrect statements regarding Eastern, specifically, Indian philosophical thinking. She laments that Śaṅkara, Nāgārjuna, Diṅnāga and Uddyotakara are not studied in the departments where Hegel, Husserl and Hume are studied. Listing several questions which stand unanswered so far in the field of consciousness studies, she draws our attention that almost all the questions have been answered offering various alternative possibilities in Śāstric texts in Sanskrit.

She feels that the knowledge of exchanges between *ātmavādins*, *anātmavādins* and *anekāntavādins* could be of crucial importance today when naturalistic thinkers are playing a dominant role in the West in the domain of consciousness studies. She also emphasizes the need for restoring balance between knowledge and power in a larger setting as well as in our educational offerings.

Prof. B. Mahadevan, in his enlightening paper, deals with inspirational leadership, which is the latest and best theory of leadership in the field of business management, and finds its roots in the teachings of *Bhagavad-Gītā*. He finds lack of spirituality and ethics, which are core values, as the root cause of several scandals that rocked India as well as many a great nations. Quoting several authorities and management *gurus*, Mahadevan speaks about paradigm shift that is taking place in the business management – from an economic focus to quality of life, spirituality and social responsibilities, from self-centredness to interconnectedness and from materialistic focus to spiritual focus, etc.

Making a critical review of two well-known management perspectives, namely, perspective of responsibility and ownership, and perspective of feeling the leadership as a great opportunity to enable others to do their best, Dr Mahadevan makes an observation that though the second perspective is the better one in all respects, its success rate is minimal.

He then proceeds to say that is why in modern management, the emerging perspective is that leaders are responsible for building organization in which people continuously expand their capacity to learn, to understand complexity and to set the vision for the organization. The six to seven recent theories, therefore, suggest that the personal traits of good leaders must include unwavering faith, significant life experiences that can spark, a strong inner development and a strong religious belief.

Dr Mahadevan traces the roots of these latest theories in the teachings of *Bhagavad-Gītā*, namely,

1. Strong need to lead by example.

2. Importance of developing a high degree of equanimity,
3. Understanding the principle of mutual dependence. He discusses them with examples from the point of view of Business Management.

Dr S. Ram Mohan continues the theme of Dr Mahadevan and finds out the roots of several modern management theories in several Sanskrit texts. He observes that the Western thinkers treated the people-oriented values, work-oriented values and spiritual values in separate compartments. In the beginning not much emphasis is given on spiritual values in managerial culture. West has understood the importance of it only after observing the phenomenal success of Japanese industry which has Zen values and holistic cultural milieu of Japan. However, says Dr Ram Mohan, these aspects have been dealt with at length in our ancient Sanskrit texts. He discusses several concepts elaborately including *antaḥkaraṇa* as the resolver of problems and *svadharma* as the way to success.

A renowned art historian Dr Vasundhara Filliozat presents fascinating episodes of *Rāmāyaṇa* which are not available in the original but have support in the form of sculpture and paintings not only in various parts of India but also in far off countries. Based upon the discourse of Sītā in the Araṇyakāṇḍa, she brings out ecological concerns of Sage Vālmīki.

Well known researcher Dr Satyapal Narang provides extensive information regarding the concept of *dāna* and how it is considered as a value and how it expanded over the centuries.

Dr Klara Gönc Moačanin, in her paper, presents a critical assessment of receptivity of Sanskrit drama and in Europe in general and in Croatia in particular. Apart from presenting hitherto unknown events of staging Sanskrit dramas in various parts of Europe in a chronological order, she evaluates each one of them with a spirit of frankness and objectivity. At times she comments that such performances were neither Indian nor European. At times they caused damage to the beauty of the original. She begins her paper with expressing the futility and near impossibility of undertaking such an exercise to read into the remote past because of intervening break of several centuries but ends with saying, "could be also a source of comparative theatrological insights as well as of emotional and spiritual inspirations". She deserves commendments for her painstaking study and frankness of presentation.

I sincerely feel that the contents of this volume will, once again, establish the relevance of Sanskrit studies for the benefit of India and the world at large.

Vempaty Kutumba Sastry

Contents

Acknowledgement

WE offer our reverential *praṇāmas* at the feet of H.H. Sri Bharati Tirtha Mahaswamiji of Sri Sringeri Sharada Peetham for inaugurating the seminar and blessing the delegates with his *anugrahabhāṣaṇam* and interacting with them individually in a special sitting. We express our gratitude to Hon'ble Justice B.N. Srikrishna for delivering the thought-provoking valedictory address. We express our indebtedness to Padmashri V.R. Gaurishankar, the Administrator of Sri Sringeri Sharada Peetham for providing logistical support in a big way to organize an International event in a small town like Śṛṅgerī.

We express our sense of gratitude to Prof. Radhavallabh Tripathy, the then Vice-Chancellor of the Rashtriya Sanskrit Sansthan, for providing funds, for delivering the scholarly Key-Note Address and for approving the publication of proceedings. Prof. A.P. Satchidananda, present Vice-Chancellor in-charge of Rashtriya Sanskrit Sansthan, was my source of strength while I was in Śṛṅgerī. Thanks are due to him for his overall support in organizing the seminar. I am glad that this volume carries his Foreword. My thanks are due to Dr Binod Kumar Singh, the Registrar of Rashtriya Sanskrit Sansthan, who has shown keen interest in getting the scholarly volume published and extended his help at every step.

Thanks to Dr K.B. Subbarayudu, the then Registrar of Rashtriya Sanskrit Sansthan for extending official support and presiding over the valedictory function. Thanks are due to Sri

Srinivasan of Surabharati of Bangalore for his invaluable service to the delegates while they were in Bangalore.

Dr S. Radha, Dr Mahabaleswar P. Bhat, Dr Subray V. Bhatta, Dr C.S.S. Narasimha Murty and Dr Ramachandrula Balaji deserve appreciation for their contribution as the Conveners of various sessions and for conducting them smoothly.

Dr Rekha Kumari provided unfailing help to me to be in correspondence with delegates several months before the seminar, in working out detailed individual itinerary and attending to all the requirements of the guests. Dr Sukla Mukherji took up the responsibility of booking of air tickets, and managed the last minute crisis efficiently. They are well acknowledged.

Dr S.N. Bhat, Dr R.C. Joisa and their team made the guests taste the recipes of South Canara to their satisfaction. Dr C.S. Bhat (accommodation), Dr R. Balaji and Dr G.I. Bhat (reception and registration), Dr Padmanabham and Dr Sahu (transport), Dr Rekha and Dr Raghavendra Bhat (venue management), and Dr M.P. Bhat and Dr Shyamsunder (temple tour) have provided excellent support. Computer programmers, Shasidhar and Ravisha, and the Ministerial staff led by Gururaja Bhat were helpful. Thanks are due to each one of them.

Shri Susheel Mittal of D.K. Printworld gave a permanent form to the deliberations through publishing the proceedings in collaboration with the Rashtriya Sanskrit Sansthan in a beautiful format. I acknowledge his efforts.

Vempaty Kutumba Sastry

1

Some Contributions of Ancient Indian Thinkers to Linguistics

George Cardona

1. Introduction[1]

PĀṆINI's greatness has been universally acknowledged. He also represents the high point of Indian thought on language and its description, the history of which extends back to predecessors of Pāṇini. It is demonstrable, moreover, that Pāṇini did more than merely accept and codify such earlier work. He subjected it to critical evaluation, accepting or rejecting aspects of what his predecessors had done in view of his own work and its aims. What pre-Pāṇinian thinkers and Pāṇini carried out in describing Sanskrit – both the current language (*bhāṣā*) of Pāṇini's time (*c.* 500 BCE) and the Vedic usage that preceded him – represents accomplishments in linguistic theory and methodology that merit being considered historically without precedent. In what follows, I shall outline briefly three such major accomplishments:

---

1 I am grateful to Prof. Vempaty Kutumba Sastry for inviting me to deliver the Rajiv Gandhi Memorial International Lecture, which I prepared under the impression that it would be delivered in English. At the time of the international seminar, however, I saw that other lectures were in Sanskrit, so that I set aside my prepared text and delivered a shortened version in Sanskrit.

1. A distinction was made between phonetics and phonology: speech production and rules describing operations that concern systematic speech units.
2. Scholars recognized posited structures from which are derived utterances found in particular texts and in the language of a community.
3. Scholars also recognized rules and possible relations among them that determined how the rules should apply.

2. Phonetics and Phonology

2.1. DESCRIPTION OF SPEECH PRODUCTION[2]

Prātiśākhyas describe how sounds are produced. The earliest detailed descriptions are found in the R̥gvedaprātiśākhya and the Taittirīyaprātiśākhya.

According to the former text, when a speaker makes an effort, the upwardly moving breath called *prāṇa* is modified in that it attains different states depending on whether the glottal aperture (*kaṇṭhasya khe*) is open (*vivr̥te*) or close (*saṁvr̥te*); it then becomes śvāsa or nāda. That is, unmodulated breath and modulated breath respectively flow through the glottal aperture when this is open and close. On the other hand, if the glottis is in between these two positions the breath flowing through the aperture becomes both śvāsa and nāda simultaneously.[3]

These three varieties of air flow are said to be the material sources (*prakr̥tayaḥ*) of articulated sounds (*varṇānām*): śvāsa for voiceless consonants (*aghoṣāṇām*), the combination of śvāsa and

---

[2] I dealt with this topic in a study to which the reader is referred for details: Cardona 1986.

[3] R̥Pr. 13.1-6, Cardona 1986: 66.

nāda for voiced aspirated stops and *h* (*soṣmoṣmaṇāṁ ghoṣiṇām*), nāda for the rest (*itareṣām*), that is, for vowels and voiced unaspirated stops, including nasals.

The Ṛgvedaprātiśākhya also states different places (*sthānāni*) at which sounds are produced, from back to front in the sound cavity: a post-velar area (*kaṇṭha* "throat"[4]) for *a*, *h* and *ḥ*;[5] the velum (*jihvāmūla*) for *ṛ*, *ḷ*, <u>*kh*</u> and stop of the *k*-set;[6] the palate (*tālu*) for *e*, stops of the *c*-set (*c ch j jh ñ*), *i*, *ai*, and *y*; the cacumen (*mūrdhan*) for *ṣ* and stops of the *ṭ*-set; the roots of the lower teeth (*dantamūla*) for stops of the *t*-set, *s*, *r*, and *l*; the lips (*oṣṭha*) for remaining sounds except for those called *nāsikya*, whose place of production is the nasal cavity.[7]

At each place of production, distinctions are made regarding how different sounds are produced. Stops involve an articulator making quick contact (*spṛṣṭam*) and then being drawn away from a place of production (*asthitam* "not remaining"). In producing semi-vowels, however, the articulator makes slight

---

4 The prātiśākhya uses derivates meaning "located at . . .", coreferential with terms referring to sounds said to be produced at the places noted: *kaṇṭhya, jihvāmūlīya, tālavya, mūrdhanya, dantamūlīya, oṣṭhya*. Extracting from these, I cite the place names: *kaṇṭha, jihvāmūla, tālu, mūrdhan, dantamūla, oṣṭha*.

5 *h* and *ḥ* are referred to as the first and fifth spirants, their position in the sound catalog for the Ṛgvedaprātiśākhya; similarly, <u>*kh*</u> is referred to as the sixth spirant.

6 *ṛ* and *ḷ* are called *jihvāmūlīya* according to the vowel segment *a* included in these complex sounds, not because the consonants *r* and *l* are velar.

7 कण्ठ्योऽकारः। प्रथमपञ्चमौ च द्वा उष्माणाम्। ऋकारल्कारावथ षष्ठ ऊष्मा जिह्वामूलीयाः प्रथश्च वर्गः। तालव्यावेकारचकारवर्गाविकाररैकारौ यकारः शकारः। मूर्धन्यौ षकारटकारवर्गौ। दन्तमूलीयस्तु तकारवर्गः। सकाररेफलकाराश्च। शेष ओष्ठ्योऽपवाद्य नासिक्यान्। नासिक्ययमानुस्वारान्। इति स्थानानि। (Ṛpr. 1.38-39, 41-45, 47-49).

contact (*dusprṣṭam*) with a place. When one produces vowels, *ṁ* (*anusvāra*), and spirants, on the other hand, the articulator does not make full contact (*asprṣṭam*) but remains for a time in proximity to a place of production.[8]

The Taittirīyaprātiśākhya begins its description of sound production saying that a primitive sound arises (*śabdotpattiḥ*) at the juncture of the throat and chest due to the movement of breath in the body and that such sound is manifested in the chest, throat, vault of the mouth, the oral cavity below this, and the nasal cavity. The air that constitutes this sound, moreover, is modified in three ways as it passes through the glottal aperture (*kaṇṭha*): if this is close or open, it becomes nāda or śvāsa, respectively, and if the aperture is midway between closure and opening, a variety of air flow called hakāra is produced. These in turn are said to be the material sources of articulated sounds (*varṇaprakṛtayaḥ*): nāda for vowels and voiced consonants (*svaraghoṣavatsu*), hakāra of *h* and fourth members of stop sets – that is, voiced aspirated stops – and śvāsa for voiceless consonants (*aghoṣeṣu*).[9]

The Taittirīyaprātiśākhya also goes into greater detail than the Ṛgvedaprātiśākhya concerning how sounds are produced at various places of production. It distinguishes how an articulator (*karaṇa*) is situated relative to a place of production (*sthāna*) for vowels and consonants. In the case of vowels, a *sthāna* is a place where approximation (*upasaṁhāra*) is carried out and the *karaṇa* is the organ which a speaker brings into proximity (*upasaṁharati*) with a place. For consonants, on the other hand, a *sthāna* is a place where contact (*sparśana*) is carried out and a *karaṇa* is the organ which a speaker causes to make contact (*sparśayati*) at a place. For example, in producing *i*-vowels, one

---

8 ṚPr. 13.8-11; Cardona 1986: 79.

9 TPr. 2.1-11; Cardona 1986: 64-65.

brings the middle of the tongue into proximity with the palate, and to produce palatal stops one causes the middle of the tongue to make contact with the palate.[10]

2.2. PHONOLOGICAL CLASSES AND OPERATIONS

Prātiśākhyas provide for sets of sounds in recognized lists to be given particular names, thereby classifying the sounds. A dichotomy is made between vowels and consonants, respectively called *svara* and *vyañjana*, and the latter are subdivided into three major groups: stops (*sparśa*), semi-vowels (*anta[ḥ]sthā, antassthā*), and spirants (*ūṣman*). Stops are further divided into five classes (*varga*) of five each, the familiar groups called *kavarga* and so on.

It is noteworthy that prātiśākhyas segregate the classes of vowels and voiced consonants, reserving the name *ghoṣavat* for the latter, although both are said to have nāda as their primitive material.[11] Thus, for example, TPr. 8.3 (तृतीयं स्वरघोषवत्परः [प्रथमः]) provides that a stop that is the first member of a stop class changes to one that is the third member of the class; that is, voiceless unaspirated stops *k c ṭ t p* change to voiced *g j ḍ d b*. The rule also specifies that the stop in question be followed by either a vowel or a voiced consonant (*svaraghoṣavatparaḥ*). Clearly, *svara* and *ghoṣavat*, both referring to voiced segments, are used to name sets of phonologically contrasting elements. Consonants are either voiced or voiceless (*aghoṣa*), but vowels are all voiced. The different sets, moreover, serve to condition different phonological operations.[12]

In the same vein, consider the term *savarṇa*. The Taittirīyaprātiśākhya states that the first nine sounds listed in

---

[10] TPr. 2.31-34, 22, 36; Cardona 1986: 78.

[11] E.g., TPr. 2.8; नादोऽनुप्रदानं स्वरघोषवत्सु। See §2.1.1 with n. 9.

[12] For additional details, see Cardona 1986: 71-77.

its sound catalogue – namely *a ā ā3, i ī ī3, r̥ r̥̄ r̥̄3* – bear the name *samānākṣara,*[13] then provides that each pair of short and long vowels is termed savarṇa with respect to each other.[14] The work goes on to say, however, that a samānākṣara preceded by a pluta vowel is not savarṇa with respect to a member of a corresponding pair.[15] Now, there is a phonetic basis for classing *a ā* and so on as sounds that are savarṇa. Indeed, Pāṇini provides that a sound which shares with another an articulatory effort at the same place in the oral cavity is called *savarṇa* with respect to that sound.[16] Saying that a sound such as *i* which is preceded by a pluta vowel is not savarṇa with another *i*, however, can hardly be based on phonetic criteria.

Consider a standard illustration. TS 6.5.84 has अग्ना३ इत्याह,[17] which is treated theoretically as deriving from the sequence अग्ना३इ। इति। आह। in the padapāṭha of this Veda. With respect to the sequence *-ā3i i-*, three rules can come under consideration, two of which let two contiguous vowels be converted to a single vowel:[18]

---

13 अथ नवादितस्समानाक्षराणि। (TPr. 1.2).

14 द्वे द्वे सवर्णे ह्रस्वदीर्घे। (TPr. 1.3).

15 न प्लुतपूर्वम्। (TPr. 1.4).

16 तुल्यास्यप्रयत्नं सवर्णम्। (A 1.1.9).

17 '(The Adhvaryu says,) "O Agni".' The mantra cited appears in TS 1.4.27, VS 8.10, and elsewhere. Details concerning how the pluta vowel of *agnā3i* should be accounted for, in Bhaṭṭabhāskara's commentary on TS 1.4.27 (TSBh. II.589.10-12) and elsewhere, need not be considered here.

18 The rules in question come under the heading of TPr. 10.1: अथैकमुभे '. . . both . . . become one.'

(a) a sequence of an *a*-vowel and a following *i*-vowel yields *e*.[19]

(b) a samānākṣara and a following savarṇa segment yield a single long vowel.[20]

(c) pada-final -*i*-vowels and -*u* respectively change to -*y* and -*v* before a vowel.[21]

(a) does not apply in -*ā3i*, since a pluta vowel is exempted from undergoing contextual changes.[22] (b) could apply in -*i*- *i*- if the contiguous vowels were classed as savarṇa with respect to each other. Consequently, one would allow *अग्ना३ ईत्याह instead of अग्ना३ इत्याह which actually occurs. The undesired result is precluded by providing (TPr. 1.4, n. 15) that a samānākṣara which would otherwise be classed as savarṇa with a following vowel is not so classed if it is preceded by a pluta vowel. Now (c) can apply to change the -*i* of *agnā3i* to -*y*. Then the pada-final -*y* is deleted.[23]

As concerns Pāṇini, it is known that he does not describe speech production. He assumes his students have a knowledge of phonetics (*śikṣā*),[24] but his sound catalogue (*akṣarasamāmnāya*) is arranged in such a way as to allow referring to sets of sounds with respect to phonological operations as formulated in the Aṣṭādhyāyī. Two examples will suffice.

The nasal stops arranged according to the sets in which they constitute the final sounds are *ṅ ñ ṇ n m*. In Pāṇini's

---

19 अथावर्णपूर्वे। इवर्णपर एकारम्। (TPr. 10.3-4).

20 दीर्घं समानाक्षरे सवर्णपरे। (TPr. 10.2).

21 इवर्णोकारो यवकारौ। (TPr. 10.15).

22 न प्लुतप्रग्रहौ। (TPr. 10.24).

23 लुप्येते त्ववर्णपूर्वौ यवकारौ। (TPr. 10.19).

24 See above with n. 16.

akṣarasamāmnāya, the nasals appear in the seventh group (*ñamaṅaṇanam*), closed by the anubandha *m*, ordered as follows: *ñ m ṅ ṇ n*. It is clear that *ñ* and *m* have been moved, while retaining the original relative order. This allows the use of the abbreviation *ṅam* required by a rule (A 8.3.32: ङमो ह्रस्वादचि ङमुण्णित्यम्।), which provides for adding initial augments *ṅ ṇ n* respectively to the initial vowel of a pada following a pada that ends with one of these consonants preceded by a short vowel; e.g., प्रत्यङ्ङास्ते "sits facing west", सुगण्णास्ते "a good astrologer is seated", तस्मिन्निति.[25] This operation does not apply to pada-final *ñ* or *m*.

There is only one sound *h* in Sanskrit, yet Pāṇini lists it twice, in the fifth (*hayavaraṭ*) and fourteenth (*hal*) sets of sounds in his catalogue. As Pāṇinīyas all recognize, the reason for this is that *h* patterns phonologically with voiced stops and with the voiceless spirants *ś ṣ*. Thus, देवदत्तस्तत्र। देवदत्तो गच्छति। देवदत्तो हसति। have *devadattas* before a voiceless dental but *devadatto* before a voiced stop and *h*-. The aorist *alikṣat* (3sg. act.) from the base *lih* "lick" (*lihanti* [3pl. pres.]) is parallel to *avikṣat* and *advikṣat* from *viś* (*viśati* [3sg. pres.]) and *dviṣ* (*dviṣanti* [3pl. pres.]). Accordingly, Pāṇini formulates a sūtra, whereby -*r* is replaced by -*u* before a voiced segment, including *h*,[26] and another sūtra, which introduces the vikaraṇa ***ksa*** after bases which end in a sound denoted by *śa**l***, that is, *ś ṣ s* and *h* and contain a penultimate *i*- *u*- or *r̥* vowel.[27]

---

25 तस्मिन्निति निर्दिष्टे पूर्वस्य। (A 1.1.66).

26 A 6.1.114: हशि च (रो: 113, उत् 111) lets -*u* replace pada-final -***ru*** before a sound denoted by *haś*, that is *h*, semi-vowels, nasal stops and other voiced stops. Details of the complete derivation of *devadatto* from *devadattas* need not be considered here.

27 A 3.1.45: शल इगुपधादनिट: क्स: (च्ले: 34).

3. Derivation and Underlying Strings

3.1. PADAPĀṬHAS AND PRĀTIŚAKHYAS

Just as a sequence अग्नाइइ। इति। आह। is posited in the padapāṭha corresponding to the saṁhitāpāṭha अग्ना३ इत्याइ in the Taittirīyasaṁhitā (see §2.2), so are other strings posited in this and other padapāṭhas to account for saṁhitā texts through derivation. Moreover, as is well known, these padapāṭhas differ from each other.

Consider, for example, the very first ṛc of the Ṛgveda, which occurs also in the Taittirīyasaṁhitā:

(1) अग्निमीळे पुरोहितंयज्ञस्य देवमृत्विजम्। होतारं रत्नधातमम्। (ṚV 1.1.1, TS 4.3.13.3).[28]

The padapāṭhas of the Ṛgveda and the Taittirīyasaṁhitā for this verse are:

(2) अग्निम्। ईळे। पुरःऽहितम्। यज्ञस्य। देवम्। ऋत्विजम्। होतारम्। रत्नऽधातमम (ṚVpp. 1.1.1).

(3) अग्निम्। ईडे। पुरोहितमिति पुरः-हितम्। यज्ञस्य। देवम्। ऋत्विजम। होतारम्। रत्नधातममिति रत्न-धातमम्। (TSpp. 4.3.123.3).

In (2) the constituents of the compound *purohitam* are recited with a break (*avagraha*) between them: पुरःऽहितम्। The Taittirīya-padapāṭha differs not only in observing what is called *parigraha*, first reciting the compound as in the saṁhitā, followed by *iti*, then the reciting the constituents with a break: पुरोहितमिति पुरः-हितम्।; there is also an accentual difference between the recitations in the two padapāṭhas. In the Ṛgveda-padapāṭha, the first syllable of *hitam*, which is originally lowpitched (*hitam*), appears as a svarita vowel. That is, the replacement by a svarita of an anudātta following an udātta in close junction applies

[28] The Taittirīya text has अग्निमीडे.

here,[29] although the two constituents are separated by a break. In the Taittirīya-padapāṭha, on the other hand, *hi̱ta̱m* of पु॒रः-हि॒त॒म् (*pu̱raḥ-hi̱ta̱m*) is recited with a low pitch. Comparably, a sequence such as *di̱vedìve*, involving āmreḍita, is accented differently in its analysed form in these two padapāṭhas. For example:

(4) उप॑ त्वाग्ने दि॒वेदि॑वे॒ दोषा॑वस्तर्धि॒या व॒यम्। नमो॒ भर॑न्तु एम॑सि।। (R̥V 1.1.7; TS 1.5.6.2).

(5) उप॑। त्वा॒। अ॒ग्ने॒। दि॒वेऽदि॑वे। दोषा॑ऽवस्तः। धि॒या। व॒यम्। नमः। भर॑न्तः। आ। इ॒म॒सि॒। (R̥Vpp. 1.1.7).

(6) उप॑। त्वा॑। अ॒ग्ने॒। दि॒वेऽदि॑व॒ इति॑ दि॒वे-दि॒वे॒। दोषा॑वस्त॒रिति॑ दोषा॑-व॒स्त॒ः। धि॒या। व॒यम्। नमः॑। भरन्तः। एति॑। इ॒म॒सि॒। (TSpp. 1.5.6.2).

दि॒वेऽदि॑वे (*di̱ve-dìve*) of (5) contrasts with दि॒वे-दि॒वे॒ (*di̱ve-di̱ve̱*) in (6).[30]

Śākalya's procedure in the R̥gveda-padapāṭha is explicable on two possible grounds. First, *pu̱raḥ-hìtam* is a pada, with one nominal ending and a single high-pitched syllable, albeit a complex one, a compound, and *di̱ve-dìve* also has a single high-pitched vowel although it has two instances of the ending *e*. In addition, it is possible that in his recitation, the break between constituents of such complexes was of a shorter duration than the break between independent padas in a string. Consequently, the phonological change that applies within a pada applies across such a break. Ātreya's procedure in the Taittirīyapadapāṭha, on

---

[29] According to R̥Pr. 3.7 (उदात्तपूर्वं स्वरितमनुदात्तं पदेऽक्षरम्।), a low-pitched (*anudāttam*) syllable (*akṣaram*) in a word changes to one with a combination of high and low pitches (*svaritam*) if it is preceded by an udātta.

[30] The first occurrence of this in the Taittirīyasaṁhitā-padapāṭha in the Poona edition has an unfortunate misprint (दि॒वेदि॑व॒ इति॑ दि॒वे-दि॒वे), which does not recur in this edition. The Mysore edition shows the proper accentuation throughout.

the other hand, reflects a recitation in which the break between constituents separated by an avagraha is the same as the one between independent padas. As a consequence, the second constituent of such complexes as *pu̱raḥ-hi̱ta̱m* and *di̱ve-di̱ve̱* does not undergo the phonological change that would apply within a pada or across pada boundaries without intervening pauses.[31]

Although Śākalya and Ātreya obviously differ in their practices, they both operate with strings that are related to saṁhitā texts. Traditionally, the Vedic saṁhitā texts are considered not to have been produced by any indvidual (*apauruṣeya*), but the padapāṭhas are viewed as human compositions. That is, the scholars in question have posited theoretical strings related to the saṁhitā texts they deal with. These posited strings, moreover, show divisions that are by no means arbitrary. They are based on principles of abstracting constituent units from saṁhitā strings.[32] These very principles also imply a corresponding set of rules whereby the saṁhitā texts are derived from the underlying elements posited in the padapāṭhas. Neither Śākalya, nor Ātreya composed such a set of rules - at least as far as can be known from available evidence - but the prātiśākhyas associated with the R̥gveda and the Taittirīyasaṁhitā formulate such rules of conversion.

3.2. PĀṆINI

Pāṇini knew Śākalya's padapāṭha to the R̥gveda, and he follows a general derivational procedure comparable to the one reflected by prātiśākhya rules. Pāṇini also differs in important

---

[31] TPr, 14.30 (उदात्तात्परोऽनुदात्तः स्वरितम्। व्यञ्जनान्तर्हितेऽपि।) provides that an anudātta that follows an udātta changes to a svarita, even if one or more consonants intervene.

[32] For studies on the principles involved, see Jha 1987 and Kulkarni 1995.

ways from his predecessors. To begin with, his grammar serves to describe not a single text such as the Ṛgveda but a language in general, including not only the speech (*bhāṣā*) of his time (*c.* 500 BCE) current in his native area (Śalātura) but also dialects spoken at that time, some of whose features had been described by other grammarians, as well as features proper to usage in Vedas (*chandasi*) and particular parts of them. In addition, Pāṇini not only operates with posited strings not found in actual usage (*alaukikāni vākyāni*) but provides for their formation by rules of affixation. Affixes (*pratyaya*) are allowed to occur with bases (*prakṛti*) – either verbal bases (*dhātu*) or nominal bases (*prātipadika*) – under several conditions: meaning condition, co-occurrence conditions, and combinations of the two.[33] For example, leaving aside accentual features, a Pāṇinian abstract string corresponding to (1) (§3.1) would be

(7) अग्नि-अम् ईड्-इ पुरोहित-अम् यज्ञ-अस् देव-अम् ऋत्विज्-अम् होतृ-अम् रत्नधातम-अम्।

This contains the verbal *īḍ* followed by the verb ending *i* (*iṭ*); the simple nominal bases *agni-*, *deva-*, *hotṛ-* followed by the nominal ending *am*; the compound bases *purohita-*, *ṛtvij-*, *ratnadhātama-* with the same ending; and *yajña-* with the nominal ending *as* (*ṅas*). At a still more abstract stage, *īḍ* is followed by a *l*-affix (*lakāra*) *laṭ* which, like all *l*-affixes, is replaced by a basic verb ending. In addition, an optional compound like *purohita-* is derived from a string *puras-**su** hita-am* whose constituents are combined to form a compound (*samāsa*).[34]

---

33 For a description of Pāṇini's derivational system, see Cardona 1997: 136-400.

34 *Puras-* itself is derived from *pūrva-* and an ending, with the taddhita suffix *asi*, and *hi-ta-* derives from *dhā-**k**ta*, with replacement of the base *dhā-* by *hi-* before the suffix ***k**ta*. Such details need not be discussed here.

The *l*-affix *laṭ* is introduced here after a base on condition that the action this denotes is referred to current time (*vartamāne*) and that an agent (*kartr̥*) of this act is to be denoted. The particular ending *iṭ* is selected because the base is marked (*īḍā̲*) to show that it takes endings of the ātmanepada set and because of the semantic condition that one agent is signified. The ending *am* is a member of the second triplet (*dvitīyā*) of nominal endings, introduced here on condition that a single direct object (*karman*) is to be signified. Since the bases *agni-*, *deva-*, *hotr̥-*, and *ratnadhātama-* are used here co-referentially (*samānādhikaraṇa*), the same ending is iterated after them.

Comparably, an utterance

(8) देवदत्तः स्थाल्यामोदनं पचति। "Devadatta is cooking rice in a pot" is derived from.

(9) देवदत्त-सु स्थाली-ङि ओदन-अम् पच्-लट्।

3.3. STATUS OF POSITED STRINGS

Pāṇinīyas are clear in expressing how they view abstract strings like (9). The position regularly maintained is that ultimately only full utterances (*vākya*) used in actual communication (*vyavahāra*) are to be granted real status. From these are abstracted words (*pada*) with meanings attributed to them and from words are abstracted bases (*prakr̥ti*), affixes (*pratyaya*), together with meanings attributed to them, as well as other elements such as augments (*āgama*). In one of the kārikās where he outlines the contents of the Vākyapadīya, Bhartr̥hari distinguishes meanings which are attributed to constituent words through abstraction (*apoddhārapadārthāḥ*), meanings which have a fixed nature (*sthitalakṣaṇāḥ*), speech units (*śabdāḥ*) which are to be explained (*anvākhyeyāḥ*) by the grammar, and those elements which serve to explain such units (*pratipādakāḥ*).[35] In his autocommentary, Bhartr̥hari explains that a meaning with a fixed nature appears in the form of a sentence meaning (*vākyarūpopagrahaḥ*). This is a single qualified entity (*viśiṣṭa ekaḥ*), an action (*kriyātmā*), whose putative parts are constructs (*kalpitoddeśavibhāgaḥ*) and which is conveyed in a grammar through the understanding of discreet constituent meanings (*vicchinnapadārthagraha-ṇopāyapratipādyaḥ*), which serve only as a means (*upāya*) for conveying the unitary qualified meaning understood from an utterance such as (8).[36] In accordance with the view that a sentential meaning is a qualified unitary meaning, Bhartr̥hari remarks that an abstracted meaning is actually totally fused (*atyantasaṁsr̥ṣṭaḥ*) in a single sentential meaning and that it is abstracted (*apoddhriyate*) from the sentential meaning once it has been given distinct status (*prakr̥tavivekaḥ san*) as a construct (*parikalpitena rūpeṇa*), that is inferred (*anumeyena*). This is only an inferred separate entity, whose form is beyond the realm of actual communication (*vyavahārātītaṁ rūpam*).[37] That is, a sentence such as (8) is actually used in normal communication, where it functions as a unit with a unitary meaning: an act of cooking qualified as occurring currently and being brought to accomplishment by particular participants. A grammarian or a speaker, depending on the resemblance of a token such as *pacati* or *odanam* in (8) and in other utterances, abstracts from any such utterance a word *pacati* or *odanam*, to which he inferentially attributes a separate

---

[35] अपोद्धारपदार्था ये ये चार्थाः स्थितलक्षणाः।
अन्वाख्येयाश्च ये शब्दा ये चापि प्रतिपादकाः।। (VP 1.24).

[36] स्थितलक्षणस्तु वाक्यरूपोपग्रहः कल्पितोद्देशविभागो विशिष्ट एकः क्रियात्मा विच्छिन्नपदार्थग्रहणोपायप्रतिपाद्यः। (VPVr̥. 1.24 [67.1-2]).

[37] तत्रापोद्धारपदार्थो नामात्यन्तसंसृष्टः संसर्गादनुमेयेन परिकल्पितेन रूपेण प्रकृतविवेकः सन्नपोद्ध्रियते। प्रविविक्तस्य हि तस्य वस्तुनो व्यवहारातीतं रूपम्। (VPVr̥. 1.14 [65.1-3]).

meaning. Once one assumes that a word such as *odanam* has separate status, one can then contrast (8) with

(10) देवतत्त: स्थाल्यां शाकं पचति "Devadatta is cooking a vegetable in a pot."

From the presence of *odanam* in (8) and the concurrent understanding that cooking here involves a rice gruel, as opposed to the absence of this term in (10) and the concurrent absence of the understanding of this meaning, one concludes that *odanam* denotes a rice gruel. However, this inference is only a construct: in reality, (8) and (10) are used as individual units of communication.

Such utterances are the true speech units to be explained (*anvākhyeyāḥ śabdāḥ*). It is not possible, however, to compose a grammar whereby each such sentence, one of an innumerable group, is described directly. Consequently, a grammarian like Pāṇini formulates a set of rules whereby units like *pacati*, *sthālyām*, *odanam*, and *śākam* are derived. These in turn are described in terms of abstracted bases and affixes, as illustrated by (9).[38]

Now, Bhartr̥hari speaks of the understanding of separate word meanings (*vicchinnapadārthagrahaṇa*) as a means (*upāya*) whereby a unitary sentential meaning is described. Elsewhere, he remarks that constituent elements and their meanings are said to be means (*upāyān pracakṣate*) because they are adopted (*upādāya*) only to be set aside (*heyāḥ*) once the ultimate objects

---

[38] Bhartr̥hari remarks that for some the highest unit of description is the utterance (*vākyāvadhikam anvyākhyānam*), for others the syntactic pada (*padāvadhikam*), an item that terminates in a nominal or verbal ending: अन्वाख्येयाश्च ये शब्दा:। केषांचित्पदावधिकमन्वाख्यानं वाक्यावधिकमेकेषाम् (VPVr̥. 1.24 [68.5-6]). Pāṇini clearly belongs to the second group, in that he derives utterances, but he does so by positing distinct padas within utterances and also derives padas by introducing affixes to bases.

have been described by means of them. Moreover, he notes that there is no fixed restriction (*niyamo nāvatiṣṭhate*) for these means.[39] In his autocommentary, he not only says that elements which are adopted for a particular end are necessarily left behind once that end has been reached,[40] but also that if students (*puruṣāḥ* "men") can be made to understand what is to be explained in another way, then different means (*upāyāntarāṇi*) also are undertaken to that end.[41]

For Bhartr̥hari, then, padas such as *devadattas*, *sthālyām*, *odanam*, and *pacati*, which are theoretically considered constituents of (8), and the constituents of these – *devadatta-su* and so on in (9) – are merely instruments whereby the true units are accounted for: utterances like (8) or words within them. These are the speech units to be explained (*anvākhyeyāḥ*), and they are divided (*vibhajyante*) into posited (*kalpitaiḥ*) pseudo-parts (*bhāgair iva*). Consequently, any set of grammatical rules (*śāstram*) set up to describe utterances through such constituents is set (*vyavasthitam*) truly far (*atidūre*) from the ultimate goal.[42] Indeed, Bhartr̥hari does not hesitate to characterize such means as ways of deceiving (*upalāpanāḥ*) young students (*bālānām*)

---

39 उपादायापि ये हेयास्तानुपायान्प्रचक्षते।
उपायानां च नियमो नावश्यमवतिष्ठते।। (VP 2.38).

40 येषां च यदर्थमुपादानं तत्सन्निधाने नियत एषां त्यागः। (VPVr̥. 2.38 [208]). The published text has *teṣāṁ* instead of *yeṣāṁ*. I have emended the text under the assumption that this is a general statement concerning entities viewed as means to ends. In his electronic edition, Aklujkar keeps *teṣāṁ* but emends *eṣāṁ* to *eva*.

41 यदि त्वन्यथापि पुरुषाः प्रतिपादयितुं शक्यन्ते तत्र तदर्थान्युपायान्तराण्यपि प्रक्रम्यन्ते।। (VPVr̥. 2.38 [209]).

42 शब्दा यथा विभज्यन्ते भागैरिव विकल्पितैः।
अन्वाख्येयास्तथा शास्त्रमतिदूरे व्यवस्थितम्।। (VP 3.14.75). I do not consider here the theological implications of the position adopted.

who are learning. The enterprise is saved, nevertheless, by adopting the position that by going via this false path (*asatye vartmani sthitvā*), one exerts oneself to attain what is true (*satyaṁ samīhate*).[43]

Pāṇinīyas at least from Bhartr̥hari onwards thus view the segments arrived at through analysing utterances only as means allowing one to describe the language, not elements with ultimate true status.[44]

4. Generalization and Grammatical Principles

To describe Sanskrit by such means, moreover, Pāṇini not only continued the methodology he inherited from predecessors of deriving utterances from abstract strings, he also accepted a theoretical stand concerning the rules which apply in such derivations. This is the principle that a grammar should be a set of rules (*lakṣaṇam*) associated with general and particular features (*sāmānyaviśeṣavat*). Patañjali makes this point forcefully,[45] illustrating it with two Pāṇinian sūtras: कर्मण्यण् (A

---

43 उपाया: शिक्षमाणनां वालानां उपलापना:।
असत्ये वर्त्मनि स्थित्वा ततः सत्यं समीहते।। (VP 2.238).

44 Pāṇini himself composed the Aṣṭādhyāyī, a set of sūtras, but has left no extant commentary in which he might have expressed his position with regard to the units with which he operates. Nor, to my knowledge, is there explicit mention in Kātyāyana's vārttikas or Patañjali's Mahābhāṣya on the fictitious status of units such as bases and affixes, although commentators consider that some of their statements reflect this position. I cannot deal with this issue in the compass of a short lecture.

45 कथं तर्हीमे शब्दाः प्रतिपत्तव्या:। किञ्चत्सामान्यविशेषवल्लक्षणं प्रवर्त्यं येनाल्पेन यत्नेन महतो महतः शब्दौघान्प्रतिपद्येरन्। किं पुनस्तत्। उत्सर्गापवादौ। कश्चिदुत्सर्ग:। कर्तव्यः कश्चिदपवाद:। कथञ्जातीयकः पुनरुत्सर्गः कर्तव्यः कथञ्जातीयकोऽपवाद:। सामान्येनोत्सर्ग:। तद्यथा कर्मण्यण्। तस्य विशेषेणापवाद:। तद्यथातोऽनुपसर्गे क:। (Bh. I.6.3-7).

3.2.1) and आतोऽनुपसर्गे कः (A 3.2.3). Both rules introduce an affix after a verbal base (*dhātoḥ*)[46] construed with a concurrently used term which refers to an object (*karmaṇi*) of the action denoted by the verb. A 3.2.1 allows ***aṇ*** to follow any base meeting this condition, but A 3.2.3 introduces ***ka*** after a base ending with *ā* (*ātaḥ*) which is not used with a preverb (*anupasarge*). The first sūtra provides for a derivate such as *kār-a-* "maker" from *kr̥*[47] construed with *kumbha* "pot": *kumbhakāra-* "pot maker"; the second accounts for a derivate such as *d-a-*[48] in *goda-* "one who gives a cow". The affixations provided by these two rules apply in related domains such that one applies in general (*sāmānyena*), the other one in a particular (*viśeṣeṇa*) sub-domain of the former. One is thus a general rule (*utsarga*), the other a related exception (*apavāda*).

A 3.2.1 and A 3.2.3 are in close proximity. However, this is not required in order to consider together a general rule and an exception to it. They may be stated in quite separate sections of the grammar yet be brought together by their intrinsic relation. For example, इको यणचि (6.1.77) is a phonological rule whereby a semi-vowel *y r l v* substitutes for a vowel denoted by the term ***ik*** – that is, *i u r̥ l̥* and their long counterparts – before another vowel; e.g. *dadhy* (← *dadhi* "yogurt"), *madhv-* (← *madhu* "honey") before *atra* "here". A 6.4.77 (अचि श्नुधातुभ्रुवां य्वोरियङुवङौ) states an operation that applies to certain stems (*aṅga*)[49] that end with *-i/ī*

[46] Both sūtras come in a section of the grammar headed by धातोः। (A 3.1.91).

[47] ***aṇ*** is marked with *ṇ* to show that it conditions vr̥ddhi replacement (A 7.2.115: अचोऽञ्णिति [वृद्धिः 114]). Additional details are not pertinent to the present discussion.

[48] ***Ka*** is marked with *k* to show that it conditions the deletion of *–ā* (A 6.4.64: आतो लोप इटि च [क्ङिति 63]).

[49] A 6.4.77 occurs in the section headed by अङ्गस्य (A 6.4.1).

or -*u*/*ū*: stems with the suffix *śnu*, verbal bases, and *bhrū* "brow". The final vowels of these stems are respectively replaced by -*iy* (*iyaṅ*) and -*uvaṅ*; e.g. *śaknuvanti* (← *śak-nu-anti*) ". . . are able", *kṣiyati* "dwells" (← *kṣi-a-ti*), *luluvatuḥ* "they two cut" (3du. pfct.) (← *lū-atus*), *bhruvoḥ* (← *bhrū-os*) "brows" (gen. loc. du.). A 6.4.77 is an exception to the more general rule A 6.1.77, applying in domains which are part of the overall domain of the latter. They are, however, stated in different sections of the Aṣṭādhyāyī: one contains rules that apply in phonological contexts, the other rules that apply to stems in particular grammatical contexts. Nevertheless, by virtue of their intrinsic relation, the two rules are brought together in a single context (*vākyaikavākyatā*).[50]

In addition to recognizing that rules and operations are related in terms of their domains, Pāṇini recognized other decision principles whereby rules are applied to arrive at appropriate results.[51]

5. Summary

It is clear and demonstrable that, by a time certainly preceding Pāṇini, ancient Indian scholars had recognized the distinction between what in modern terminology are called phonetics and phonology. They describe speech production with accuracy and in detail. In addition, these scholars arrived at the position that one can posit strings which serve, through the application of phonological rules, to arrive at final texts of the saṁhitās.

---

50 Pāṇinīyas recognize this principle, although Pāṇini does not explicitly formulate it. The principle is formulated overtly in R̥Pr. 1.53 (न्यायैर्मिश्रानपवादान् प्रतीयात्।), which states that one should understand exceptions together (*miśrān* "mixed") with the general rules — here called *nyāya* — to which they are related.

51 Principles observed in Pāṇini's grammar are described briefly in Cardona 1997: 401-27.

Pāṇini inherited the fruits of such thinking and built upon them, devising a grammar in which utterances of Sanskrit are accounted for through a derivational system which begins with semantic relations and in which abstract strings are posited to derive utterances of actual usage. Pāṇini also operated with a set of decision principles to guide the proper application of the rules of the grammar. In all of these aspects, ancient Indian scholars merit our recognizing their impressive accomplishments.

References and Abbreviations

A: *Aṣṭādhyāyī*.

Abhyankar, K.V. 1962-72. *The Vyākaraṇa=Mahābhāṣya of Patañjali* edited by F. Kielhorn, revised and furnished with additional readings, references, and select critical notes, third edition. श्रीभगवत्पतञ्जलिविरचितं व्याकरणमहाभाष्यम् एफ् कीलहोर्न इत्यनेन संशोधितम् . . . अभ्यंकरोपाह्व-वासुदेवशास्त्रिसुत-काशिनाथेन संदर्भग्रन्थनिदर्शनैः दुर्बोधस्थलव्याख्यानकारिणीभिः टिप्पणीभिश्च परिष्कृतम्. Three volumes. Poona: Bhandarkar Oriental Research Institute.

Bh.: *Mahābhāṣya*. See Abhyankar, K.V.

Cardona, George, 1986, Phonology and phonetics in ancient Indian works: the case of voiced and voiceless elements, in Krishnamurti, Bh. (editor), Colin Masica and Anjani Sinha (associate editors), *South Asia Languages: Structure, Convergence and Diglossia*, Delhi: Motilal Banarsidass, pp. 60-80.

———, 1997, *Pāṇini, His Work and Its Traditions*, vol. I: *Background and Introduction*, 2nd edn., Delhi: Motilal Banarsidass.

Jagdishlal Shastri, 1971, *Vājasaneyi-Mādhyandina-Śukla-Yajurveda Saṁhitā with the Mantra-bhāṣya of Uvaṭa, the Vedadīpa-bhāṣya of Mahīdhara, Appendices, an Alphabetical List of Mantras and a short Introduction* वाजसनेयि-माध्यन्दिन-शुक्ल-युजुर्वेद-संहिता श्रीमदुवटाचार्यविरचितमन्त्रभाष्येण श्रीमहीधराचार्यकृतवेददीपभाष्येण च समन्विता, Delhi: Motilal Banarsidass.

Jha, V.N., 1987, *Studies in the Padapāṭhas and Vedic Philology*, Delhi: Pratibha Prakashan.

Kulkarni, Nirmala R., 1995, *A Grammatical Analysis of the Taittirīya*

Padapāṭha, Pre-Pāṇinian Grammatical Traditions, Part II, Sri Garib Oriental Series 192, Delhi: Sri Satguru Publications.

Mahadeva Sastri, A. and K. Rangacharya, 1894-98, तैत्तिरीयसंहिता भट्टभास्करमिश्रविरचितभाष्यसहिता *The Taittirīya Saṁhitā of the Black Yajurveda with the Commentary of Bhaṭṭa Bhāskara Miśra*, 10 vols., Mysore Oriental Library Series, Mysore: Government Branch Press, repr. 1986, Delhi: Motilal Banarsidass.

Mangal Deva Shastri, 1931, *The Ṛgveda-Prātiśākhya with the Commentary of Uvaṭa* edited from original manuscripts, with introduction, critical and additional notes, English translation of the text, and several appendices, vol. II: *Text in Sūtra-Form and Commentary with Critical Apparatus* उवटकृतभाष्यसहितं श्रीशौनकीयम् ऋग्वेदप्रातिशाख्यम् . . ., Allahabad: The India Press.

Rangacharya, K. and R. Shama Shastri, 1906, *The Taittirīya Prātiśākhya with the Commentaries: Tribhāṣyaratna of Somayārya and Vaidikābharaṇa of Gārgya Gopāla Yajvan*, with an English Introduction, and Sanskrit Introduction by K. Raṅgācārya तैत्तिरीयप्रातिशाख्यम् सोमयार्य-विरचित-त्रिभाष्यरत्नाख्यव्याख्यया गार्ग्यगोपाल-यज्वविरचित-वैदिकाभरणाख्यव्याख्यया च सहितम् आङ्ग्ल-भूमिकया कस्तूरिरङ्गाचार्यप्रणीतया संस्कृतभूमिकया च समुपबृंहितम् . . . Bibliotheca Sanskritica 33, Mysore: Government Branch Press, repr. 1985, Delhi: Motilal Banarsidass.

Rau, Wilhelm, 1977, *Bhartṛhari's Vākyapadīya, Die Mūlakārikās nach den Handschriften herausgegeben und mit einem Pāda-Index versehen*, Abhandlungen für die Kunde des Morgenlandes Band XLII, 4, Wiesbaden: Steiner.

ṚPr.: *Ṛgvedaprātiśākhya*. See Mangal Deva Shastri.

ṚV: *Ṛgveda*. See N.S. Sontakke, et al.

ṚVpp.: *Ṛgveda-padapāṭha*. See N.S. Sontakke, et al.

Sontakke, N.S. et al., 1933-51, ऋग्वेदसंहिता श्रीमत्सायणाचार्यविरचितभाष्यसहिता *Ṛgveda-Saṁhitā with the Commentary of Sāyaṇācārya*, 5 vols., Poona: Vaidic Samshodhan Mandal.

Sontakke, N.S. and T.N. Dharmadhikari, 1970-2010, कृष्णयजुर्वेदीया तैत्तिरीयसंहिता पदपाठयुता भट्टभास्कर-सायणाचार्य-विरचित-भाष्याभ्यां समेता *Taittirīya Saṁhitā with the Padapāṭha and the Commentaries of Bhaṭṭa*

Bhāskara Miśra and Sāyaṇācārya, 4 vols., in eight parts, Poona/Pune: Vaidika Saṁśodhana Maṇḍala.

Subramania Iyer, K.A., 1966, *Vākyapadīya of Bhartr̥hari with the Vr̥tti and the Paddhati of Vr̥ṣabhadeva Kāṇḍa I Critically Edited*. . . . Deccan College Monograph Series 32, Poona: Deccan College.

——, 1983, श्रीभर्तृहरिविरचितं सवृत्तिवाक्यपदीयद्वितीयकाण्डम् पुण्यराजकृतटीकोपेतम् *Vākyapadīya of Bhartr̥hari (An ancient Treatise on the Philosophy of Sanskrit Grammar) Containing the Tīkā of Puṇyarāja and the Ancient Vr̥tti Edited . . . with a Foreword by Ashok Aklujkar, Kāṇḍa* II., Delhi: Motilal Banarsidass.

Taittirīyaprātiśākhya. See K. Rangacharya and R. Shama Shastri.

TS: *Taittirīyasaṁhitā*. See N.S. Sontakke and T.N. Dharmadhikari, A. Mahadeva Sastri, and K. Rangacharya.

TSpp.: *Taittirīyasaṁhitā Padapāṭha*, See N.S. Sontakke and T.N. Dharmadhikari, A. Mahadeva Sastri, and K. Rangacharya.

TSBh: *Bhaṭṭabhāskara's Commentary on the Taittirīyasaṁhitā*. See N.S. Sontakke and T.N. Dharmadhikari, A. Mahadeva Sastri, and K. Rangacharya.

VP: *Vākyapadīya*. See Rau.

VPVr̥.: *Vākyapadīya vr̥tti*. See Subramania Iyer.

VS: *Vājasaneyisaṁhitā*. See Jagdishlal Shastri.

2

Some Speculations on the Contribution of Sanskrit to the Development of World Thought

Radhavallabh Tripathi

I AM extremely grateful to my esteemed colleague Vempaty Kutumba Sastry for giving me this opportunity to join this august gathering of veteran scholars from various parts of India and other countries. I also congratulate him for having chosen a pertinent theme for discussions in this seminar. Now that you have seen this serene place, and also heard to His Holiness Swami Bharatitirthaji, you all will agree with me that the Śṛṅgerī Campus of the Rashtriya Sanskrit Sansthan is the most suitable place for holding this seminar. This campus is not only one of the best centres of traditional Sanskrit learning, it also has all the potential to emerge as an international hub of knowledge where modern thought and technology will go hand-in-hand with the in-depth study of Śāstras.

When Ramanuj Devnathan, one of the principals in the service of Rashtriya Sanskrit Sansthan, was at the helm of affairs in this campus, we decided to institute an international lecture series in this campus. Scholars of repute like Pierre Sylvain Filliozat, Vasundhara Filliozat, Allisson Butch and Sheldon Pollock have so far delivered lectures under this series. As a sequel to this prestigious a lecture series, you have just heard a lecture by George Cardona, one of the most outstanding Sanskrit scholars of our times.

A university campus is known by its faculty and students. I am happy to note that the students of Śṛṅgerī Campus have displayed extraordinary talents and have made achievements that can bring glory to any institution. This also speaks of the quality and sincerity of the teachers of this campus. I would like to dedicate the following two stanzas I have just composed to the teachers and students of this campus:

मृत्पिण्डोपमशिष्यं भ्रमयंश्चके स्वकीयशेमुष्याः।
रचयति पात्रविशेषं गुरुरुत्तमकुम्भकारसमः।।

वितरति विद्यां प्राज्ञे प्रतिभामादीपयंस्तदीयां सः।
जडमपि शिष्यं प्रज्ञापदवीं योग्यो गुरुस्तु नयेत्।।

Only yesterday I participated in the inaugural ceremony of Choice Based Credit System – which is a reincarnation of the *gurukula* system in a modern context. We are now in a position to say with confidence that Sanskrit is preparing to meet the new global challenges, and the twenty-first century has opened the gates of immense possibilities in Sanskrit world.

It is in the backdrop of this that this seminar has assumed an added significance for me and I hope that the deliberations of this seminar will not only bring out the contributions made by Sanskrit to intellectual traditions and theories at global level in the past, they will also envisage the possibilities of further contributions that the knowledge systems of Sanskrit – the Śāstras as we call them – can still make at the global level.

I hope that the post-modern scenario of today's world and post-colonial scenario in our country will also be taken into account with a view to create a hermeneutics of Sanskrit-based knowledge systems (the śāstric traditions of Sanskrit) and some of the modern theories. Perhaps you will agree with me that the Indian theories of language as propounded in works of Patañjali, Bhatr̥hari, Nāgārjuna, Kauṇḍabhaṭṭa or Nāgeśa have assumed greater significance in the so-called post-modern world. Wittgenstein is one of the well-known philosophers of twentieth century. He has discussed his idea of language in his first work *Philosophical Investigations*. There Wittgenstein opined that language is shaped and influenced by socio-economic factors. But years after, when he had come into contact with Indian philosophers like K.J. Shah and Ramchandra Gandhi, in his last work he revised his opinion and said that language also shapes society and the reality. What he said falls in line with these thoughts of Vedic seers and *ācāryas* of Sanskrit traditions:

वागेव विश्वा भुवनानि जज्ञे
इदमन्धं तमः कृत्स्नं जायेत भुवनत्रयम्।
यदि शब्दाह्वयं ज्योतिरासंसारन्न दीप्यते।।
वाचामेव प्रसादेन लोकयात्रा प्रवर्तते।

Names of some of the great intellectuals of twentieth century along with their works can be cited to bring out how directly or indirectly Sanskrit-based knowledge systems have been responsible in shaping various ideologies of global thought. Even with my very superficial knowledge in this area, I can say that much of the corpus of writings by Ferdinand de Saussure would not have materialized without his acquaintance with Indian theories of language. In the realm of aesthetics, the discussion on the concept of *sahr̥daya* in Sanskrit poetics has become even more significant considering the modern theories of reader's response in literary criticism as advanced by some post-modern critics like Rolland Barth; and the concept of symbolism as advanced by Sussan Langer is replenished in the light of her acquaintance with the theories of *rasa* and *dhvani*. Harold Coward in his well-known work on *Derrida and Indian Philosophy*[1] finds correspondences between Bhartṛhari and Derrida as well as Nāgārjuna and Derrida. He also discusses the challenges that Indian theories can pose before a post-modern thinker. Various precepts of *Nāṭyaśāstra* are now being validated through Brecht, Stanislavsky, Grotovsky, Peter Brook and others.

The dialogue between diverse traditions and their interacting with each other leads to the advancement of thought process and stimulates the process of theory-building. In this process, it is likely that even our Śāstric traditions would get rejuvenated and perceptions for future be evolved. Sri Aurobindo in his *Future Poetry* is for building up foundations of a future aesthetics based on spirituality, acquainted as he was with both the Eastern and the Western traditions of thought. I would like to mention here the wonderful experimentations made by Daya Krishna in the last decades of twentieth century. Daya Krishna, himself one of the modern philosophers from our country, conducted some workshops involving dialogues between modern philosophers on one hand and the traditional *paṇḍita*s on the other. In the Pune symposium, the theory of proposition postulated by Bertrand Russell was presented before the traditional Sanskrit *paṇḍita*s, through extempore Sanskrit translation of its exposition in English. The *paṇḍita*s were asked to respond to it from their own stand or system. The English translations of what *paṇḍita*s like Badarinath Shukla said in Sanskrit in reaction to the theory of proposition were presented before the modern philosophers in an extempore way. The modern philosophers were amazed to find the śāstric traditions of Sanskrit so receptive and alive to new ideas. It was during the course of such interactions with

---

[1] Harold Coward, *Derrida and Indian Philosophy*, State University of New York, 1990.

modern philosophers that Pt Badarinath Shukla, one of the great Naiyāyikas of the past century, presented his own theory of *dehātmavāda*. During past three decades, this *dehātmavāda* as postulated by Pt. Shukla has been subjected to criticism from some corner or the other in academic circles, the very controversy generated through it sufficiently proves the vivacity and potential with which Sanskrit continues to be a medium for intellectual discourse.

The theme chosen for this international seminar also envisages looking to the past. In India the past in the form of a heritage has ever been a living source of inspiration. "We - the people of India - have always held in high esteem the cultural heritage of this land." This was the first sentence of a verdict by the Supreme Court of India in a case related to Sanskrit in the curriculum of Central schools. In fact, we define ourselves in terms of our past. Amartya Sen describes this inexorability of past in our life in this way:

> We live in the present, but that is a tiny bit of time, it passes as we talk. The current moment, as vivid as it is, does not tell us much about who we are, how we can reasonably see ourselves, and where we would place our loyalties if and when we face divisions. Our identities are strongly influenced by the past.[2]

It is natural to feel to be a part of the past. The tendency to derive wisdom, life and sustenance from past is a mark of the health of a society. On the other hand, the tendency to glorify past without viewing it in a holistic framework can be deterrent to the health of a society, though it becomes necessary in a certain phase of history.

It is here that I have some reservations regarding the theme selected for this International seminar. A number of

---

[2] Amartya Sen, *On Interpreting India's Past*, p. 1.

seminars have been organized in recent decades in India (and similar seminars are in planning as well) that had themes like Sanskrit in Global Perspectives and Values in Sanskrit Literature. The organizers/participants of such seminars had certain presumptions in their mind, viz.: (i) that India has been the only cradle of civilization in some hoary past (sometimes with great confidence the periodicity of inception of civilization in our country was taken back to a several hundred millennia on basis of certain mathematical/astrological calculations or mythological references); and (ii) that India has been the *jagadguru* (teacher of the world) as it had attained a developed culture when other countries were uncivilized.

The validity of these presumptions is subject to examination, and the Indian scholars airing such views should have studied ancient cultures of China, Iran and Greek also before making any claims with regard to the superiority or antiquity of Indian civilization. Also, the basic principle of reporting, i.e. "hearsay does not equal eye-witness"[3] must be regarded as equally applicable to any research. When Manu expressed a wish that all human beings of this *pr̥thivī* (globe) should learn their *caritra* (behaviour) from the first-borns of this *deśa* (nation),[4] he did not have the same idea of *pr̥thivī* and *deśa* which we have in our minds now.

The tendency towards glorification of past and greatness of Indian culture that dominated the socio-political scenario in our country during the nineteenth and the first half of the twentieth century was helpful in inculcating the spirit of renaissance and provided an impetus to the struggle for freedom. Such a tendency might not have been with us right from the beginnings of our

---

3 Edward S. Sachau (2005), *Alberuni's India*, Preface, p. 3.

4 *Manusmr̥ti*, II.20.

civilization, but it did surface, as a part of defence structure, at the onslaughts of foreign invasions or foreign rules during the first or the second millennium CE. While it provided inputs for resisting the foreign rule and also served as a cover to save our society from the overpowering feelings of inferiority, it also tended to make us recluses and created hindrances in opening any dialogue with alien cultures.

Mahāpaṇḍita[5] Alberuni (ACE 973–1048) who regarded Indians as "excellent philosophers, good mathematicians and astronomers",[6] has made a brilliant exposition of the barriers "which separate the Hindus from the Muslims and make it so particularly difficult for a Muslim to study any Indian subject".[7]

---

5 I have chosen this epithet for Alberuni with a distinct concept of *mahāpaṇḍita* in mind. A scholar with mastery in one Śāstra, with in-depth knowledge of a particular cultural, a particular literary or intellectual tradition can be a *paṇdita*, and a scholar with expertise in many disciplines with in-depth knowledge in diverse cultures, diverse literary or intellectual traditions is a *mahāpaṇḍita*. Alberuni, Darashikoh and Rahul Sankrityayana are *mahāpaṇḍitas*. Rahul Sankrityayana was formally conferred with the title of *mahāpaṇḍita* by the *paṇḍitas* of *Kāśī*, but they did not define what a *mahāpaṇḍita* meant to them.

6 Edward S. Sachau (2005) *Alberuni's India*, Editor's Preface, p. xvii.

7 Some of these barriers according to Alberuni are – (i) The enormous range and richness of the language (Sanskrit) of the aliens or Hindus, (ii) the use of "a neglected vernacular" (meaning perhaps Prakrit) and the use of the classical one only by "the upper and educated classes", (iii) difference of alphabets, phonetics and pronunciations in Arabic and Sanskrit, (iv) carelessness of the scribes of the manuscripts, (v) the misty and constrained phraseology in metrical compositions, (vi) difference in religion and belief between Hindus and Muslims, (vii) the Hindu's directing "their fanaticism against those who do not belong to them – against all foreigners". They call them *mleccha*, i.e. "impure and forbid having any connection with them", and (ix) an unreceptive attitude. – ibid., p. 17

To quote him, "The Hindus believe that there is no country but theirs, no nation like theirs, no kings like theirs, no religion like theirs, no science like theirs."[8] On the other hand, Alberuni also presents an analysis of shortcomings and limitations of the foreign reporters who intend to study India and enumerates the reasons as to why and how they present false accounts with regards to the culture and customs of this country.

Contrary to the unreceptive attitude towards aliens and the tendency to subsist upon self-glorification that surface in the course of history in our society, an openness for dialogue with other cultures and a desire to make the world a place better than ever have been the marks of our culture. It is in this background that the idea of *saṁskṛti* is spelled out in *Yajurveda* – *sā prathamā saṁskṛtir viśvavārā*. Aitareya Mahīdāsa in his *Aitareya Brāhmaṇa* dealt with the application of this concept of *saṁskṛti* in the realm of *śilpa* (art). He also defined *śilpa* as a continuous process of culturation of the self (*ātmasaṁskṛti*). He said that all *śilpas* lead to *ātmasaṁskṛti* (self-purification). There are two types of *śilpas* – *daiva* (the divine) and *mānuṣa* (the human). The world as created by God is *daivaśilpa* and a piece of art produced by *anukṛti* or re-doing this *daivaśilpa* is *mānuṣaśilpa*.[9]

The interconnectivity of the whole universe and an indispensable relationship between the divine and the human as well as human (divine?) participation in the divine (human?) activity that is subsequently termed as *līlā* – these ideas form a world-view that is distinct from the world-views in some other

---

[8] Sachau, op. cit., p. 22.

[9] . . . . देवशिल्पानामनुकृतीह शिल्पमधिगम्यते। हस्ती, कंसो वासो हिरण्यम्। अश्वतरी रथः। – *ऐतरेयब्रा.* XXX.1 vol. III, p. 131.

आत्मसंस्कृतिर्वाव शिल्पानि। छन्दोमयं वा। एतैर्यजमान आत्मानं संस्कुरुते। – *एतरेयब्रा.* XXX.1 vol. III, p. 132.

cultures. They also present the idea of man participating in the process of making the universe better than ever. There is no place for a heliocentric universe in this view – man and God stand almost on equal footing sharing the same functions. The universe is viewed through the metaphor of a tree – the great *aśvattha vr̥kṣa*, where the roots, trunk, branches, leaves, flowers and fruits are all interconnected. There was no scope for the introducing the "individual" and the idea of "freedom" in this tradition. It is not that the individuality is altogether denied. Each leaf of a tree has its own existence, it gets its sap from the tree in its distinct way, and yet it is the leaf as long as it remains a part of the tree.

In view the complementarities in this universe, certain noble thoughts and ideals were evolved and practised in our country that can be said to form the corpus of Indian contributions to world culture. Since man is not alone and is not a mere individual, he has some obligations. He stands in obligation to the other parts of the Cosmic Man – the universe, because he subsists upon them. Therefore he is advised to repay his *r̥ṇas* (debts) to them – to the deities, to the forefathers, to the teachers and to the *mahābhūtas* (elements).

The universe to us has been multi-centric, rather than uni-centric, therefore there has been pluralism. The seers visualize the multi-layered structure of this world, find it multi-lingual and inhibited by people of diverse faiths. This acceptance of pluralism leads to democratic values and harmony:

- जनं बिभ्रती बहुधा विवाचसं नानाधर्माणं पृथिवी यथौकसम् . . . .
- समानो मन्त्रः समितिः समानी . . . .
- समानी प्रपा सह वोन्नभागः . . . .
- कृण्वन्तो विश्वमार्यम्।

- यत्र विश्वं भवत्येकनीडम् . . . .
- आ नो भद्राः क्रतवो यन्तु विश्वतः . . . .
- पुमान् पुमांसं परिपातु विश्वतः . . . .

The values of non-violence and compassion came to be practised in this tradition and the message of non-violence and compassion was also conveyed at global level by the missionaries of Buddhism. The ideas of non-violence and compassion were present in other cultures also. Pythagoras in Greece had spoken about the ideology based on non-violence and compassion. But the ideology was developed to the subtle levels in actual practice here and therefore the missions of Aśoka and others helped in establishing a world-religion based on non-violence and compassion.

The holistic approach to life and world is envisaged in several concepts, beliefs and practices that are envisaged in Sanskrit traditions.

We are living in times when Sanskrit studies are facing a crisis, perhaps the most difficult one in history. There are challenges and problems to be faced and solved. And yet the efflorescence is breathing with immense potential as well. I hope that the deliberations of this international conference will not only spell out the contribution of Sanskrit to global thought, they will also rejuvenate all of us to be ready and well equipped for meeting global challenges.

Bibliography

Aitareya Brāhmaṇa, with Sāyaṇa's Commentary, 3 vols., 2nd edn., New Delhi: Rashtriya Sankrit Sansthan, 2006.

Sachau, Edward C., *Alberuni's India*, ed. with notes and indices, Delhi, 2005.

Sen, Amartya, *On Interpreting India's Past*, Asiatic Society Calcutta, 1994.

3

The Rāmāyaṇa in World Literature

John Brockington[1]

WHATEVER one's views about how the *Rāmāyaṇa* ascribed to Vālmīki originated, the story of Rāma is undoubtedly one of the most widely spread and popular not only within India but throughout the rest of Asia. Indeed, of all the epics composed in various parts of the world, it is the *Rāmāyaṇa* which has spread most widely, throughout India, Central Asia and South-East Asia, and been current over the longest time-span. In this paper I shall only be able to cover a little of what my title suggests but I hope to do so in a way that illustrates the significance of the story and, in order to give my remarks more cohesion, I shall focus on the impact of religion and sovereignty on the *Rāmāyaṇa* tradition and concentrate on its spread in South-East Asia, even so discussing only a few selected texts.

The general outlines of the story have remained largely unchanged since it was first told around the fifth century BCE, but its popularity has ensured that it was re-told with an ever-increasing number of narrative additions. Within India, many tellers made the story a religious epic, identifying Rāma as

---

[1] An earlier version was delivered as a joint paper by Mary Brockington and myself at the conference "Ramayana: Reinterpretation in Asia", organized by the Asian Civilisations Museum, Singapore, 17-18 July 2010; I gladly acknowledge my indebtedness to Mary Brockington's major input to all this work.

an *avatāra* of Viṣṇu and eventually as God; for others, Śiva or even the Goddess played the more important role. For the Sikh guru Gobind Singh Rāma's military activities provided a useful example to his followers at the start of the eighteenth century, while much earlier Jain tellers had been troubled by some of the more aggressive or fantastic elements in the old story, but used its popular appeal to propagate their own value, modifying what they found objectionable. Other tellers retained the original view of Rāma as a secular human hero.

The story became popular in South-East Asia at an early date,[2] and similar factors applied there. In countries dominated by Buddhist ideals, or eventually by Islam, tellers made significant modifications to render the actions of a foreign deity appropriate to their new audiences. The amount of material available is vast and complex (so complex that I retain the Sanskrit names of the characters to minimize confusion),[3] so today I will discuss – as I indicated – only a few representative examples of such modifications, considering what impact they have had on the established narrative. I begin with a Buddhist version from Myanmar.

Buddhist versions: Rāma Vatthu (Myanmar)

The Myanmar *Rāma Vatthu*, composed in the seventeenth century, has a thoroughly Buddhist appearance, while keeping close to the general outline of the Sanskrit *Rāmāyaṇa*. As in

---

[2] It was known in Java from at least the tenth century CE, and from at least the eleventh in Myanmar.

[3] Each published text represents only one version, not the totality of the tradition current in any particular area; because a feature occurs (or is absent) in one published text, we must not assume that it was or was not known in the same area or language group at the same date. The Muslim versions known collectively as the *Hikayat Seri Rama* are especially complex; see Barrett 1963.

some other South-East Asian adaptations, Rāma is presented as a *bodhisattva*,[4] a largely superficial modification, easily achieved, since the *bodhisattva* doctrine has analogies with the *avatāra* system. The consequences for the detailed outworking of the plot are more substantial. For example, the episode in which Sītā attests her chastity throughout her captivity by entering a fire which does not burn her has been retained, but there is no role for any gods.[5] The ending, too, is different: instead of Rāma's suicide and triumphal return to heaven as Viṣṇu, with a defiant Sītā, resentful at having been unjustly exiled by Rāma, back in the care of the Earth from which she was born – appropriate in

---

4 Ohno 1999: 81-83, 91, 94, 157; see also 106. Rāma is also presented as a *bodhisattva* in U Aung Phyo's *Rama Thagyin*, U Toe's *Rama Yagan* and Saya Htun's *Alaung Rama Thagyin* from Myanmar (Thein Han 1973: 74; Ohno 1999: 1-2), in *Lanka Xihe* from Yunnan and the Mon *Loik Samoing Ram* (Ohno 1999: 23).

From an early date in Sri Lankan tradition, an appropriate selection of episodes from the *VRm* had been adapted and given the framework of a *jātaka*; this *Dasarathajātaka* (Cowell IV 1901: 78-82, tr. W.H.D. Rouse, studied in Mary Brockington 2002: 139-41) became popular in South-East Asia, but remained distinct from the other Buddhist adaptations, which were based on the full Sanskrit version. Tellings also incorporated into a *jātaka* frame include the NE Thai *Rāmajātaka*, and Lao versions A and B (Ohno 1999: 23; Lafont 2003: Phuk 1; Vo 1971: 19 and 61).

Other versions, such as the Thai *Ramakien*, the Khmer *Rāmakerti*, and Lao version C retain the convention that Rāma is an incarnation of Viṣṇu/Nārāyaṇa (Olsson 1968: *passim*; Pou 2007: I, 16-17; Vo 1971: 77-78).

5 *VRm* 6.104-6; Ohno 1999: 160. In 1775, slightly later than the *Rāma Vatthu*, U Aung Pho ended his *Rama Thagyin* with the death of Rāvaṇa, allowing his audience to assume a happy reunion for the hero and heroine, without the distasteful suspicions of the purification by fire and Sītā's subsequent banishment and final disappearance, although these episodes do occur in works by later Myanmar authors (Thein Han 1973: 76-77). →

Vaiṣṇava tellings – Sītā allows herself to be persuaded to return to Rāma and the couple live in harmony for thousands of years and die of natural causes,[6] a conventionally sentimental happy ending more suited to the Buddhist ethos.

Whereas the virtues extolled in the early Sanskrit *Rāmāyaṇa* are those of the kṣatriyas, in the *Rāma Vatthu* more force is given to morality in general. The introduction of Buddhist values can be detected as early as the tenth-century Javanese *Rama Kakawin*, much of which closely follows or even translates Bhaṭṭi's Sanskrit *Rāvaṇavadha* (sixth to seventh century). Rāvaṇa reacts violently to Vibhīṣaṇa's good advice and kicks him. Bhaṭṭi's Vibhīṣaṇa mildly replies with more good advice before leaving court to defect to the enemy, but the Javanese text inserts a long sermon on the Buddhist virtue of forbearance, all the more pointed because this time Rāvaṇa has kicked his brother on the head; but Vibhīṣaṇa still defects.[7]

In the *Rāma Vatthu*, characters are repeatedly said to observe and preach specifically Buddhist codes of conduct;[8] distasteful

→ The purification by fire has been completely eliminated from Lao versions B and C in favour of an immediate happy reunion between Rāma and Sītā (Vo 1971: 58, 81).

6 *VRm* 7.100 and 7.88; Ohno 1999: 176-77; also Lao versions A, B and D and presumably C (Lafont 2003: Phuk 10; Sahai 1976: 74; Vo 1971: 60, 83).

7 *VRm* 6.10; Santoso 1980: 14.60-70; Fallon 2009: 295-97. Much later, Mādhava Kandalī's Assamese Vibhīṣaṇa is sustained during similar provocation by his adherence to *dharma* (Nagar 2000: II, 57).

Rāvaṇa also kicks Vibhīṣaṇa on the head in the *Rāma Vatthu*, but there is little evidence of "forbearance" in the angry words with which Vibhīṣaṇa leaves (Ohno 1999: 147).

8 Daśaratha's admonition to Rāma (Ohno 1999: 96-97) would have been thought unnecessary in the Sanskrit original.

episodes such as the bereaved blind ascetic's curse on Daśaratha,[9] the mutilation of Śūrpaṇakhā,[10] repeated examples of Rāvaṇa's lust and generally immoral behaviour,[11] and the possibility of incest,[12] are minimized or eliminated; and there is less killing, of men or animals.[13]

---

[9] *VRm* 2.58.43-47; Ohno 1999: 78-82, 105. For a detailed examination of this episode in Rāma and *jātaka* tradition see Mary Brockington 2010.

[10] *VRm* 3.17.18-24. In the *Rāma Vatthu*, in Lao version A and in the *Lanka Xihe* from Yunnan she is not lustful and so she is not mutilated, and Rāma and Lakṣmaṇa are not guilty of cruel joking; her resentment is fuelled by grief at the death of her sons (Ohno 1999: 118; Lafont 2003: Phuk 6; Ohno 1999: 37; see also *Rama Thagyin*, Thein Han 1973: 74). In Lao versions B and D the abduction takes place immediately after the wedding, eliminating the court intrigues, the mutilation and the consequent slaughter (Vo 1971: 34; Sahai 1976: 44), although all are retained in Lao version C (Vo 1971: 79).

[11] The numerous concubines in Rāvaṇa's harem have been respectably married to him, not abducted as they are in *VRm* 7.24.1-17; and the order to execute Hanumān is excused on the grounds that he is a mere robber, not an official envoy (*VRm* 5.49-50; Ohno 1999: 74, 137).

[12] For details see below.

[13] Few of the *VRm* duels in the battle for Laṅkā are replicated (Ohno 1999: 143-57; *Rama Thagyin*, Thein Han 1973: 75). Sugrīva chooses to fight Vālin personally in single combat rather than raise an army to wage war against his brother to avoid the loss of innocent life (Ohno 1999: 122).

In the *VRm* the sage Viśvāmitra's sacrifices are polluted by attacks from the *rākṣasas* Mārīca and Subāhu and their companions; Rāma and Lakṣmaṇa kill all but Mārīca (who survives to become the decoy golden deer). In the *Rāma Vatthu* no rituals are mentioned, and the sage is pestered by a crow and wishes to be rid of it without killing it, so Rāma merely blinds the repentant crow in one eye, as in the Vālmīki episode with which it has been conflated (Ohno 1999: 86-89; see also *Rama Thagyin*, Thein Han 1973: 74; *VRm* 1.18 and 29;

→

The rituals that play a significant role in the Indian *Rāmāyaṇas* were, where possible, eliminated in line with Buddhist sensibilities. In most Indian tellings, from about the first century CE onwards, a horse-sacrifice brings about the birth of Rāma and his brothers to their childless parents by means of the *pāyasa* given to their mothers. In the *Rāma Vatthu* there is no sacrifice, and the boys are born when the queens are given bananas by a sage.[14] This episode, tenuously and illogically, mitigates the horror of the curse imposed on the king for accidentally killing a hermit.[15] The motif of birth to a childless couple procured by fruit (in India often a mango) had become internationally widespread. A variant is used again by the same teller to explain the birth of Rāvaṇa and his brothers to a pious virgin ascetic

---

→ 5.36.12-33); in Lao version A even the blinding is eliminated, and Rāma frightens the crows into submission by twanging his bowstring (Lafont 2003: Phuk 3).

14 *VRm* 1.11-15; Ohno 1999: 81-84; also *Rama Thagyin*, Thein Han 1973: 73-74. Lao versions A, B, C and D all omit any mention of a birth sacrifice (Lafont 2003: Phuk 3; Vo 1971: 23 and 78; Sahai 1976: 36).

In a fusion of the two approaches, later in *Rāma Vatthu* the childless Janaka intends to perform a birth sacrifice for a son; instead, the sages he has commissioned find him a daughter, Sītā, by pseudo-natural means (Ohno 1999: 85; see n. 30 below). Similarly, in Lao version B Rāvaṇa's invulnerability results from a prediction, not from his own *tapas* (Vo 1971: 22).

15 *VRm* 2.58.43-47. In the *Rāma Vatthu* and Lao version A Daśaratha's fate is merely a prediction, not a specific curse (Ohno 1999: 80; Lafont 2003: 51); in the *Rāma Vatthu*, as in Kālidāsa's Sanskrit *Raghuvaṁśa* 9.80, the childless Daśaratha welcomes the prediction that he will at last have a son.

In the *Lanka Xihe* from Yunnan the whole point of the original episode is lost. Daśaratha is not cursed, but nurses the hermit boy back to health, and it is the boy who advises Daśaratha how to obtain sons (Ohno 1999: 35).

woman and a god.[16] Such an auspicious origin for the villain is not found in their source, which concentrates on Rāvaṇa's might, but the Buddhist versions tend towards morality tales, with an originally virtuous Rāvaṇa corrupted because he neglects the Precepts of Conduct, and then leads his subordinates astray by his bad example.[17] At the last moment he repents, recognizing Rāma as a *bodhisattva*, and begs forgiveness, but it is too late and Rāma kills him.[18] The plot-line is paramount.

Another horse-sacrifice plays an important part at the end of the Sanskrit text, leading to the discovery of Rāma's long-lost sons Kuśa and Lava.[19] Many of the later tellers, both within and outside India, elaborate this episode into a violent encounter with the boys during the horse's preliminary wanderings and lose sight of the animal's eventual slaughter; perhaps this is why

---

[16] She presents the god with mangoes, and he makes her pregnant by stroking her stomach (Ohno 1999: 20, 69-70; cf. *Rama Thagyin*, Thein Han 1973: 73). This motif is also found in *Lanka Xihe* from Yunnan and Lao version A (Ohno 1999: 34; Lafont 2003: Phuk 1); cf. *VRm* 7.9.

The stomach-stroking motif is used by narrators of other Buddhist tales including the *Sāmajātaka* (Shaw 2006: 286), when the story-line demands an ascetic woman must bear a child without infringing a vow of celibacy, and awkwardly adapted in the *Mahābhārata* to preserve the unmarried Kuntī's virginity when she conceives Karṇa (3.291.23).

[17] Ohno 1999: 75.

[18] Ohno 1999: 157; see also *Rama Thagyin*, Thein Han 1973: 75-76.

In a number of Indian Vaiṣṇava texts, Rāvaṇa and others go to heaven or achieve *mokṣa* by being killed by Rāma; see for example Vālin and Rāvaṇa in the Kāśmīrī version of Prakāśa Rāma (Nagar 2001: 45 and 87), and Mārīca in the Assamese version of Mādhava Kandalī (Nagar 2000: I, 220). Mārīca's happiness to be killed by Rāma and be reborn as a god also appears in Tibetan Buddhist tradition (de Jong 1989: 23-24).

[19] *VRm* 7.82-86.

the Myanmar teller felt able to retain this form of the recognition scene in *Rāma Vatthu*.[20]

Muslim Versions: Hikayat Seri Rama (Malay), Maharadia Lawana (Philippine)

The Malay *Hikayat Seri Rama* (a vast, sprawling compilation popular in much of Indonesia as well as the present Malaysian peninsula) and *Maharadia Lawana*, a briefer, more unified version recorded in the Philippines, at the furthest extent of the area, whose teller often replaces earlier elements with international motifs and shows no interest in moral issues, both demonstrate that the Muslim elements found in the extant manuscripts are little more than a veneer over an already-established core. Whatever additions are made, the fundamental narrative remains the same.

The Malay version must have been Islamicized much later than the corresponding Buddhist transformation of the Sanskrit *Rāmāyaṇa*.[21] It is not clear just what was the nature of the tradition underlying the Islamicization process,[22] but one late

---

20 Ohno 1999: 168-71; in Lao version C the horse is explicitly sacrificial, but intra-family killing is avoided (Vo 1971: 82).

In Lao version A the boys kill their father (Rāma is subsequently revived) after encountering a wandering horse, but it is not part of a sacrifice (Lafont 2003: Phuk 10). Other Buddhist tellers remodel the episode to lessen the violence; in Lao versions B and D no sacrificial horse is involved (Vo 1971: 60; Sahai 1976: 69-71). The Yunnan *Lanka Xihe* presents a fusion of the Lao A and B episodes (Ohno 1999: 42).

21 "The bulk of the material in the Malay saga reached the Malay world between the thirteenth and the seventeenth centuries" (Barrett 1963: 543); the earliest known manuscript (itself a late recension) was in existence in 1612 (Saran and Khanna 2004: 150, n. 5).

22 References to Rāma's identity with Viṣṇu imply a Hinduized substrate but details suggest a certain amount of influence from Buddhist sources; one example is that in one manuscript, although Rāvaṇa himself is born naturally, he sends his parents flowers from →

copyist specifically recorded his intention of exercizing from his *Hikayat* text "All that is not good";[23] his attempts were only partially successful. Islam has no analogue to the *avatāra* or the *bodhisattva* systems; accordingly neither in the *Hikayat* nor in *Maharadia Lawana*, are the heroes identified as divine; heavenly figures are given appropriate new identities as Allah, Nabi Adam and the angel Gabriel, but traces of Rāma's identity with Viṣṇu and other examples of reincarnation remain.[24] Popular narrative features are remodelled to correspond: the ritual performed by the sage to produce Daśaratha's children is retained and even elaborated, but there is no reference to the slaughter of a horse or the intervention of a deity;[25] Sītā's demonstration of purity by fire is retained, but without divine intervention;[26] and the fight that leads to Kuśa and Lava being recognized takes place during a hunt rather than a horse sacrifice;[27] all three episodes are absent from *Maharadia Lawana*.

Sītā's parentage raises difficult moral questions. In the

→ which are born Śūrpaṇakhā, Kumbhakarṇa and Vibhīṣaṇa (Barrett 1963: 540; cf. p. 34, n. 3 in this article).

[23] It is interesting to note that Indian Muslims have not always shared these inhibitions; Mughal patrons were prepared to commission beautiful paintings and translations of the Sanskrit text as prized possessions; see also Narayanan 2001 and Richman 2008: 193-20 for south Indian Muslims' sometimes ambivalent appropriation of the Rāmāyaṇa tradition.

[24] For the growing impact of Islamization, see Saran and Khanna 2004: 136 and Barrett 1963, esp. pp. 532 and 543.

[25] *VRm* 1.11-15. Nevertheless, Daśaratha is advised by another sage to supplement that ritual with the slaughter of 1,000 elephants (Zieseniss 1928: 10); significantly, the episode is missing from the later of the two sources analysed there.

[26] *VRm* 6.104-6; Saran and Khanna 2004: 222.

[27] Saran and Khanna 2004: 223; see above, n. 19.

earliest version of the Sanskrit *Rāmāyaṇa* she is born naturally to Janaka and his wife; at a later stage her origin is a mystery, and she is regarded as the daughter of Earth.[28] In the earliest Buddhist version, the Pāli *Dasarathajātaka* from Sri Lanka, she is full sister of Rāma but also his wife; neither Janaka nor Rāvaṇa appears in this version.[29] Texts from Tibet and Mongolia belonging to the differing Mahāyāna tradition make her unambiguously the daughter of Rāvaṇa and his wife, using the widespread narrative motif of the child destined to bring about the death of its father, but do not address the moral implications of Rāvaṇa's lust for her;[30] the Myanmar *Rāma Vatthu* avoids the imputation of incest implicit in both situations, and makes her the reincarnation of a *gandharvī* outraged by Rāvaṇa, found at birth by Rāvaṇa who has her cast into the water, which leads to her being found and reared by Janaka.[31] If the Muslim redactors of the Malay tradition

[28] Sītā is Janaka's birth daughter at *VRm* 2.82.11; 5.11.16 and 5.19.4. He is said to have found her in a furrow at 1.65.14-16 and 2.110.26-30; cf. 7.88.

[29] *Dasarathajātaka*: Cowell IV (1901): 78-82, tr. W.H.D. Rouse, studied in Mary Brockington 2002: 139-41.

[30] Tibetan: de Jong 1989: 16; 1993: li; liii; Mongolian: de Jong 1993: xliv. Sītā is also Rāvaṇa's daughter in Lao version D (Sahai 1976: 37).

Lao version C appears to tolerate the possibility of brother/half-sister marriage: Sītā is the daughter of Daśaratha and a 4th wife, expelled from Ayodhyā at birth as result of a gloomy prediction by astrologers, thrown into the sea and adopted by a hermit (Vo 1971: 79). Version B removes the relationship one generation by making Sītā Rāma's niece, daughter of Rāvaṇa and Rāma's sister, his wife (Vo 1971: 28).

The idea that Sītā is the daughter of Rāvaṇa and his wife Mandodarī is widespread in Indian tradition too.

[31] Ohno 1999: 75-76, 84-85; this conflation of the Vedavatī and Rambhā episodes (*VRm* 7.17 and 7.26.9-47) with her birth in many later vernacular texts as Mandodarī's daughter is also found in →

recorded in *Hikayat Seri Rama* found the representation of incest, real or potential, distasteful, they did not feel able to eliminate it, and developed an even more complicated and fantastic threefold paternity-line: Rāma is the son of Daśaratha and Mandodarī (usually Rāvaṇa's wife), and Sītā is the daughter of Daśaratha and a replica Mandodarī (so half-sister to Rāma) but is thought to be the daughter of Rāvaṇa and so is cast out to be found and reared by Janaka.[32]

This acceptance of fantasy is not complete; some magic elements are rationalized or explained, although not necessarily eliminated.[33] One example is that while in the Sanskrit text Rāvaṇa seeks to persuade the captive Sītā that Rāma is dead and undermine her resistance by presenting her with an illusory head of Rāma, produced by magic, in the *Hikayat* he shows her two real heads, pretending that they are those of Rāma and his brother.[34] The *Maharadia Lawana* narrative reflects an even greater tension between domestication and extreme fantasy.[35] The bow contest is now replaced by two suitor tests: to kick a

---

→ the Myanmar *Rama Thagyin*, Yunnan *Lanka Xihe* and Lao version A (Thein Han 1973: 73; Ohno 1999: 35-36; Lafont 2003: Phuk 3).

32 Saran and Khanna 2004: 218; Zieseniss 1928: 11-13. For a similar motif in the Thai *Ramakien*, see n. 37 below.

33 There is also a noticeable tendency towards rationalization in the Indian Jain tellings (John Brockington 1985: 266-69).

34 *VRm* 6.22-23; Saran and Khanna 2004: 221. A certain amount of fantasy is retained in a parallel episode in the Thai *Ramakien*: Indrajit transforms a *rākṣasa* awaiting execution for cowardice into an illusory Sītā, decapitates him/her and sends the head to Rāma (Olsson 1968: 227-29); cf. *VRm* 6.68.

35 The extant version dates from the mid-seventeenth to early nineteenth centuries, according to Juan R. Francisco (1980: 175). The setting envisaged is an island community, and Rāvaṇa's crimes are little more than inciting mischief by spreading gossip.

football, and to kill a monster; heroes, heroine and villain are apparently all conceived by natural means, but Hanumān is born as the son of Rāma – but not Sītā – in an impossible time frame, without sex or – specifically – adultery (he is conceived as the result of a particularly painful dream).[36]

Issues of Sovereignty: Ramakien (Thai)

The Thai *Ramakien* is neither Hindu nor Buddhist, but a non-devotional, secular narrative, although Buddhist sensibilities are not ignored. The Rāma story is presented to Buddhists in other forms: in Buddhist rituals and painted on Buddhist temple walls in Bangkok.[37] Similarly a modern Thai-inspired set of paintings in the Buddhist temple of Wat Bo at Siem Reap, Cambodia, portray the life of Rāma. In the written text the position found in the *Rāma Vatthu* is reversed; Rāma is not a *bodhisattva* but an incarnation of Viṣṇu, and he is fully conscious of his identity throughout.

The relative status of Śiva and Viṣṇu is ambivalent. Śiva scarcely figured in the earliest Sanskrit *Rāmāyaṇa*, but was given an increasing role in later Śaiva adaptations. Non-Hindu versions left sectarian rivalry behind in favour of narrative development. Some of Śiva's prominence in these versions is an accident of plot: while Viṣṇu is on earth fulfilling his duty as an *avatāra*, Śiva necessarily appears as the authority figure in heaven, as he does in most of the *Ramakien*. At the end he uses this authority to bring about the reconciliation betweeen Rāma and Sītā that is introduced into several South-East Asian versions, not just as a

---

[36] Francisco 1994: 155-57. Hanumān is the son of Rāma (and sometimes of Sītā) following a complicated series of transformations in Lao versions B and C, and in two differing forms in the *Hikayat Seri Rama* (Vo 1971: 36; 78; Zieseniss 1928: 20-21; Saran and Khanna 2004: 150 n. 9, 219).

[37] Reynolds 1991: 55-59.

romantic happy ending, but in order that as Viṣṇu and Śrī they may later resume their proper function in heaven as a united, divine couple.[38] The exception to the portrayal of Śiva as pre-eminent is an episode that takes place before the incarnation, when Mt. Kailāsa, his home, is knocked askew by an enemy and only Rāvaṇa is strong enough to straighten it; the cunning demon tricks the gullible supreme god into giving him his wife Umā as a reward, and it is the intervention of the even more cunning Viṣṇu that induces Rāvaṇa to return Umā and accept a less dangerous reward.[39]

The text now standard was composed, or commissioned, by King Phutthayotfa Chulalok, who took the title Rāma I (1737–1809),[40] but the basic subject matter was certainly not new to Thailand: at least four centuries before, all written versions were lost when the older capital Ayuthaya was destroyed by the Burmese in 1767 (Ayuthaya, of course, was named after Ayodhyā, so much had the narrative become indigenized). The newly-established Thai rulers had a pressing need to demonstrate the legitimacy and power of their rule, and made use of the surviving oral sentiment to bolster their position, even calling themselves "Rāma", a process that helps to explain some of *Ramakien*'s more striking features.

---

[38] The Thai version of Sītā's parentage, in which Kakanasun steals rice from Daśaratha's *yajña* and gives it to Mandodarī, again presents the idea that Sītā is both Rāma's sister and Rāvaṇa's daughter (Olsson 1968: 65-68); the doubly incestuous implications are evidently less important than the need to present Sītā as an incarnation of Śrī.

[39] Olsson 1968: 38-40.

[40] This version was completed in 1797, but his predecessor, King Taksin of Thonburi, was responsible for the earliest known written rendering (*c.* 1775).

The text they commissioned was sometimes romantic,[41] robust in its attitude,[42] and often rather racy,[43] with elaborate innovations, and without the Muslim and Jain tendency to rationalize but rather with a greater emphasis on the fantastic. Accounts of sacrifices are not eliminated but minimized: the birth ritual is retained (without mentioning the slaughter of a horse); a horse is involved in the recognition of Kuśa and Lava, but any sacrificial context is only implicit.[44] The exiles' long journey in the forest conversing with sages is truncated in favour of military exploits, so the abduction takes place early in the exile and Sītā spends almost fourteen years in captivity (making more credible Rāma's harsh suspicions of her fidelity).[45] The non-devotional context made it possible to develop the conflict between the harsh, even savage, Rāma and the assertive, resentful Sītā after their return from killing Rāvaṇa;[46] both give

---

[41] Rāma and Sītā's eyes meet accidentally before the suitor test and they both fall in love; their wedding night is described in detail, but with delicate sensuality (Olsson 1968: 81-82).

[42] For instance, Śūrpaṇakhā is mutilated (Olsson 1968: 103-04).

[43] Hanumān, for instance, makes love to at least six females, including Rāvaṇa's wife (Olsson 1968: 136-37, 161-64, 168-69, 281-88, 298-99). The son born to him by the Queen of the Fish results from one of these casual sexual encounters, rather than a drop of his sweat as in Prakāśa Rāma's Kāśmīrī narrative and in Lao version D (Nagar 2001: 82; Sahai 1976: 60-61). Another conquest, Benjakai, remains faithful to him throughout, aiding him in later episodes, and is eventually given to him as his wife as a reward for his service (Olsson 1968: 254, 331-32).

[44] Olsson 1968: 62, 389-98.

[45] *VRm* 6.103; Olsson 1968: 310.

[46] Rāma is a harsh and impetuous ruler, quick to order executions: of Hanumān and another *vānara* (later reprieved) for squabbling at the building of the causeway, of Sītā for her supposed infidelity, and of his unrecognized ten-year-old son for attacking Hanumān →

way to intensely human passions far removed from the gentle other-worldliness of their Sanskrit originals.

The chief feature, however, is the considerable dynastic emphasis, with a seemingly endless series of fights as new allies unknown to the Sanskrit *Rāmāyaṇa* perform their duty of aiding or avenging Rāvaṇa, carrying on the conflict in ever more fantastic but repetitive ways into the next generation. In many texts Rāma's sons are recognized when they show themselves capable of killing the otherwise invincible Hanumān, Rāma's brothers, and even Rāma himself (all the casualties are soon brought back to life). It can be no accident that this episode appears in the Thai text without the death of the king, however temporary.[47] The morality propagated in this narrative is that of fidelity to the king.[48]

→ (Olsson 1968: 166-67, 378, 392-95). Sītā, who has learned to value her independence during her exile, furious at being tricked into returning to Ayodhyā, is vehement in her refusal to be reconciled after what she considers to have been a legal divorce (Olsson 1968: 404-05).

47 Olsson 1968: 396-98. For this episode in the *Rāma Vatthu*, see above, p. 40.

48 A similar tactic was employed by those regimes (also newly established), who much earlier commissioned the Śaiva temple at Prambanan in Java (*c.* CE 850) and the Khmer Angkor Wat (the state temple of Sūryavarman II, 1113-*c.* 1150). It is no accident that the role of Vibhīṣaṇa (who defects to the enemy and eventually replaces Rāvaṇa as king) is minimized, and the death of Rāvaṇa (a king, even if he was wicked) avoided as far as possible in these visual texts, while the loyal devotion of sons, brothers, courtiers and allies who sacrifice their lives gloriously for their monarch – right or wrong – is celebrated. The frieze demonstrating significant events in the reigns of previous monarchs commissioned by a new king of a different line at the Vaikuṇṭha Perumāl Temple in Kāñcī (late eighth century CE) is another testimony to the need to create →

Conclusion

The Myanmar, Malay, Philippine and Thai versions are not Hindu tales; nor are the Jain versions, any more than the Śaiva versions are Vaiṣṇava. The *Rāma Vatthu* is aimed at a Buddhist audience, the *Hikayat Seri Rama* and *Maharadia Lawana* have an Islamic overlay, and the *Ramakien* is an action-packed thriller with a relaxed view of moral conventions, portraying an authoritarian king as its hero, composed by a Buddhist for a Buddhist audience but dominated by issues of sovereignty. Why did generations of tellers of so many different religious persuasions choose to translate or adapt this Vaiṣṇava Hindu text – a text so unacceptable that they had to introduce repeated modifications to make it suit their purpose or culture? Basically, it is because the narrative is paramount. Throughout the journey from the Gaṅgā basin to the Philippines, despite all the additions and religious and cultural constraints, the narrative has been felt to be so important that the main plotline and fundamental details such as the golden deer could not be discarded.

The attraction of a good story, well told, cannot be overestimated.

Sanskrit proper names with vernacular variants of main corresponding characters

VRm	*South-East Asian variants*
Rāma	Phra Lam; Lamma; Langma; Mangandiri
Sītā	Sida; Sinta; Xila; Malano Tihaia/Malaila Ganding
Janaka	Kannaka; Chanok; Maharisi Kali; Kassahpahrahsi
Kuśa and Lava	Kusi and Tilawi/Tabalawi; Kusa and Lona; Sengvath and Loma; Mongkut and Lop; Put and Rup; Bout and

→ an auspicious symbol of the enduring political power aspired to by newly-established warrior monarchs.

	Houp
Daśaratha	Dasaratta; Thataratha; Tadalata; Totsarot
Viṣṇu	Mahabisnu; Narai
Śiva	Betara Guru; Isuan; Isur
Kailāsa	Krailat
Viśvāmitra	Bisvamitr; Swamit; Kotampa; Bodaw
Sugrīva	Sugrit; Sukreep/Paya Waiyawongsa; Thugyeik; Kaling Phalichanh
Vālin	Bali; Balia; Pali; Galin; Kakat; Thirat; Sangkhip; Parimok
Hanumān	Anumone; Anuchit; Houlaman; Hvolahman; Laksamana
Rāvaṇa	Lawana; Rab; Rabahnasvn; Dasagiri; Totsakan; Phommachak; Pengmajia
Mandodarī	Mandudaki; Mantaly; Monto; Chantha/Soudtho
Vibhīṣaṇa	Bhibhisana; Bibusanam; Bibhek; Pipek; Phik Phi; Piyasha; Totsa Kiree Wong
Śūrpaṇakhā	Samanakha; Surapandiki; Dalihada; Trighata; Tharikhata; Gambi
Indrajit	Inderajata; Indacitta; Intorachit; Yindaxida; Ronapak
Laṅkā	Theinko

Bibliography

TEXTS, TRANSLATIONS AND SUMMARIES

Barrett, E.C.G., 1963, "Further Light on Sir Richard Winstedt's 'Undescribed Malay Version of the Ramayana'", *Bulletin of the School of Oriental and African Studies*, **26**: 531-43.

Brockington, John and Mary Brockington (tr.), 2006, *Rāma the Steadfast: An Early Form of the Rāmāyaṇa*, London: Penguin Books.

Cowell, E.B. et al., 1895-1907, *The Jātaka or Stories of the Buddha's former births*, 6 vols., Cambridge: Cambridge University Press [repr. 1995,

3 vols., Oxford: Pali Text Society].

Fallon, Oliver (tr.), 2009, *Bhatti's Poem: The Death of Rávana*, New York: New York University Press and JJC Foundation.

Francisco, Juan R., 1994, "From Ayodhya to Pulu Agamaniog: Rama's Journey to the Philippines", Quezon City: Asian Center, University of the Philippines [reprinted without the notes from: "Maharadia Lawana", *Asian Studies* (University of the Philippines, Quezon city) 7(2), August 1969: 186-249].

Goldman, Robert P. et al. (tr.), 1984-, *The Rāmāyaṇa of Vālmīki: An Epic of Ancient India*, 7 vols., Princeton Library of Asian Translations, Princeton: Princeton University Press.

de Jong, J.W. (ed. and tr.), 1989, *The Story of Rāma in Tibet: Text and Translation of the Tun-huang Manuscripts*, Tibetan and Indo-Tibetan Studies 1, Stuttgart: Franz Steiner.

——, 1993, "The Story of Rama in Tibet", in *A Critical Inventory of Ramayana Studies in the World*, ed. K. Krishnamoorthy, Satkari Mukhopadhyaya and S. Jithendra Nath, II, pp. xxxviii-lvii, New Delhi: Sahitya Akademi [article previously published in Asian Variations in Ramayana: Papers presented at the International Seminar on 'Variations in Ramayana in Asia: Their Cultural, Social and Anthropological Significance', New Delhi, January 1981, ed. K.R. Srinivasa Iyengar, pp. 163-82, New Delhi: Sahitya Akademi, 1983].

Lafont, Pierre-Bernard (tr.), 2003, *Phommachak: Rāmāyana tay lōe de Muang Sing (Haut Mékong)*, présentation et traduction du tay lōe par Pierre-Bernard Lafont, Paris: Centre 'Histoire et Civilisations de la Péninsule Indochinoise [Lao version A (Muongsing)].

Mahābhārata (tr.), 1973-, *The Mahābhārata*, tr. J.A.B. van Buitenen, James L. Fitzgerald et al., Chicago: Chicago University Press., II, 1975. The Book of the Assembly Hall, 2 and The Book of the Forest, 3: tr. J.A.B. van Buitenen.

Nagar, Shanti Lal (tr.), 2000, *Mādhava Kandalī Rāmāyaṇa, composed in Assamese*, 2 vols., I, pp. 110-11, 207. Rāmāyaṇa in Regional Languages 1. New Delhi: Munshiram Manoharlal.

—— (tr.), 2001, *Rāmāvatāracarita, composed in Kashmiri by Śrī Prakāśa Rāma Kuryagrāmī*, Rāmāyaṇa in Regional Languages Series 2, New Delhi: Munshiram Manoharlal.

Ohno, Toru (tr.), 1999, *A Study of Burmese Rama Story with an English*

Translation, Osaka: University of Foreign Studies.

Olsson, Ray A. (tr.), 1968, *The Ramakien: A Prose Translation of the Thai Ramayana*, Bangkok: Praepittaya.

Pou, Saveros (tr.), 2007, *Rāmakerti I "La Gloire de Rāma": Drame épique médieval du Cambodge*, tr. Saveros Pou and Grégory Mikaelian, Paris: L'Harmattan.

Sahai, Sachchidanand (tr.), 1976, *Rāmāyaṇa in Laos: A Study in the Gvāy dvórahbī*, foreword by Suniti Kumar Chatterji, New Delhi: D.K. Publishers [Lao version D], re-issued 2004 as Lao *Rāmāyaṇa*: Gvāy dvóraḥbī, rendering into English from 'Lāv' language: a comparative study, Delhi: B.R. Publishing Corporation.

Santoso, Soewito (ed. and tr.), 1980, *Ramayana Kakawin*, 3 vols., Śata-piṭaka Series, Indo-Asian Literatures 251, New Delhi: Sharada Rani.

Saran, Malini and Vinod C. Khanna, 2004, *The Ramayana in Indonesia*, New Delhi: Ravi Dayal.

Shaw, Sarah (tr.), 2006, "The Story of Sāma: Sāma Jātaka (540)", in *The Jātakas: Birth Stories of the Bodhisatta*, pp. 274-310, New Delhi: Penguin India.

Thein Han, U., 1973, "The Ramayana in Burma", *Studies in Indo-Asian Art and Culture*, **2**: 71-83.

Vālmīki *Rāmāyaṇa* (*VRm*), 1960-75, *The Rāmāyaṇa of Vālmīki*, crit. edn. by G.H. Bhatt and U.P. Shah, 7 vols., Baroda: Oriental Institute.

Vo, Thu Tịnh, 1971, "Phra Lak — Phra Lam, version lao du Ramayana indien et les fresques murales du Vat Oup Moung, Vientiane, par Vo Ṭhu Tinh, clichés de Raymond Guerin", *Bulletin des Amis du Royaume Lao*, **6**: 1-94. [Lao versions B (Vientiane) and C (Luang Prabang)] reprinted as Phra Lak Phra Lam: le Ramayana Lao, Collection Littérature Lao 1 Vientiane: Vithagna, 1972; 3rd edn., 1985, Paris: Sudestasie.

Zieseniss, A., 1928, *Die Rāma-Sage bei den Malaien*, Hamburg: Friederichsen and de Gruyter, Eng. tr. 1963, Burch, P.W. (tr.), *The Rama Saga in Malaysia*, Singapore: Malaysian Sociological Research Institute.

STUDIES

Brockington, John, 1985, *Righteous Rāma: The Evolution of an Epic*, Delhi: Oxford University Press.

Brockington, Mary, 2002, "'Once upon a time . . .': the *Rāmāyaṇa* in Traditional Tales", in *Indian Epic Traditions: Past and Present*, Papers presented at the 16th European Conference on Modern South Asian Studies, Edinburgh, 5-9 September 2000, ed. Danuta Stasik and John Brockington, pp. 133-58, *Rocznik Orientalistyczny* 54.1.

——, 2010, "Daśaratha, Śyāma, a brāhman hunter, and Śrāvaṇa: the tale of four tales (with pictures)", in *From Turfan to Ajanta: Festschrift for Dieter Schlingloff on the Occasion of His Eightieth Birthday*, ed. Eli Franco and Monika Zin, pp. 89-116, Rupandehi (Nepal): Lumbini International Research Institute.

Francisco, Juan R., 1980, "The Ramayana in the Philippines", in *The Ramayana Tradition in Asia*, Papers presented at the International Seminar on The Ramayana Tradition in Asia, New Delhi, December 1975, ed. Venkatarama Raghavan, pp. 155-77, New Delhi: Sahitya Akademi.

Narayanan, Vasudha, 2001, "The Ramayana and Its Muslim Interpreters", in *Questioning Rāmāyaṇas: a South Asian Tradition*, ed. Paula Richman, pp. 265-81, New Delhi: Oxford University Press.

Reynolds, Frank E., 1991, "*Rāmāyaṇa*, *Rāma Jātaka*, and *Ramakien*: A Comparative Study of Hindu and Buddhist Traditions", in *Many Rāmāyaṇas: The Diversity of a Narrative Tradition in South Asia*, ed. Paula Richman, pp. 50-63, Berkeley: University of California Press.

Richman, Paula (comp. and ed.), 2008, *Ramayana Stories in Modern South India*, Bloomington: Indiana University Press.

4

The Sanskrit Phonetic Tradition and Western Phonetics

Hans Henrich Hock

Introduction

THE impact of the knowledge of Sanskrit and its grammatical tradition on Western linguistics is well known and is dealt with in virtually all books on the history of linguistics (e.g. Morpurgo Davies 1992; Robins 1997). What has received less coverage, and especially less DETAILED coverage, is the influence of the Sanskrit phonetic tradition on Western phonetics. The most comprehensive discussion so far is that of Allen (1953).

The goal of this paper is to provide a more detailed discussion, focusing both on the positive contributions of the Sanskrit tradition and the more problematic ones, as well as the way in which a slow merger of the Sanskrit tradition and earlier Western approaches led to the field of articulatory phonetics as we now know it.

The rest of the paper is organized in five major parts. Part one deals with the issue of voicing and aspiration, an area where the Sanskrit tradition has made the greatest and most positive contributions. Part two is devoted to the classification and phonetic identification of consonants. Part three takes up the issue of vowel classification and the development of a "glottal" or resonance-based theory. Part four discusses later developments reflecting the influence of the grammatical tradition. Part five presents a summary and conclusions.

1. Voicing and Aspiration

The Western tradition, going back in large measure to Dionysius Thrax (second-first century BCE), managed to make a systematic distinction between voiced and voiceless stops and, for Greek, voiceless aspirates, by providing labels to differentiate the consonants as classes; see [1]. The terminology used, however, is generally acknowledged to lack phonetic sophistication (see the discussion and references in Allen 1953: 36-37). Two of the Greek terms make at least some impressionistic or auditory sense – *psilón*, lit. "bare, smooth", for the voiceless stops, and *daséon*, lit. "thick, shaggy, rough", for the voiceless aspirates, but the third term – *méson*, lit. "middling" – does not, nor does Dionysius Thrax's further explanation of the term provide any help, namely that it is "more *daséon* than *psilón* and more *psilón* than *daséon*'.[1]

[1] Toútōn psíla mèn tría, κ, π, τ, daséa dè tría, θ, φ, χ, mésa dè tría, β, γ, δ.[2] Mésa dè eírētai, hóti tôn mèn psilôn estì dasútera, tôn dè daséōn psilótera (Dionysius Thrax, ed. Uhlig 1883: 12-13)

---

1 The only way the term *méson* and the explanation "more *daséon* than *psilón* and more *psilón* than *daséon*" could be made sense of is if the voicing "buzz" associated with voiced elements was considered to be comparable to the "rough" character of aspiration, so that voiced stops could be considered to have some degree of "roughness", but not the same degree as the voiceless aspirates; but no such explanation is traditionally provided. Moreover, note that such an interpretation would conflict with the more recent Western impressionistic label "soft" to refer to voiced consonants.

2 Allen (1953: 36) reverses the order of the "middling" stops, placing δ before γ.

> Of these, there are three smooth consonants – *k, p, t*, three rough – *th, ph, kh*, three middling – *b, g, d*. They are called middling because they are rougher than the smooth ones, and smoother than the rough ones.

The terminology did not improve when transferred to Latin, as *tenuis, aspirata*, and *media*; in fact the term *tenuis*, lit. "thin, stretched", fails to capture the impressionistic appropriateness of the Greek *psilón*. Moreover, since Latin does not have a native category of voiceless aspirates, the term *aspirata* came to be used even for spirants, a usage that persisted to the time of Grimm (see e.g. Grimm 1822: 12; Gabelentz and Loebe 1848: 38; see Allen 1953: 36-37 for general discussion).

The Latin terminology persisted into the early modern period. But at that time, it coexisted with other, merely impressionistic labels, which lack any discernible phonetic substance. In central and northern Europe, the prevailing terms were Germ. *hart* (Danish *haard*) "hard" for voiceless and *weich* (Dan. *blöd*) "soft" for voiced (see e.g. Rask 1818: 48; Kühner 1934: 19, who uses these terms beside the Greek and Latin ones).[3] Attempts at providing a phonetic account for the difference between voiced and voiceless are rare, and typically mistaken. For instance, Wallis (1653: 13) claims that in voiced stops, the breath is equally divided between the nose and the throat.[4] A

---

[3] In English writings, the terms *surd* and *sonant* are often used; but to judge by the entries in the *Oxford English Dictionary*, the use of both terms, in reference to voiceless and voiced, goes back to Max Müller (dated 1868). Earlier uses, of the eighteenth century, use *surd* without a contrasting *sonant*, in contexts such as *mute, surd*, or *vocal* (1767), where it is not at all clear that the word designates "voiceless" or has any clear phonetic basis. (The corresponding modern French terms are *sourd* and *sonore*, with presumably similar ancestry.)

[4] Si Spiritus, inter nares & fauces aequaliter divisus, occlusis Labiis →

major exception is Hart (1569) who, in addition to "hard" and "soft", uses the terms "breathed, unsounded" vs. "inward, sounded" to distinguish voiceless from voiced. Here the terms "unsounded" and "sounded" seem to be on the right phonetic track, but unfortunately, Hart's work made no impact on the development of Western phonetics.[5]

Here the Sanskrit tradition is clearly superior, recognizing that the glottis (*kaṇṭha*) is involved in the distinction between voiced and voiceless speech sounds, with opening for the voiceless and closing or narrowing (or "adduction") for the voiced. Consider, e.g. the passages in [2]/[3] and [4]/[5]. What is especially worthy of note is that *h*, i.e. voiced *h* [ɦ], as well as the *h*-like element of voiced aspiration, is defined as different from both voicing and voicelessness. See especially [4c], which characterizes the articulation of *h* as being intermediate between voicing and voicelessness; and while [2b] may not be as explicit, it says essentially the same thing. It is not clear whether this characterization was based on actual observation of the vocal folds in action, or whether it was informed by the auditory quality of voiced *h*. Referring to Westermann and Ward 1933: §250, Allen notes that the breathy voice characteristic of voiced *h* is in fact produced by the glottis being part open and part adducted. What is clear is that in this characterization the Sanskrit phoneticians were far ahead of European scholars. Consider in this context the incredulous, uninformed, and

→ intercipiatur; formatur consona B . . . (If the breath, equally divided between nose and throat, is interrupted by the closed lips, the consonant b is formed . . . .)

5 It is only in recent linguistic historiography that Hart's approach was rediscovered. The same appears to be true for Kempelen's clear understanding (1791) of the articulatory basis of voicing and voicelessness.

uncharitable remarks by Whitney (1862, 1868) reproduced in [6].

[2] a. *vāyuḥ prāṇaḥ koṣṭhyam anupradānaṁ kaṇṭhasya khe vivṛte saṁvṛte vā - āpadyate śvāsatāṁ nādatāṁ vā vaktrīhāyām* (ṚP 13.1-2)

Air, breath, emission from the chest in the opening of the throat results in voicelessness or voicedness during vocal activity depending on its being open or close [i.e. in close contact or adducted]

b. *ubhayaṁ vāntarobhau* (ṚP 13.3)

or (if the throat is) in between the two (i.e. open and adducted), (it results in a mixture of) both kinds.

[3] a. *śvāso 'ghoṣāṇām* (ṚP 13.4)

Breath (is the characteristic) of voiceless (consonants),

b. *itareṣāṁ tu nādaḥ* (ṚP 13.5)

but of other (consonants), voicing,

c. *soṣmoṣmaṇāṁ ghoṣiṇāṁ nādaśvāsau* (ṚP 13.6)

of *h* and the voiced aspirates, both voicing and voicelessness.

[4] a. *saṁvṛte kaṇṭhe nādaḥ kriyate*

Voice is produced with the glottis in close contact (TP 2.4)

b. *vivṛte śvāsaḥ*

Breath [= voicelessness] with (the glottis) open (TP 2.5)

c. *madhye hakāraḥ*

h in an intermediate position (TP 2.6; thus explained in the commentary).

[5] a. *nādo 'nupradānaṁ svaraghoṣavatsu*

Voice is the characteristic of vowels and voiced (consonants) (TP 2.8)

b. *hakāro hacaturṣu*

In *h* and the voiced aspirates it is *h* (as defined in 4c above) (TP 2.9)

c. *aghoṣeṣu śvāsaḥ*

In voiceless (consonants) it is breath (TP 2.10).

[6] a. I confess myself unable to derive any distinct idea from this description, knowing no intermediate utterance between breath

and sound, excepting the stridulous tone of the loud whisper, which I cannot bring into any connection with an *h* (Whitney 1862: 348).

b. That intonated and unintonated breath should be emitted from the same throat at once is physically impossible (Whitney 1868: 52).

Moreover, unlike the Romans and later Western scholars such as Grimm, the Sanskrit phoneticians clearly distinguished between spirants (*ūṣman*) and aspirates (*soṣman*). At the same time, they did not explicitly define or characterize the *ūṣman* that accompanies the aspirates. The definition of voiced aspirates in [5a] might suggest otherwise, but the element *h* that characterizes them clearly is not the same as the SPEECH SOUND *h*, which in fact is defined as having *h*, i.e. having voiced *h*-quality. Rather, it must designate a consonant FEATURE, on a par with the features of voicing and voicelessness. Notice in this regard that there is no corresponding definition of voiceless aspirates as having voiceless *h*-quality.[6] (This issue is discussed further in Part 3.)

---

[6] According to a minority position, some (*eke*) say that the aspiration of voiceless aspirates is a homorganic spirant (see [i] below); and Deshpande (1997: 110-11) seems to accept this as the earlier conceptualization of voiceless aspirates. The statement in [i] below, however, goes along with more general attempts at a featural analysis of the sounds of Sanskrit (see Part 3 for discussion), a fact which does not suggest great antiquity of the view expressed here. Moreover, while it is certainly conceivable that there was some articulatory and/or acoustic/auditory overlap between stop and aspiration, it is not likely that this was a widespread phenomenon. Otherwise one would expect widespread changes of the sort *ph* > *pφ*>*φ* or *f* in later Indo-Aryan. True, for the labial, such changes are found in some of modern Indo-Aryan, but they seem to be recent; and there is no evidence for the widespread occurrence of similar changes in the other stops. →

In the early nineteenth century the Sanskrit phonetic tradition became familiar to Western scholars, first through recasts of grammars such as the *Siddhāntakaumudī* (e.g. Colebrooke 1805, Carey 1806, Wilkins 1808) and only later through editions of original phonetic treatises (e.g. Weber 1858; Whitney 1862, 1868); see further in Part 4. It is from that point onward that Western publications begin to use calques of the Sanskrit terminology, even if at first still in competition with the classical European one. Thus, Bopp (1833) uses the Sanskrit classification in discussing Sanskrit phonetics (24), but continues to use the Latin terms for Greek and Latin (96) and varying between the two terminologies for Germanic (78 vs. 85-86). By the time of Schleicher, the Sanskrit-based classification becomes more generally accepted, not just for Sanskrit but for Indo-European linguistics, and even for Lithuanian (see e.g. Schleicher 1861: 8 as well as 1856). However, the classical Western terminology continues to be used by many linguists, even though those using it will be increasingly aware that *tenuis* "really" means voiceless, and *media* voiced.

Finally, it is worth mentioning that the Prātiśākhyas make a distinction between "voiced" as a phonetic feature (*nāda*) and "voiced" as a phonological one (*ghoṣin, ghoṣavat*). The former characterizes all voiced speech sounds, including the vowels, the latter applies only to the consonants, where the opposition voiced: voiceless is distinctive (at least in the stops). On this

---

→ [i] *āhur ghoṣaṁ ghoṣavatām akāram eke 'nusvāram anunāsikānām soṣmatāṁ ca soṣmaṇām ūṣmaṇāhuḥ sasthānena ghoṣiṇām ghoṣiṇaiva* (R̥P 13.15-17)

Some call *a* the voice of voiced (consonants), *anusvāra* of the nasal ones; and they call the aspirateness of the (voiceless) aspirates a spirant of the same position, (and) of the voiced (aspirates, a spirant) of (the same) voicedness (i.e. *h*).

issue see the detailed discussion by Cardona (1986).[7] (See also Part 4 below.)

2. The Classification of Consonants

As is well known, the order of elements in the Sanskrit *varṇa* or *akṣara samāmnāya* proceeds in the direction of the air stream, starting with the glottis and velum and ending with the labials. Modern (Western) phonetics normally proceeds in the opposite direction, starting with the labials and ending with the velars, and the glottals. In this part of my paper I briefly outline the influence of the Sanskrit system on Western linguistics and the way that the competition between that system and pre-existing Western classifications was resolved.

Given the general impact of Sanskrit phonetics on Western linguistics, it is not surprising that its classification (starting from the glottals and velars) was accepted by many linguists. This includes not only Indo-Europeanists like Schleicher (1856, 1861), but also some classicists (e.g. Kühner 1834: 19), and even scholars working on non-Indo-European languages such as Böhtlingk[8] 1851 on Yaḳuts. Moreover, it formed the basis for early attempts at devising cross-linguistic or universal transcriptional systems or phonetic alphabets, starting with

---

[7] Deshpande (1997: 58-59) disagrees with this view, focusing on the statement in [i] (n. 6 above). But the crucial defining feature here does not seem to be the word *ghoṣa*, but *akāra*, which is defined elsewhere as *kaṇṭhya*, i.e. glottal, in R̥P 1.38, and which comes to be used as a featural designation of voice. Moreover, elsewhere the *R̥k Prātiśākhya* makes a clear distinction between the phonetically defined *nāda*, which is common to vowels and voiced consonants, and *ghoṣin*, which defines the class of voiced CONSONANTS and is, itself, defined in terms of the larger concept *nāda*; see [2] and [3] above.

[8] Böhtlingk was of course also editor of Pāṇini's grammar, as well as co-editor of the important "St. Petersburg Dictionary" of Sanskrit.

Jones (1788) and continuing to Lepsius (1855/1863).

The Sanskrit model, however, competed with two pre-existing systems. One had the order that prevails in modern phonetics – labial : dental : velar, with variation in terminology. For instance, Wallis (1653: 13-14) uses the terms labiae : palatum : guttur, and Rask (1818: 48) uses Danish terms that translate as labial : lingual : palatal. Grimm (1822: 10) followed Rask's classification (using the terms labial : dental : guttural), and his model is no doubt responsible for the fact that others working on Germanic linguistics operate with the same system (e.g. Stamm 1858: 296). This system seems to have been especially widespread in English publications, where we find it from a very early time; in addition to Wallis (see Wilkins 1668; Holder 1669; as well as the influential Bosworth 1823). The attractive feature of this "English" classification is that it starts with the most easily observed consonants, the labials. A further, reinforcing element may have been that Wallis, Wilkins, and Holder were involved in speech education efforts for the deaf, a context in which lip reading is an important factor.

The second pre-modern Western system seems to go back to Dionysius Thrax's grouping of letters – *k : p : t; th : ph : kh; b : g : d*; see example [1] repeated for convenience. This is, of course, simply the order in which the respective letters appear in the Greek alphabet. Moreover, there is no phonetic principle of ordering, except the accidental one that the letters designating labial and velar stops always occur next to each other. The order of the dental, however, varies: in two of the classes it precedes, in one it follows. In some generalized fashion this system is found in a number of early modern linguistic and philological publications, mainly on Greek and Latin (see Schneider 1819: 198 (*ch : ph : th*); Matthiae 1808: 12 (guttural : labial : lingual)). It is however also found in Gabelentz and Loewe's treatment of Gothic (1843: 39) and Hahn's grammar of Old High German (1852: 10).

[1] Toútōn psíla mèn tría, κ, π, τ, daséa dè tría, θ, φ, χ, mésa dè tría, β, γ, δ. Mésa dè eírētai, hóti tôn mèn psilôn estì dasútera, tôn dè daséōn psilótera (Dionysius Thrax, ed. Uhlig 1883: 12-13).

Of these, there are three smooth consonants – *k, p, t*, three rough – *th, ph, kh*, three middling – *b, g, d*. They are called middling because they are rougher than the smooth ones, and smoother than the rough ones.

Some early nineteenth-century publications employ a combined approach. For instance, Buttmann (1833: 11-12) gives the classification labial : lingual : palatal ("according to articulation") and *ph : kh : th; b : g : d; p : k : t* (according to "quality" [Eigenschaften]). And Bopp (1833) adopts the Sanskrit system for Sanskrit as well as generally for Germanic; but he follows Grimm's classification (labial : dental : guttural) in discussing "Grimm's Law"; and for Greek and Latin he retains the system of Dionysius Thrax. In his case, however, the use of the latter system seems to have some linguistic justification, in that dental stops change to *s* before *t* in Greek, while labials and velars remain stops.

Still, of the three different systems the classical Greek one is the weakest from the perspective of (articulatory) phonetics. It is therefore not surprising that it faded out.

What seems to have eventually favoured the "English" classification (beginning with the labials) over the Sanskrit one seems to be the fact that the early attempts at cross-linguistic or universal phonetic alphabets by scholars like Jones and Lepsius were superseded by British phoneticians – Ellis (1848), Bell (1867), and Sweet (1880-81) – who played a major role in the developments leading to the International Phonetic Alphabet and who, naturally, were partial to the "English" phonetic tradition.

Beyond the overall classification of consonants, a few other issues deserve mentioning. One is the characterization of *r* as retroflex in many of the Śikṣās; see e.g. [7]. This retroflex classification has been accepted in Western publications such as Wackernagel (1896: 209). In fact, Wackernagel considers the retroflex value to be original and the characterizations in the Prātiśākhyas to reflect linguistic change. The historical evidence of the Sanskrit phonetic and grammatical tradition suggests exactly the opposite; for the Prātiśākhyas, which as a class precede the extant Śikṣās, classify *r* in terms that must be interpreted as indicating alveolar, not retroflex pronunciation; see e.g. [8] and Allen (1953: 53-54). As argued in Hock 1991, the difference can be explained as reflecting a phonetic characterization in the Prātiśākhyas vs. a phonological classification in the later grammatical literature and the Śikṣās, a classification which focuses on the fact that *r*, like retroflex *ṣ*, triggers the change of dental *n* to retroflex *ṇ* (with certain restrictions), as in *brahmaṇā* (with retroflex) vs. *ātmanā* (with unchanged dental).[9]

[7] *syur mūrdhanyā r̥-ṭu-ra-ṣā dantyā ḷ-tu-la-sā smr̥tāḥ* (PŚ (i) 17)
r̥, the retroflex stops, *r*, *ṣ* should be retroflex; *ḷ*, the dental stops, *l*, *s* dental.'

[8] *dantyānāṁ jihvāgraṁ prastīrṇam* | . . . *rephasya dantamūlāni* (AP 1.24, 28)

---

[9] Varma suggests that there may have been dialectal variation between alveolar and retroflex articulation of *r* (1929: 8-9), but there is no attested evidence in favour of such variation. (The varying outcome of *rt* as *tt* or *ṭṭ* in Prakrit may reflect different developments of an intermediate stage with alveolar**t̲t̲*, resulting from assimilation of dental *t* to the preceding alveolar *r̲*; see Hock 1996.)

Of the dentals, the tip of the tongue, stretched forward (is the articulator). . . . Of *r*, the tooth roots.

A second issue concerns the classification of the *antastha* consonants or "semi-vowels" *y* and *v* as palatal and labial. If the sounds were in fact phonetically semi-vowels, in the sense of glides, a proper characterization would have been as front-velar and rounded-back-velar respectively. Now, for *v*, the Prātiśākhyas suggest that it was, in fact, no longer a glide but rather a labiodental consonant; see [9] and the discussion in Allen (1953: 57). Moreover, some texts characterize both *v* and *y* as involving some degree of contact; see [10].

[9] a. *oṣṭhāntābhyāṁ dantair vakāre* (TP 2.43)

In the case of *v*, (contact is made) by the ends of the (lower) lip and the teeth.

b. *vo dantāgraiḥ* (VP 1.81)

Of *v*, (production is) by the tip of the teeth (and the lips).

[10] a. *spr̥ṣṭam asthitam* | *duspr̥ṣṭaṁ tu prāg ghakārac caturṇām* | *svarānusvāroṣmaṇām aspr̥ṣṭaṁ sthitam* (R̥P 13.10-12)

(Consonants) have contact that is not stationary; the four sounds before *h* (i.e. *y, r, l, v*) have incomplete contact; the vowels, *anusvāra*, and the breathings (*h, ḥ*) have no contact and are stationary.

b. *tālau jihvāmadhyābhyāṁ yakāre* | . . . *oṣṭhāntābhyāṁ dantair vakāre* (TP 2.39, 43)

[with *anuvr̥tti* of *sparśayati* "one makes contact" from 2.35]

In the case of *y*, (contact is made) by the middle (edges) of the lip; in the case of *v*, by the ends of the teeth and the lips.

We can conclude, then, that *v* was labiodental, and not a back-rounded semi-vowel; its classification as a labial consonant therefore was appropriate. The exact phonetic interpretation of the statements regarding *y* is less clear – what precisely was the (incomplete) contact of *y* in the palatal area? Varma (1929: 126-28) notes that some of the Śikṣās provide for the realization of *y* as *j* under certain circumstances; but if the basic value of *y* had been identical to that of *j*, one would expect some of the Prātiśākhyas to have stated so. Perhaps we should think of something like Northern German fricatival [ʝ] instead of [y] (IPA [j])? Or is the "contact" classification simply analogical to that of the related "semi-vowel" *v*? Unfortunately, the statements in the Prātiśākhyas are not clear enough to answer these questions.

3. Vowel Classification and the Development of a Resonance or "Glottal" Theory

The classification of *y* and *v* as palatal and labial consonants (rather than front- and back-rounded glides) seems to be responsible for the fact that the *i*- and *u*-vowels are likewise classified as palatal and labial, respectively; see e.g. [11]. It appears that in this case the classification was not made on purely articulatory-phonetic grounds. True, the lip rounding of *u*-vowels might lead to a classification as labial, but this would ignore the primary articulation in the back-velar area. And there does not seem to be any articulatory justification for classifying front-velar *i*-vowels as palatal. Rather, the motivation seems to have been the well-known alternation between *i*- and *u*-vowels on one hand and *y* and *v* on the other (as in *prati-gacchati : praty-agacchat*), combined perhaps with an attempt to extend to the vowels the classificatory system established for the consonants.

[11] a. *tālavyāv ekāracakāravargāv ikāraikārau yakāraḥ śakāraḥ . . . śeṣa oṣṭhyo 'pavādya nāsikyān* (R̥P 1.42, 47)

e, palatal stops, *i, ai, y, ś* are palatal . . . the rest is labial excepting the nasals.

b. *tālau jihvāmadhyam ivarṇe . . . oṣṭhopasaṁhāra uvarṇe* (TP 2.22, 24)

For the *i*-vowels, the middle of the tongue (approximates) the palatal, there is approximation of the lips for the *u*-vowels.

As far as I can tell, there is no evidence in the Prātiśākhyas that *i*- and *u*-vowels had ever been classified in any other way. So this classification seems to be ancient.

The case is very different as regards the *a*-vowels and the *svarabhakti* component of the syllabic liquids.

Circumstantial evidence suggests an early classification of *a* as velar. As I have argued in Hock 1992, following a suggestion by George Cardona, the best account for the classification of the syllabic liquids *r̥* and *ḷ* as *jihvāmūlīya* or *jihvāmūla* (see [12]-[14]), supported by evidence in the *Vājasaneyī Prātiśākhya*, is that these were articulated as in [15], with ¼-*mātrā svarabhakti* [^{a}]-vowel elements flanking a non-syllabic ½-mātrā liquid element, and that *jihvāmūlīya* refers to the articulation of the *svarabhakti* elements – only the liquid element in the middle is identified with the ordinary pronunciation of the liquid as dental or alveolar. This interpretation resolves the difficulties that arise if the term *jihvāmūlīya* is interpreted as indicating a uvular [*R*]-pronunciation which, given the general descriptions in the Prātiśākhyas would require the highly improbable pronunciation in [15'], switching from uvular to alveolar and back to uvular articulation.

[12] *r̥kāra-lkārāv atha ṣaṣṭha ūṣmā jihvāmūlīyāḥ prathamaś ca vargaḥ* (R̥P 1.41)

r̥, *ḷ*, *x*, and the velar stops are articulated at the base of the tongue.

[13] *r̥-x-kau jihvāmūle* (VP 1.165)

r̥, *x*, and the velar stops are articulated at the base of the tongue.

[14] *jihvāmūlam r̥varṇasya kavargasya ca bhāṣyate* । *yaś caiva jihvāmūlīya ḷvarṇaś ceti te smr̥tāḥ* (commentary on AP 1.20)

The base of the tongue is declared (the articulator) of the *r̥*-vowels, the velar stops; also *jihvāmūlīya* and *ḷ* are considered such.

[15] *r̥* = [$^{a}r^{a}$]

l̥ = [$^{a}l^{a}$]

[15'] *r̥* = [$^{\text{R̥}}r^{\text{R̥}}$] (??)

Crucially, this interpretation requires the assumption that at the stage that the syllabic liquids came to be characterized as *jihvāmūlīya*, *a*-vowels were classified as velar. Moreover, since the term *jihvāmūlīya* is used in reference to the syllabic liquids even in the earliest Prātiśākhya texts, this classification must have been the oldest one that we can infer.[10]

By the time of the extant Prātiśākhyas, the classification of the *a*-vowels has changed. The *Taittirīya Prātiśākhya* in effect characterizes the position of the *a*-vowels as the most neutral state of the speech organs [16]. A further step appears to lie in the characterization of *a* as glottal [17]. As Allen (1953: 59) notes, this characterization can be understood "if we assume that it was viewed as a 'neutral' vowel in the sense of involving no special intra-buccal articulatory effort". Significantly, however, this classification no longer is articulatorily based but instead focuses on the neutral RESONANCE of the *a*-vowels. A fringe benefit of this re-classification would have been that the articulatorily questionable characterization of *i*- and *u*-vowels as "palatal" and "labial" could now have been justified in terms of resonance. However, the Prātiśākhyas did not take advantage of this opportunity and continued to operate with an articulatory basis for the palatal or labial classification of *i* and *u*.

[16] *avarṇe nātyupasaṁhatam oṣṭhahanū nātivyastam . . . anādeśe praṇyastā jihvā* ǀ *akāravad oṣṭhau* (TP 1.12, 20-21)

In the *a*-vowels, lips and jaw are not (to be) too closed nor too separated. . . . In the absence of instructions (to the contrary), the tongue is stretched out and the lips are in the position of the *a*-vowels.

---

[10] In this assessment I differ from Hock (1992).

[17] *kaṇṭhyo 'kārah* (R̥P 1.38)
a is glottal.

The reason for this fact may lie in the fact that the identification of *a* as glottal gave rise to the next step – grouping *a* together with the (articulatorily) glottal *h* and *visarga*; see [18] (the continuation of [17]), as well as [19].

[18] *prathamapañcamau ca dvau ūṣmaṇām* (R̥P 1.39)
and also the first and fifth spirants (i.e. *h* and *ḥ*).

[19] *a-ha-visarjanīyāḥ kaṇṭhe* (VP 1.71)
a, *h*, and *visarjanīya* (are produced) in the throat.

This, in turn, made it possible that "some" (*eke*) proposed an even "bolder" identification of *a* as the "voice" of voiced consonants, in tandem with the characterization of *anusvāra* as the "voice" of nasals; of homorganic spirants as the "voice" of (voiceless) aspirates, and of *h* as the "voice" of the voiced aspirates; see [20]. As Allen (1956: 59-60) as well as Cardona (1986) note, here we have arrived at a sophisticated, even if speculative feature theory of Sanskrit phonetics, most of which is couched in glottal terms.

[20] *āhur ghoṣaṁ ghoṣavatām akāram eke 'nusvāram anunāsikām soṣmatāṁ ca soṣmaṇām ūṣmaṇāhuḥ sasthānena ghoṣiṇām ghoṣiṇaiva* (R̥P 13.15-17)
Some call *a* the voice of voiced (consonants), *anusvāra* of the nasal ones; and they call the aspirateness of the (voiceless) aspirates a fricative of the same position, (and) of the voiced (aspirates, a fricative) of (the same) voicedness (i.e. *h*).

A final development seems to have been the classification of the velar stops as *kaṇṭhya*, i.e. as glottal too; see e.g. [21]. The exact motivation for this change is difficult to discern. Perhaps the fact that some textual traditions retained an echo of the original classification of *a*-vowels and the velar stops as velar (see [22]) provided an analogy.

[21] a. *kaṇṭho 'kuhavisarjanīyānām* (CV (ii) 3)

(The place of articulation) of *a*-vowels, velar stops, *h*, *ḥ* is glottal.

b. *a-ku-ha-visarjanīyāḥ kaṇṭhyāḥ* (PŚ (ii) 1.1 ≈ PŚ (ii) 1.2 ≈ ĀŚ 1.2)

The *a*-vowels, velar stops, *h*, *ḥ* are glottal.

[22] *kavarga-avarṇa-anusvāra-jihvāmūlīyā jihvyā ekeṣām* (PŚ (iii) 1.6 = AŚ 1.5)

The velar stops, *a*-vowels, *anusvāra*, and *x* are velar according to some.

It is the resulting classification of *a*-vowels and velars as *kaṇṭhya*, of *i*-vowels, *y*, and palatals as palatal, and of *u*-vowels, *v*, and labials as labial (see [23]) which reached the Western world through the grammars of Colebrooke (1805), Carey (1806), Wilkins (1808), and the like, with "guttural" commonly translating *kaṇṭhya*. And for a long time it dominated Western vowel classifications, not only in publications on Sanskrit, such as Whitney 1989, but also in Indo-Europeanist and other publications, such as Bopp 1833 and Schleicher 1861; see e.g. [23].

[23] Phonetic system Schleicher (1861: 8)

Consonanten								Vocale	
momentane laute				dauerlaute					
	nicht aspirierte stumm	nicht aspirierte tön.	aspiratae tönend	spirauten stumm	spirauten tönend	nassale tön.	r-laute tön.		
gutt.	*k*	*g*	*gh*					*a*	*aa* (*â*) *âa* (*â*)
pal.					*j*			*i*	*ai* *âi*
lingu.							*r*		*au* *âu*
dent.	*t*	*d*	*dh*	*s*		*n*			
lab.	*p*	*b*	*bh*		*v*	*m*		*u*	

This system even influenced Western articulatory phonetics – in spite of the fact that its classification of *a*-vowels as guttural, *i*-vowels as palatal, and *u*-vowels as labial is articulatorily inappropriate. The classification is found, e.g. in Ellis (1848) (see [24]) and even as late as the 1900 and 1932 revisions of the International Phonetic Alphabet (IPA); see e.g. [25]. An articulatorily more appropriate classification, in terms of "front" : "centre" : "back" is found as early as Sweet 1902 and seems to, indirectly, inspire Ellis's earlier organization. While the 1932 revision of the IPA incorporates some of this classification, it seems to have been fully adopted only in (1989); see Maître Phonétique (1933) vs. International Phonetic Association (1989). Even to the present day, some publications refer to front vowels as palatal (e.g. Harris and Kaisse 1999; Hoole 1999). (The classification guttural, however, was abandoned quite early, and the labial one more recently.)

[24] Vowel system of Ellis (1848: 23)

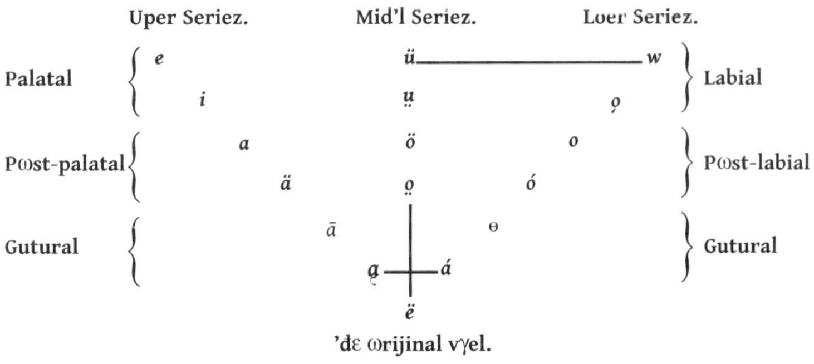

[25] IPA 1932 (International Phonetic Association 1933)[11]

	Bila bial	*Labio-dental*	*Dental/alveolar*	*Retro-flex*	*Palato-alveolar*	*Alveolo-palatal*	*Palatal*	*Velar*
Plosive	p b		t d	ʈ ɖ			c ɟ	k g
Nasal	m	ɱ	n	ɳ			ɲ	ŋ
Lateral Fricative			ɬ ɮ					
Lateral Non-fricative			l	ɭ			ʎ	
Rolled			r					
Flapped			ɾ	ɽ				
Fricative	ɸ β	f v	θ ð s z ɹ	ʂ ʐ	ʃ ʒ	ɕ ʑ	ç ʝ	x ɣ
Frictionless Continuant	w ɥ	ʋ	ɹ				j (ɥ)	(w)

Vowel		Front	Central	Back
Close	(y ʉ u)	i y	ɨ ʉ	ɯ u
Half-close	(ø ɵ o)	e ø	ɵ	ɤ o
			ə/ɜ	
Half-open	(œ ɔ)	ɛ œ		ʌ ɔ
		æ	ɐ	
Open	(ɒ)		a	ɑ ɒ

[11] Post-velars and some vowels omitted for easier display.

For the vowels, then, the influence of the Indian phonetic tradition was less helpful than for the consonants.

Moreover, to my knowledge, the interesting glottal and resonance-based theories of the Prātiśākhyas had no influence on Western phonetics. These are issues that Western phonetics had to explore and define for itself. In fact, only a few authors, such as Allen (1953) and Cardona (1986), have understood – and appreciated – the theories of the Prātiśākhyas.

4. Later Developments and the Influence of the Grammatical Tradition

The major reason for the Western lack of appreciation of the glottal and resonance-based theories is no doubt the fact that they were sidelined even in the post-Prātiśākhya tradition of Sanskrit grammar and the Śikṣās that grew out of (or along with) that tradition.

On the positive side, that tradition is characterized by the introduction of a new concept, that of effort or force of articulation (commonly characterized as *mahāprāṇa* "great-breathed" vs. *alpaprāṇa* "little-breathed").[12] On the less positive side, we find a tendency to lump the phonetic concepts *śvāsa* or *nāda* together with the phonological terms *aghoṣa* or *ghoṣavat* and to further link these with the concept of greater or lesser effort. Moreover, reflecting the focus of the grammatical tradition on

---

[12] This notion has some precedent in a passage of the *Taittirīya Prātiśākhya*, according to which the feature *śvāsa* is stronger in the voiceless aspirates and spirants; see [i]. But note that no such claim is made for the voiced aspirates.

[i] *bhūyān prathamebhyo 'nyeṣu* (TP 2.11)

(*śvāsa*) in the others (i.e. in voiceless aspirated stops) is greater than in the first stop series (i.e. voiceless unaspirated).

grammar, rather than phonetics, voiced and voiced aspirated stops are lumped together, reflecting their similar grammatical (phonological) behaviour, but ignoring their difference in articulatory terms (see the passages in [26] and [27]). The passage in [28] uses a slightly different terminology (*śvāsa/nāda* "voiceless/voiced" vs. *īśacchvāsa/īśannāda* "slightly voiceless/ slightly voiced"), but the effect is the same. Further, in some passages, the terms *ghoṣavat : aghoṣa* are used even in reference to the vowels, in contrast to the Prātiśākhya restriction of the terms to the consonants; see [29] with the clarifying commentary in [30].

[26] *vargāṇāṁ prathamadvitīyāḥ śaṣasavisarjanīyajihvāmūlīyopdhmānīyā . . . vivr̥takaṇṭhāḥ śvāsānupradānā aghoṣāḥ* । *varg[āṇāṁ] prathame 'lpaprāṇā itare sarve mahāprāṇāḥ* । *vargāṇāṁ tr̥tīyacaturthā antasthā hakārānusvārau . . . saṁvr̥takaṇṭhā nādānupradānā ghoṣavantaḥ* । *varg[āṇāṁ] tr̥tīyā antasthāś cālpaprāṇā itare sarve mahāprāṇāḥ* (ĀŚ 4.2-5)

The first and second stop series (i.e. voiceless unaspirated and aspirated), *ś*, *ṣ*, *s*, *visarjanīya*, *x*, *φ*, are open-throat, have *śvāsa* as their basis, and are voiceless. The first series (i.e. voiceless unaspirated stops) are small-breathed, all the rest great-breathed. The third and fourth stop series (i.e. voiced unaspirated and aspirated), the semi-vowels, *h*, and *anusvāra* are (produced) with close-throat, have *nāda* as their basis, and are voiced. The third series and the semi-vowels are little-breathed, all the rest great-breathed.

[27] *. . . santi hyāsyād bāhyāḥ prayatnāḥ . . . vivārasaṃvārau śvāsanādau ghoṣavadaghoṣatā alpaprāṇatā mahāprāṇatā iti* । *tatra vargāṇāṁ prathamadvitīyā vivr̥takaṇṭhāḥśvāsānupradānā aghoṣāḥ* । *eke 'lpaprāṇā apare mahāprāṇāḥ* । *tr̥tīyacaturthāḥ saṁvr̥takaṇṭhā nādānupradānā ghoṣavantaḥ* । *eke 'lpaprāṇā apare mahāprāṇāḥ . . .* (*Mahābhāṣya* 1.1.4 on Pāṇini 1.1.9)

There are processes that are external to the oral cavity. . . . (These are) openness and closure (of the glottis), *śvāsa* and *nāda*, voicelessness and voicedness, little-breath and great-breath. Then the first and second groups of stops (i.e. the voiceless stops) are characterized as open-throat, having *śvāsa* as their basis, voiceless. Some are little-breathed, others great-breathed (i.e. unaspirated vs. aspirated). The third and fourth groups of stops (i.e. the voiced stops) are characterized as close-throat, having *nāda* as their basis, voiced. Some are little-breathed, others great-breathed (i.e. unaspirated vs. aspirated).

[28] *ñamo 'nunāsikā nahro nādino hajhaṣaḥ smr̥tāḥ* | *īṣan-nādā yaṇo jaśca śvāsinas tu khapādayaḥ* | *īṣac chvāsāṁś caro vidyād gordhāmaitat pracakṣate* | (PŚ (i) 39-40)

ñam (= the nasals) are nasal, *h* and *jhaṣ* (= voiced aspirates) have *nāda*, (but) not *h* combined with *r*; *yaṇ* (= *y, r, l, v*) and *jaś* (= voiced stops) are pronounced with light *nāda*; *khap* (= voiceless stops, in effect voiceless aspirates, because of the following restriction) and the voiceless spirants have *śvāsa*; *car* (= voiceless unaspirated stops) have light *śvāsa*. This is called the foundation of speech.

[29] *atha yatra ekaḥ pacatīty ekaḥ pūrvaparayor hrādena pracchādyate* (MBh. 1.4.4 on Pāṇini 1.4.109)

Now when there is one (stop, as the *c* in) *pacati* (in contact with a voiced element[13]), then that one is covered over by the sound of the preceding and following (vowels).

[30] *dvayor akārayor ghoṣavator madhye cakāro ghoṣavān iva lakṣyate* (KPr on MBh 1.4.4)

Between two voiced (*ghoṣavat*) *a*-vowels, the *c* (in *pacati*) is heard as voiced (*ghoṣavat*) as it were.

5. Conclusions

As we have seen, the phonetic tradition of the Prātiśākhyas was far ahead of Western linguistics, as regards the distinction voiced : voiceless and the nature of voiced *h* and voiced aspiration on one hand and the sophisticated resonance-based and glottal vowel theories on the other. Especially the insights regarding voicing exerted a decisive and lasting influence.

Western linguistics, however, first became familiar with the Sanskrit tradition through recasts of the grammatical tradition.

---

13 See the *sparśaghoṣasaṁyoge* of the preceding vārttika.

As a consequence, it adopted the post-Prātiśākhya terminology in which the terms *ghoṣavat/ghoṣin* and *aghoṣa* were used for both consonants and vowels and, moreover, the term *ghoṣavat/ghoṣin* was used both for simple voiced consonants and for voiced aspirates and *h*.

Even so, the impact even of this more limited understanding of voicing and aspiration on Western linguistics was profound, in that it provided a phonetically meaningful, articulatory basis for distinguishing voiced and voiceless speech sounds. The legacy of this impact is seen in the continued use of Western calques of the Sanskrit terms *ghoṣavat/ghoṣin* and *aghoṣa*, such as English *voiced* and *voiceless*, or German *stimmhaft* and *stimmlos*.

In other cases, the impact of Sanskrit phonetics was only temporary, especially concerning the ordering of consonant classes from velar/glottal to labial. Interestingly, when Chinese adopted the Sanskrit phonetic tradition, it also changed the order to start with the labials (see Norman 1988: 30-31).[14]

Finally, in some cases the influence of the Sanskrit phonetic on the West was less than optimal. This is the case not only for the characterization of *i*- and *u*-vowels as palatal and labial, and the late classification of velars, *a*-vowels, and glottals as *kaṇṭhya*, translated as guttural, which was only slowly replaced by an articulatorily more appropriate classification. The post-Prātiśākhya definition of *r* as retroflex likewise was not particularly insightful. The same holds true, although for different reasons, for the retention of the term *jihvāmūlīya* for syllabic *r̥* (and *l̥*) after the *a*-vowels were no longer classified as velar, since this led to speculations that there were Sanskrit varieties in which *r̥* was uvular.

[14] Interestingly, however, the Japanese (kana) syllabary, presumably based on Chinese, starts with the velars, and so does the Korean (hangul) script.

On balance, however, it is clear that knowledge of the Sanskrit phonetic tradition transformed Western phonetics tremendously – for better or for worse. It is difficult to imagine what would have happened without that knowledge.

Textual References

AP: *Atharvaveda Prātiśākhya.* Cited from Whitney 1862; see also Deshpande 1997.

ĀŚ: *Āpiśali Śikṣā*, ed. Yuddhiṣṭhira Mīmāṁsaka in *Śikṣāsūtrāṇi*, 2nd edn., Bhāratīyaprācyavidyāpratiṣṭhāna, Saṁ 2028.

CV: *Candra-Vr̥tti*, ed. Yuddhiṣṭhira Mīmāṁsaka in *Śikṣāsūtrāṇi*, 2nd edn., Bhāratīyaprācyavidyāpratiṣṭhāna, Saṁ 2028.

KPra: *Kaiyaṭa Pradīpa.* Contained in Vyākaraṇa-mahābhāṣyam: Śrīkaiyaṭakr̥tapradīpena Nāgojībhaṭṭakr̥tena Bhāṣya-pradīpoddyotena ca vibhūṣitam, ed. Vedavrata Śāstrī, 5 vols., Rohtak: Harayāṇā-Sāhitya-Saṁsthānam, 1961-63.

MBh: *Mahābhāṣya*: Vyākaraṇamahābhāṣyam, ed. Franz Kielhorn, 3rd edn. Kashinath Vasudev Abhyankar, 3 vols., Pune: Bhandarkar Oriental Research Institute, 1962.

PŚ: *Pāṇinīya-Śikṣā*: (i) śloka-version, ed. Rudraprasād Avasthī with the commentary "Pradīpa", Haridāsa Saṁskr̥tagranthamālā, 59, Varanasi, 1972; (ii/iii) two sūtra-versions ("laghupāṭha" and "vr̥ddhapāṭha"), ed. Yuddhiṣṭhira Mīmāṁsaka in *Śikṣāsūtrāṇi*, 2nd edn., Bhāratīyaprācyavidyāpratiṣṭhāna, Saṁ 2028.

R̥P: *R̥gveda-Prātiśākhyam*, ed. Vīrendra Kumār Varmā, Banaras Hindu University, 1970.

RT: *R̥ktantram*, ed. Surya Kanta, Delhi: Meherchand Lachhmandas, 1970 (originally published 1933).

TP: *Taittirīya Prātiśākhya.* Cited from Whitney 1868.

VP: *Vājasaneyī Prātiśākhya.* Cited from Weber 1858.

References

Allen, W. S[idney], 1953, *Phonetics in Ancient India* (London Oriental Series, 1), London/New York/Toronto: Oxford University Press.

Bell, Alexander Melville, 1867, *Visible Speech: The Science of Universal*

Alphabetics, London/New York: Simpkin, Marshall & Co. and Trübner.

Böhtlingk, Otto von, 1851, *Über die Sprache der Jakuten*, St. Petersburg: Kaiserliche Akademie der Wissenschaften.

Bopp, Franz, 1833, *Vergleichende Grammatik des Sanskrit, Zend, Griechischen, Lateinischen, Litthauischen, Gothischen und Deutschen*, vol. 1, Berlin: Dümmler.

Bosworth, Joseph, 1823, *The Elements of Anglo-Saxon Grammar*, London: Harding, Mayor, Lepard.

Buttmann, Philipp, 1833, Griechische Grammatik, 14th edn., Berlin: Mylius.

Cardona, George, 1986, "Phonology and Phonetics in Ancient Indian Works: The Case of Voiced and Voiceless Elements", in: *South Asian Languages: Structure, Convergence, and Diglossia*, ed. Bh. Krishnamurti et al., pp. 60-80, Delhi: Motilal Banarsidass.

Carey, William, 1806, *Grammar of the Sungskrit Language, composed from the works of the most esteemed grammarians, to which are added examples for the exercise of the student, and a complete list of the dhatoos*, or roots, 2 vols., Serampore: Mission Press.

Colebrooke, Henry Thomas, 1805, *A Grammar of the Sanscrĭt Language*, vol. 1, Calcutta: Honorable Company's Press.

Deshpande, Madhav M., 1997 (ed. and tr.), *Śaunakīyā Caturādhyāyikā: A Prātiśākhya of the Śaunakīya Atharvaveda*, Cambridge, MA/London: Harvard University Press.

Ellis, Alexander John, 1848, *Essentials of Phonetics: Containing the Theory of a Universal Alphabet*, London: Pitman.

Gabelentz, Hans Conon von der and Julius Loebe, 1843, *Ulfilas: Veteris et novi testamenti versionis gothicae fragmenta quae supersunt . . . cum glossario et grammatica linguae gothicae*, Leipzig: Brockhaus.

Grimm, Jacob, 1822, *Deutsche Grammatik*, vol. 1, 2nd edn., Göttingen: Dieterich.

Hahn, Karl August, 1852, *Althochdeutsche Grammatik*, Prag: Calve.

Harris, James W. and Ellen M. Kaisse, 1999, "Palatal Vowels, Glides and Obstruents in Argentinian Spanish", Phonology, **16**: 117-90.

Hart, John, 1569, *An Orthographie: Conteyning the Due Order and Reason, howe to Write or Paint Thimage of Mannes Voice, Most Like to the Life or*

Nature, London: William Seres.

Hock, Hans Henrich, 1991, "Dialects, Diglossia, and Diachronic Phonology in Early Indo-Aryan", in: *Studies in the Historical Phonology of Asian Languages*, ed. W.G. Boltz and M.C. Shapiro, pp. 119-59, Amsterdam/Philadelphia: Benjamins.

——, 1992, "Were r̥ and ḷ Velar in Early Sanskrit?", in: *Vidyā-Vratin: Professor A.M. Ghatage Felicitation Volume*, ed. V.N. Jha, pp. 69-94 (Sri Garib Dass Oriental Series, 160), Delhi: Sri Satguru Publications.

——, 1996, "Subversion or Convergence?: The Issue of pre-Vedic Retroflexion Reconsidered", *Studies in the Linguistic Sciences* **23**(2): 73-115.

Holder, William, 1669, *Elements of Speech: An Essay of Inquiry into the Natural Production of Letters: with an appendix concerning persons deaf and dumb*, London: J. Martyn.

Hoole, Philip, 1999, "Articulatory-acoustic relations in German Vowels", in: *ICPhS99: Proceedings of the 14th International Congress of Phonetic Sciences, San Francisco, 1-7 August 1999*, ed. J.J. Ohala, Y. Hasegawa, M. Ohala, D. Granville, and A.C. Bailey, pp. 2153-56, Berkeley/Los Angeles: University of California Press.

International Phonetic Association, 1933, Le Maître Phonétique, vol. 42, Bourg-la-Reine: International Phonetic Association.

——, 1989, "Report on the 1989 Kiel Convention", *Journal of the International Phonetic Alphabet*, **19**(2): 67–80.

Jones, Sir William, 1788, "Orthography of Asiatick Words in Roman Letters", *Asiatick Researches*, **1**: 1-56.

Kempelen, Wolfgang von, 1791, *Mechanismus der menschlichen Sprache nebst Beschreibung einer sprechenden Maschine*, Wien: Degen.

Kühner, Raphael, 1834, *Ausführliche grammatik der griechischen sprache*, Hanover: Hahn.

Lepsius, Richard, 1855, *Das allgemeine linguistische Alphabet: Grundsätze der Übertragung fremder Schriftsysteme und bisher noch ungeschriebener Sprachen in europäische Buchstaben*, Berlin: Hertz.

——, 1863, *Standard Alphabet for Reducing Unwritten Languages and Foreign Graphic Systems to a Uniform Orthography in European Letters*, Revised English translation of Lepsius 1855, London/Berlin: Williams & Norgate/Hertz.

Matthiae, August, 1808, *Griechische Grammatik zum Schulgebrauch*, Leipzig: Crusius.

Morpurgo Davies, Anna, 1992, *Nineteenth-century Linguistics* (= *History of Linguistics*, vol. 4, ed. Giulio Lepschy), London/New York: Longman.

Norman, Jerry, 1988, *Chinese*, Cambridge: University Press.

Rask, Rasmus Christian, 1818, *Undersøgelse om det gamle Nordiske eller Islandske Sprogs Oprindelse*, København: Gyldendal.

Robins, Robert Henry, 1997, *A Short History of Linguistics*, 4th edn. London: Longman.

Schleicher, August Wilhelm, 1856, *Handbuch der litauischen Sprache*, Prage: Calve.

——, 1861, *Compendium der vergleichenden grammatik der indogermanischen Sprachen*, vol. 1, Weimar: Böhlau.

Schneider, Konrad Leopold, 1819, *Ausführliche mit möglichst sorgfältiger Benutzung der vorhandenen Hülfsmittel und nach neuen Untersuchungen verbesserte Grammatik der lateinischen Sprache*, Berlin: Reimer.

Stamm, Friedrich Ludwig, 1858, *Ulfila: oder, die uns erhaltenen Denkmäler der gothischen Sprache: Text, Grammatik und Wörterbuch*, Paderborn: Schöningh.

Sweet, Henry, 1880-81, "Sound Notation", *Transactions of the Philological Society*, 177-235.

——, 1902, *A Primer of Phonetics*, 2nd edn., Oxford: Clarendon Press.

Uhlig, Gustauus, 1883, *Dionysii Thracis ars grammatica*, Lipsiae (Leipzig): Teubner.

Varma, Siddheshwar, 1929, *Critical Studies in the Phonetic Observations of Indian Grammarians*, London: Royal Asiatic Society; repr., 1961, Delhi: Munshiram Manoharlal.

Wackernagel, Jakob, 1896, *Altindische Grammatik*, 1, Göttingen: Vandenhoeck & Ruprecht.

Wallis, John, 1653, *Grammatica linguae anglicanae, cui praefigitur de loquela sive sonorum formatione tractatus grammatico-physicus: et (nunc primum) subjungitur praxis grammatica*, Oxford.

Weber, Albrecht, 1858 (ed. and tr.), "Das Vājasaneyi-Prātiśākhyam", *Indische Studien*, **4**: 65-171, 177-331.

Westermann, Diedrich Hermann and Ida C[aroline] Ward, 1933,

Practical Phonetics for Students of African Languages, London: Oxford University Press.

Whitney, William Dwight, 1862 (ed. and tr.), "The Atharva-Veda Prâtiçâkhya, or Çâunakîyâ Caturâdhyâyikâ: Text, Translation, and Notes", *Journal of the American Oriental Society*, 7: 333-616.

——, 1868 (ed. and tr.), *The Tâittirîya-Prâtiçâkhya, with its commentary, the Tribhâshyaratna: Text, Translation, and Notes* (Journal of the American Oriental Society 9), New Haven: American Oriental Society.

——, 1889, *Sanskrit Grammar*, Cambridge, MA: Harvard University Press.

Wilkins, John, 1668, *An Essay Towards a Real Character, and a Philosophical Language*, London: Gillibrand and Martin.

Wilkins, Sir Charles, 1808, *A Grammar of the Sanskrĭta Language*, London: Black, Parry, and Kingsbury.

5

Ardhamātrālāghava

Pierre-Sylvain Filliozat

EVERYONE knows the *paribhāṣā* "*ardhamātrālāghavena putrotsavaṁ manyante vaiyākaraṇāḥ* (by saving half a *mātrā* Grammarians feel the joy of getting a son)" (*Paribhāṣenduśekhara* of Nāgojībhaṭṭa, 122, BORI, Poona, 1962). It is attached to *Aṣṭādhyāyī* and the celebrity of Pāṇini's work is largely due to the brevity that the saying extols. The purpose of this communication is to examine in which circumstances such a principle of economy of enunciation has come in usage and in which field of intellectual activity it has been used. Economy of enunciation implies economy of thinking, both principles and their applications are to be taken into consideration.

The principle of "lightness" of enunciation entails a maximal reduction of the number of signifiers to only those which are necessary to convey a message. When there are several signifiers for one and same signified, the choice should be of the shortest signifier. A refinement is to create artificial signifiers shorter than the natural ones, i.e. technical terms such as the Pāṇinian *pratyāhāras*. A principle of economy of signifiers has a companion in a principle of signification: every element in a message has necessarily a meaning or purpose and is sufficient to convey it.

These two principles are couched in a traditional stanza. See *Viṣṇudharmottara* III.5.1:

svalpā/alpākṣaram asaṁdigdhaṁ sāravad viśvatomukham ।
astobham anavadyaṁ ca sūtraṁ sūtravido viduḥ ॥

Sūtra experts know it to have minimal letters, no ambiguity, to contain the essential, to face all sides, to be without interruption, to be non-liable to criticism.

In fact, *paribhāṣā* in its metaphoric formulation is the last one in the list of Puruṣottama and the last commented by Nāgeśa. It is not seen in the fifteen other lists so far known.[1] We may have a doubt regarding the antiquity of the formulation, but we have no doubt about the early appearance of the principle in *vyākaraṇa* tradition. Patañjali applies it literally, when he discusses the respective *lāghava* and *gaurava* of the formulation *iṇaḥ* vs. *yvor* in the *sūtra* 6.4.77: "*aci śnudhātubhruvāṁ yvor iyaṅuvaṅau* (before an ending beginning with a vowel, *iyaṅ, uvaṅ* appear in the place of *i ī, u ū* final of an *aṅga* ending by *śnu*, of a *dhātu*, of *bhrū*)". The formulation *yvor*, used by Pāṇini in *yvor iyaṅuvaṅau*, is of three-and-half *mātrās*. Another formulation could be *iṇaḥ* which is of three *mātrās*. The difference is a half of a *mātrā*. Patañjali concludes:

so 'yam evaṁ laghīyasā nyāsena siddhe sati yad garīyāṁsaṁ yatnam ārabhate tad jñāpayaty ācāryaḥ pareṇa na pūrveṇeti ।

Since, when the operation succeeds with a lighter formulation, the *ācārya* undertakes a heavier one (by half a *mātrā*), he reveals that the *pratyāhāra iṇ* has the later *ṇ* in the *Māheśvarasūtras* not the former one.

– *Mahābhāṣya*, Kielhorn edn., I.35

Apart of the satisfaction the grammarian could derive from such an economy of wording, he took it as a very powerful tool

[1] See the table of *paribhāṣās* in *Paribhāṣāsaṁgraha* (*A Collection of Original Works on Vyākaraṇa Paribhāṣās*), ed. critically K.V. Abhyankar, Poona: Bhandarkar Oriental Institute, 1967.

to extract new or hidden information from Pāṇini's *sūtras*. The utility of the economy principle has contributed a lot to its popularity, since it has been used and abused in the long history of *Aṣṭādhyāyī* interpretation. Patañjali has fully endorsed the principle as a tool of argumentation. He has not referred to the pleasure of achieving *lāghava* at any cost. The comparison with the birth of a son may be one of the maxims traditionally transmitted in Sanskrit schools.

What is the origin and motivation of such preoccupation with brevity of speech?

There is a natural human attitude in favour of two types of *lāghava* – brevity of thought and brevity of expression. Both have been cultivated with fervour, from Vedic times. Even before Pāṇini, *Kalpasūtras* cared consciously for abridged short formulas. That can be shown in the field of the early geometry of fire altars made of bricks in the oldest *Śulbasūtras*. We have to consider that Baudhāyana, Pāṇini, Kātyāyana, etc. worked in an oral society and composed their manuals for memorization and practical applications that required economy. A noteworthy feature of the *sūtra* genre is that it is purely oral. A *sūtra* formulation is a short, spoken object, we can say a mental object, when it is memorized. There is no necessity to write it, in order to use it practically. Whether Pāṇini knew the existence of writing or not is debated. But we can assert that he did not use it for composing his *Aṣṭādhyāyī*. There is no graphic and written device among the numerous devices of abbreviations he has used. And that differentiates drastically Pāṇini's formalization from the modern one which relies mostly on graphic devices, parentheses, etc.

Orality and memorization were constraints for searching brevity of expression, and even for elaborating modes of interpretation. From the moment abbreviations and formalization go beyond the natural devices of shortening expression, procedures of expanding the compact material must be elaborated. *Sūtras* must be memorized and knowledge of their comprehension and extension must be acquired through a commentary. Patañjali says it:

> *na kevalāni carcāpadāni vyākhyānaṁ vṛddhiḥ āt aij iti* ।
> *kiṁ tarhi* ।
> *udāharaṇaṁ pratyudāharaṇaṁ vākyādhyāhāra ity etat samuditaṁ vyākhyānaṁ bhavati* ।

> The commentary is not the mere set of words *vṛddhiḥ, āt, aic*. What then? Example, counter-example, filling up of the sentence, all together are the commentary. – *Mahābhāṣya* I.11

A ritual origin has been a further motivation for the quest of *lāghava* and the procedures of interpretation based on it. We read it again in the well-known words of Patañjali:

> *na yathā loke tathā vyākaraṇe* ।
> *pramāṇabhūta ācāryo darbhapavitrapāṇiḥ śucāv avakāśe prāṅmukha upaviśya mahatā yatnena sūtraṁ praṇayati sma* ।
> *tatrāśakyaṁ varṇenāpy anarthakena bhavituṁ kiṁ punar iyatā sūtreṇa* ।

> In grammar it is not like in the world. The *ācārya* who possesses authority, having a purificatory *darbha* grass on the hand, sitting in a pure place, facing the east, with a great effort, has composed the *sūtras*. In these conditions, it is impossible that even one phoneme is purposeless, a fortiori one *sūtra* of this length.
>
> – *Mahābhāṣya* ad 1.1.1, Kielhorn edn., I.39

There are several points to underline in this passage. The effort of composition of the *sūtra* is acknowledged. A religious ritual accompanied the task of the author. Taken literally the designation of *ācārya* refers to an orthodox "practitioner". The author is sacralized for his orthopraxis. Intellectual power and spiritual background confer authority *prāmāṇya* to the *sūtra*. And when Patañjali says it cannot be *anarthaka*, he takes *artha* in the sense of purpose, since he holds a *gaurava* of half a *mātrā* as a *jñāpaka*, a revealer of an information. The information obtained from the presence of this half *mātrā* phoneme is not a meaning of that half *mātrā*. The half *mātrā* phoneme is meaningless by itself. But it can be said that it has a purpose, which is to reveal the said information.

Pāṇini is the most illustrious user of the *lāghava* principle, he is not the inventor. His intellectual approach derives probably from those of previous grammarians and beyond the domain of speech from the field of ritual, i.e. the old *Kalpasūtras*. In our documentation they are the first to offer brief *sūtras*. They offer the first instances of general rules, which are the prominent tools of brevity of thought. A simple example is the *Śulbasūtra* rule for the square of the diagonal in *Baudhāyana-*, *Āpastamba-Śrautasūtras*. After giving a few triplets of numbers a, b, c so that $a^2 + b^2 = c^2$, such as 3, 4, 5; 7, 24, 25; 15, 36, 39, etc. they give the general rule, nowadays familiar under the name of Pythagoras theorem:

> *dīrghasyākṣṇayārajjuḥ pārśvamānī tiryaṅmānī ca yat*
> *pṛthagbhūte kurutas tad ubhayaṁ karoti* ।
>
> The diagonal of a rectangle produces both [the squares] that the flank side and the transverse side produce separately.
>
> – *Āpastamba* I.4

The general rule achieves an economy of thought and expression, when compared to the enumeration of instances. We can assert that these ancient thinkers were well aware of this principle of economy, since they have coined technical words for the concepts of general rule and exception, *utsarga* and *apavāda* as means of economy. This is echoed in a well-known passage of Patañjali's *Mahābhāṣya*. After stating that teaching correct words straightaway is "lighter" than teaching them through mentioning corrupt words, he raises the question whether the enumeration word by word could be done and shows that it is not at all the possible means, through the story of Bṛhaspati teaching Indra in this way and their failure to reach the end. Then he expresses in clear terms the right method:

> *kiṁ cit sāmānyaviśeṣaval lakṣaṇaṁ pravartyam, yenālpena yatnena mahato mahataḥ śabdaughān pratipadyeran* ।
> *kiṁ punas tat ?*
> *utsargāpavādau* । *kaś cid utsargaḥ kartavyaḥ kaś cid apavādaḥ* ॥
>
> *kathaṁjātīyakaḥ punar utsargaḥ kartavyaḥ kathaṁjātīyako 'pavādaḥ* ।
>
> *sāmānyenotsargaḥ kartavyaḥ* ।
> *tad yathā "karmaṇy aṇ"* । 3.2.1
> *tasya vieśeṣeṇāpavādaḥ* । *tad yathā "āto 'nupasarge kaḥ"* ॥ 3.2.3
>
> An instrument of knowledge [here, a set of formulae] containing the general and the particular must be undertaken; that is a small effort by which [students] will learn words by great groups.
>
> But what is that [instrument of knowledge]?
>
> Assertion and denial. One assertion must be done, and a denial. – *Mahābhāṣya* Paspaśā, Kielhorn edn., I.6

– But an assertion of what sort should be done, a denial of what sort?

– An assertion through the general should be done, for example "when the object [is the complementary word, after a root] there is *aṇ*", a denial through a particular case of it, for example "after *ā*-ending [root], if there is no preverb, there is *ka*".

The use of the word *lakṣaṇa* in this context requires an examination, as it plays an important role in many disciplines. *Dhātupāṭha* mentions two possible roots *lakṣa darśanāṅkanayoḥ* "to look, to mark" *parasmaipadin* and *lakṣa ālocane* "to examine" *ātmanepadin*. The word *lakṣaṇa* is derived with the suffix *lyuṭ* (*ana*) after the first according to Bhānujī Dīkṣita's commentary on *Amarakośa*. The meaning *darśana* "to see" is possible in the present context. The meaning *ālocana* "to examine, to consider" is also very appropriate. The derivative *lakṣya* means "the object to be seen, considered, aimed at"; for instance it refers to the target aimed at by a hunter. In the present passage we understand *lakṣaṇa* as referring to the process of aiming at an entire domain of objects. It is different of the mere sight of an individual. Aiming at an entire domain implies the recourse to the general and the particular.

There is a history of *lāghava*. It started with the care for brevity of expression in the genre of *sūtras*. *Aṣṭādhyāyī* is famous in this respect, but not unique. Pāṇini has been surpassed by competitors in his own field, such as Śākaṭāyana in *Kātantra*, Anubhūtisvarūpācārya in *Sārasvatavyākaraṇa* and Bopadeva in *Mugdhabodha*. In other disciplines there are noteworthy, very condensed *sūtras*, such as *Chandaḥsūtra* of Piṅgala.

With the advent of writing in the sphere of intellectual activities, new devices of abbreviation came into usage. This can be shown in the works of mathematicians. The Sanskrit *Pāṭī-Gaṇitaśāstra*, right from the time of Āryabhaṭa, has combined all the advantages of mental operating, oral expression and writing. Graphic signs for numbers, graphic disposition of operations designed on sand or with chalk on a board, erasing, etc. have gradually found a prominent place in practice of calculus. The first graphic device of abridgement of expression in *gaṇita* is the representation of numbers with a single sign, different of letters, for the atomic numbers. In a first period there were primary signs for 1 to 9, 10, 100 and 1,000. Other numbers were expressed with combinations of primary signs (fig. 1).

VALEUR	ARAMÉO-INDIEN	KHAROSTRĪ de Niya	VALEUR	BRĀHMĪ d'Aśoka	Inscr. de Nānāghāt	Inscr. de Nāsik	VALEUR	NĀNĀGHĀT	NĀSIK	VALEUR	KUSĀNA
1	/	⎮⎮⌐	1		•	—	300			1	—
2	//		2		:	=	400			2	=
3	///		3			≡	500			3	≡
4	//// X	X	4	+		+⨉	700			4	
5	//// IX	IX	5			h	1000			5	
6	//X		6				2000			6	
7	///X		7				3000			7	
8	XX		8				4000			8	
9	/XX		9				6000			9	
10			10				8000			10	
11			13				10000			20	
20			20				20000			30	
30			40				70000			40	
50			50							50	
70			70							60	
100			80							70	
110			100							80	
200			200							90	
1000			356							100	

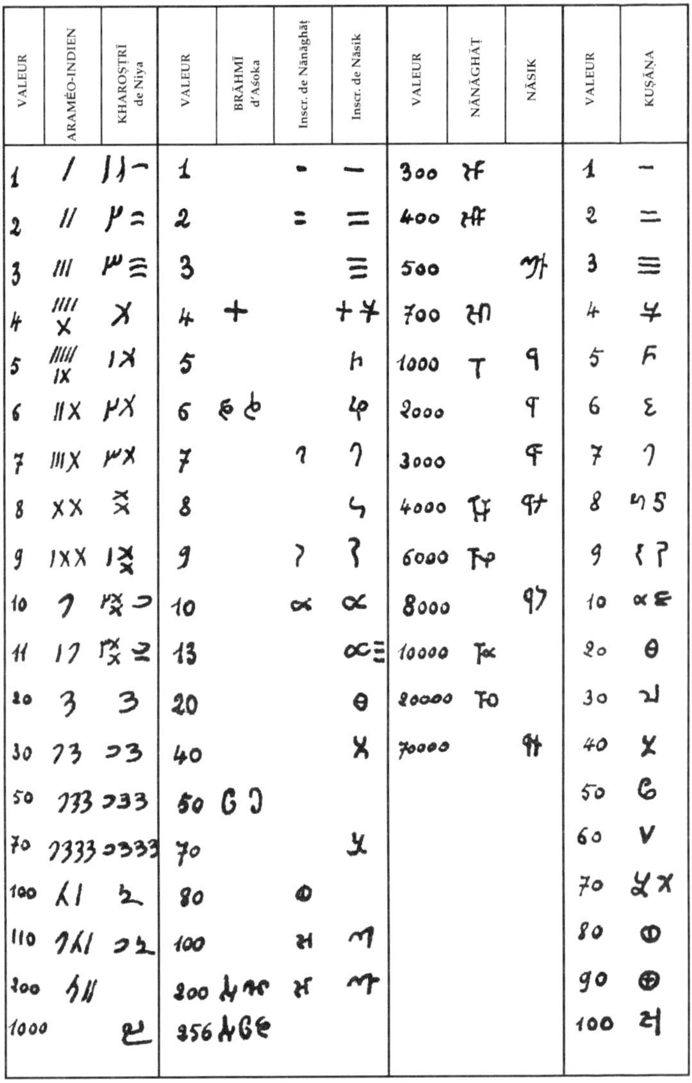

fig. 1: Oldest system of writing numbers

From the fifth century a still more simple method added 0 to the 9 atomic numbers, a value of a power of 10 was ascribed to the places of the writing of ciphers and for numbers above 9 one could proceed by combinations of only ten primary signs. Later works such as the Bakhśāli manuscript and manuscripts of commentaries display interesting graphic dispositions of numbers with frames for written operations, new signs such as a dot or what we call now "plus sign" for negative numbers, etc.

The introduction of written formalization in mathematics has not suppressed the oral habits of formalization of *paṇḍitas* engaged in mathematical and astronomical research. Āryabhaṭa composed a manual of astronomical calculations in mnemonic verses, especially in *āryā* meter. Written numbers cannot enter into a verse. He imagined a code to transpose a written number in pronounceable phonemes, preserving the shortness of the written form. In writing, the place of the cipher is significant: it shows it is a number of units, of tens, of hundreds, etc. First Āryabhaṭa fixed phonemes for places: starting from right each vowel refers to two places, odd called *varga* and even called *avarga*. Similarly the consonants from *k* to *m* denote the numbers 1 to 25 and are called *varga*; the eight consonants *y* to *h* denote 30, 40 and so on up to 100 and are called *avarga* (*fig.* 2). A *varga* consonant combined with a vowel denotes its number in the place denoted by the vowel in its *varga* place: *khu* denotes 2 placed in *varga u*, i.e. 20 000. An *avarga* consonant combined with a vowel denotes its number in the place denoted by the vowel in its *avarga* place: *yu* denotes 30 placed in *avarga u*, i.e. 3 00 000. Astronomers often deal with huge numbers. Āryabhaṭa transformed 158 crore 22 lakh 37 thousand and 5 hundred into *ṅiśibuṇḷṣkhṛ̥*. Even in verse it does not look poetical, or easy to pronounce. To decode it, it is practically necessary to write. Āryabhaṭa used it, but had no follower.

au *ai* *o* *e* *ḷ* *ṛ* *u* *i* *a*

0 0 0 0 0 0 0 0 0 0 0 0 0 0 0 0 0 0

A V A V A V A V A V A V A V A V A V

fig. 2: Āryabhaṭa's code for writing numbers with letters

In a sharp contrast another code of transposing written numbers in phonemes, the *kaṭapayādi* system enjoyed a great success and longevity. No inventor is known. It must have been elaborated after the time of Āryabhaṭa, when the place-based numeration system had become current in Jyotiṣa. *Kaṭapayādi* means "beginning with *k, ṭ, p* or *y*". One starts from anyone of these four letters and gives to each letter in the order the value 1 to 9; *ñ* and *n* denote 0. In a cluster of consonants, only the last one has a numerical value:

1	2	3	4	5	6	7	8	9	0
k	kh	g	gh	ṅ	c	ch	j	jh	ñ
ṭ	ṭh	ḍ	ḍh	ṇ	t	th	d	dh	n
p	ph	b	bh	m					
y	R	l	v	ś	ṣ	s	h	ḷ	

A lot of possibilities are given to transpose with a variety of phonemes a sequence of ciphers as it is written. It is possible to compose meaningful words at the same time one writes a number. A rather legendary author, at an early date, Vararuci, has composed 248 short sentences called *vākyas* to denote the longitudes of the moon. He has thus realized the shortest possible text, easily memorized, because the numbers coincide with common words. For example the 26th *vākya* is: *dhanyā vidyeyaṁ syāt* (may this knowledge be beneficent), which denotes the numbers 11-14-19. The three numbers denote successively one of the twelve *rāśis*, one of the thirty *tithis* sharing this *rāśi*, one of the sixtieth part of a *tithi* (*nāḍī* or *ili*). A procedure is defined to calculate mentally, everyday, on the basis of the memorized *vākyas*, the position of the moon, *tithi* and *nakṣatra*. It is of common use in orthodox circles of *paṇḍitas* in Kerala.

This is a true example of *lāghava* in oral expression, but depending on writing, one could ask the question: what is the advantage of converting the written number into the oral symbol? The *kaṭapayādi* is a code different from Āryabhaṭa's code, which was conceived chiefly for verse composition. The *vākyas* are not versified. Their main difference is the simplicity of the code and the possibility of forming meaningful sets of words. This is favourable to mental calculation. First it renders memorization easier. The letters of the code are shorter names of the ciphers. A *vākya* is another way of reading the written number, equally short, whereas the natural names have an appalling length for high numbers. Then a well-trained person will not require reconverting in writing. The shorter reading is a help for mental calculation, as the shorter spoken expression of numbers is less embarrassing than the long natural enunciation. This is a good case of *lāghava* helping mental work.

There is one more advantage to the *lāghava* in the *vākyas* of Vararuci, i.e. a *maṅgala* value. Many of them have been skilfully composed so as to yield an auspicious meaning. When they are not complete sentences, the given words have an expectative, which a *paṇḍita* will easily fill up *maṅgalārtham*. For example the first *vākya* is *gīr naḥ śreyaḥ* filled up with a word like *dadyāt* to obtain the meaning "may Sarasvatī give us the best".

With *śabdalāghava* goes *arthalāghava*, economy of mental work has been appreciated in all intellectual circles, for calculation, for reasoning and for argumentation. Naiyāyikas have attached such an importance to the quality of *lāghava*, that they often declare the lightest argument as their *siddhānta*.

Without neglecting *śabdalāghava* Navya-Nyāya has cultivated *arthalāghava* more than any other school. I extract from the Vyutpattivāda a simple example. Gadādhara, on the basis of Pāṇini's *sūtra* 2.3.2, "*karmaṇi dvitīyā*" defines the second nominal ending (accusative) as expressing *karmatva* "the property of being object of action" and not *karman* "the object" itself. Why? Gadādhara says:

> *karmaṇaś ca na tathātvam, karmaṇi nāmārthasya grāmāder abhedānvayasaṁbhave 'pi dhātvarthagamanādinā tadanvayāsaṁbhavāt, gauravāc ca* ।
>
> The object is not the meaning of the second ending, because, even if there is the possibility of a relation of identification of the village, meaning of the noun, with the object, there is no possibility of such relation with the action to go, meaning of the verb root, and because of heaviness of interpretation.

In the example *grāmaṁ gacchati* (he goes to the village) there are three elements: the village, meaning of the noun *grāma*; the idea of object of action, meaning of the second ending; the action to go, meaning of the verb. The question is to find how they accord between themselves. The village is the object; the relation between them is identity (*abheda*) and that relation is direct. But the village does not have a direct relation with the action. One could say that there is a direct relation (*nirūpakatvasaṁbandha*) between the property of being a *karman* and the action to go, and that property resides in the village. By a chain of relations (*paramparā*) the village gets related to the action to go. Here comes the notion of *gaurava*. The *paramparā* relation is a laborious view. Gadādhara prefers to say that the rule *karmaṇi dvitīyā* refers to the *karmatva* "property of being object of action". This is a metonymic mode of expression: the mention of the *dharmin* signifies *dharma*; and it is well accepted as a common power of words. By saying that the second ending means *karmatva*, it is possible to say that *karmatva*, which accords with the village by the relation of being borne by it, accords with the action to go by the direct relation of being a describer of it. In this way the word *grāmam* agrees with the verb *gacchati*. The final knowledge obtained from the sentence is:

> *grāmaniṣṭhakarmatānirūpakaṁ gamanam*
>
> The action to go having regard to the property of being object residing in the village.

Only immediate relations are now involved and the three elements are disposed in a simple scheme harmonizing the whole. This is not *śabdalāghava*. This is *arthalāghava*. No economy of thought is devoid of importance, when a complex theory has to be framed out of a multiplicity of elements. The case of the second ending is one among many in the project of Vyutpattivāda which is to harmonize all concepts observed in the understanding of language as a source of knowledge. The lightest way of harmonizing disparate elements is to build the theory with immediate relations.

The pleasure derived from *lāghava* is also manifest in literature. Sanskrit has a fine device of abbreviation which is the compound word. Pāṇini registers as optional the ability to express an idea in a syntactically connected set of words, the *vigrahavākya*, or in a *samāsa* which drops all syntactic connectors, *vibhakti*s, etc. Such a device exists in natural language. In ancient Sanskrit literary texts, Vedic religious poetry, the *vākya* mode of expression is much more frequent than the compound and *samāsa*s compound two or three words at the most. In course of time *samāsa*s have grown longer and longer, and have been given more and more prominence over the *vigrahavākya* mode. The literary advantage of *samāsa* is brevity and density of poetical effects. More is said in shortened words. More is implied and open to interpretation. More is left to imagination. Poetry is the realm of *vyañjanā* (suggestion). There is a relationship between *lāghava* and *dhvani*. This is *śabdalāghava* and *arthalāghava* combined together to the highest degree possible in natural language. And the pleasure we have in reading and savouring long *samāsas* tells the worth of *lāghava*.

In his *Kādambarī*, Bāṇa Bhaṭṭa describes the reception of a skilled and learned parrot in the court of King Śūdraka. Pomegranate seeds are offered to him. They are qualified with a *samāsa* of twelve words:

> *hari-nakhara-bhinna-matta-mātaṅga-kumbha-mukta-rakta-ārdra-muktā-phala-tviṁṣi khaṇḍitāni dāḍima-bījāni*
>
> Meaning word for word in the same order: "lion-rent-intoxicated-elephant-bump-released-blood-humid-pearl-fruit-glow separated pomegranate-seeds".

Pomegranate seeds have brightness similar to the glow of a pearl wet of the blood released from the frontal globes of a rutting elephant, rent by the claws of a lion. According to poets' convention there are pearls in the frontal globes of the elephant. Lions are told to kill elephants by jumping on their back and tearing out the frontal globes of the Indian elephant. Pearls tainted by blood fall on the ground. The image speaks by itself to describe the red seed which has always a clear spot of transparency. Why such a violent image? The context explains it. The parrot is brought from the forest. And that is suggested by the wild character of the image. An explanation expressed in full words would have ruined the beauty of the compound. The close proximity of the words, achieved in the compound form, reinforces, intensifies the striking contrast of the image.

Lāghava is an essential quality, cultivated by Sanskrit *paṇḍitas*' circles with full awareness of its value. It is met with occasionally in literatures of the West. The concept of general rule and exception is there. But there are not so many instances of caring for economy of words. There was not the same awareness to its price. Formalization became a must in mathematics and allied sciences at a late period, in the seventeenth century with Leibnitz and others. Nowadays the Indian model of rejoicing at the economy of half of a short vowel is celebrated all over the world.

6

Rāmāyaṇa and the Elements of Ecology

Vasundhara Filliozat

Rāmāyaṇa is one of the most famous epics in the world and Vālmīki is the author. *Rāmāyaṇa* is known to be one of the longest and most ancient epics. It is one of the biggest Kāvyas in Sanskrit and easy to understand. Usually this poetical work is given to the beginner to learn Sanskrit. It is not only popular in India but also abroad in countries such as Thailand, Cambodia, Bali and Sri Lanka. It has even travelled to Guadeloupe and Martinique, French West Indies islands. Before coming to the main aim of the article we would like to give some interesting episodes which are not in the original text but current in oral traditions.

Some popular episodes that a common man narrates are not in the original *Rāmāyaṇa*. Take for example in the Sundara-Kāṇḍa when Hanuman gives Rāma's ring to Sītā, he was happy having accomplished his duty. So he starts dancing and jumping from tree to tree in the Aśokavana. That disturbed the peaceful atmosphere of the garden. So Rāvaṇa sends his men to arrest Hanumān and bring him to his court. To insult Hanumān Rāvaṇa does not give him a seat. Hanumān decides to take revenge on this and coils his tail and sits on it, making his seat higher than that of Rāvaṇa's throne. This episode is not in the original *Rāmāyaṇa*. In Paṭṭaḍakal there is a temple to God Lokeśvara built by Lokamahādevī, queen of Vikramāditya II's of Bādāmī Cāḷukya dynasty in the eighth century CE. Many episodes from the epic have been carved on one of the pillars of the *raṅgamaṇḍapa* in which there is the episode of Hanumān in the court of Rāvaṇa seated on his coiled tail. It shows that the interpolation of this anecdote must have been done before the eighth century.

One more such anecdote tells how the two brothers Vālin and Sugrīva came to have monkey faces. To know the story we have to see *Pampāmāhātmya*, a *sthalapurāṇa*, where local stories about different parts of the famous pilgrim centre Hampi are related. To enhance the importance of the site each and every *tīrtha*, lake and place, stories have been told.

In the area near the western gate of the site there is a hillock called Somādri and a lake Somatīrtha. Once Sage Gautama with his three children went to Hampi to attend the fair. Of the three children the elder one was a girl and the younger two were boys. On the way, as the boys were of tender age and it was hot the father with much compassion, took the boys on his shoulders and began to walk. The girl did not appreciate it. She murmured:

> Ah! What a father! He makes his own daughter to walk in the hot sun and carries others' children on his shoulders.

On hearing this, the angry father asked her the meaning of what she murmured. To know the truth, the girl said:

> Dip your children in the water of Somatīrtha and you will understand the meaning of what I murmered.

No sooner the boys came out of the lake than their faces turned into that of monkeys and the girl came out unaffected. The father was flabbergasted by this transformation and questioned his wife Ahalyā to tell the truth. She confessed that the elder son is born to Indra and the younger to Sun-god, but the daughter is his. The mother was not happy with the denunciation of her daughter and cursed her too to have the face of a monkey. This girl is Añjanā, mother of future Hanumān.

This story is not in the original *Rāmāyaṇa* either. A detailed account of it is found in Pampāmāhātmya, Madhyabhāga, Pūrvārdha, chapter 110. The same episode is so common in Cambodia that it is even interpreted in the murals of the Royal Palace at Phnom Penh.

Often south Indians get confused when a north Indian vegetable called *sītāphala* is served. *Sītāphala* for a south Indian is the custard apple; it is a fruit and cannot be cooked. South

Photo courtesy: Mme. Marie Gamonet

Indians are wonderstruck at the idea of cooking *sītāphala* as a vegetable. For north Indians, especially the Delhites, *sītāphala* means a vegetable and that is "pumpkin".

Once while going through the book *Namma hoṭṭeyalli Dakṣiṇa America* (*South America in Our Stomach*) by the famous botanist of Karnataka B.G.L. Swamy, son of D.V. Gundappa a poet of yester years, read a story told by his grandmother. This book is in Kannaḍa. The story, according to his grandmother, is from *Rāmāyaṇa.* When Sītā was carried away by Rāvaṇa and kept her as a prisoner in the Aśokavana in his capital Laṅkā, Rāma and Lakṣmaṇa were going in search of the princess. On their way the two young princes met Śabarī, a woman of hunters' community. She was a great devotee of Rāma. Happy to see the idol of her devotion, she invited them to her hut and served fruits. The story is the same as in *Rāmāyaṇa.* She used to taste the fruits before offering them. She did not serve one of the fruits. Rāma asked her why she did not offer it. She answered: "This fruit will be served to you by Sītā. So I have kept it for her." The grandmother of Swamy ended her story by saying that since then this fruit is called *sītāphala*. Swamy's grandmother did not know the source of this story. Further, he writes that the custard apple is from South America, how can it be known in the times of Rāma. Probably, our author also did not know what *sītāphala* in the north is. This episode of *sītāphala* is also not in the original *Rāmāyaṇa*. From which version of the epic Swamy's grandmother learnt is also unknown to us.

Many such anecdotes are current in different parts of India but their sources are unknown. It will be nice if a collection of such anecdotes can be published one day.

There is an interesting portion in the third *kāṇḍa* that is in the Araṇya-Kāṇḍa (Forest Chapter) of *Rāmāyaṇa* by Vālmīki. The context is that the princely family is in exile. Rāma and Sītā along with Lakṣmaṇa are at Pañcavaṭī. As the title of the *kāṇḍa* chapter suggests, the princely family is in the forest. The worries of Vālmīki about the conservation of the flora and fauna of the forest are expressed through the speech of Sītā.

Here Sītā is worried. She is worried because Rāma and Lakṣmaṇa belong to the kṣatriya warrior class. That means that they are always with their weapons. Sītā fears that when one is always with weapons he is naturally tempted to use them. Ascetics live with their disciples in their monasteries. By and large, forests are ideal places for monasteries. So the sages live in forests. It is believed that the peaceful atmosphere dances in the monasteries of these sages. There is no enmity between the cruellest animals such as tigers and soft-natured deers.

Vālmīki's worry is expressed through the words of Sītā in the following ten verses in the Pañcavaṭī of Araṇya-Kāṇḍa:

tvam hi bāṇadhanuṣpāṇir bhrātrā saha vanaṁ gataḥ ।
dr̥ṣṭvā vanacarān sarvān kaccit kuryāḥ śaravyayam ।। 1 ।।

You carry a bow and arrows in hands, move around in the forest, on seeing the forest dwelling beings, you will make use of your arms, needlessly.

kṣatriyāṇām iha dhanur hutāśasyendhanāni ca ।
samīpataḥ sthitaṁ tejobalamuchrayate bhr̥śam ।। 2 ।।

The arc placed near a kṣatriya, (is like) combustible placed near fire, favours the power.

evam etat purāvr̥ttaṁ śastrasaṁyogakāraṇaṁ ।
agnisaṁyogavad dhetḥ śastrasaṁyoga ucyate ।।3 ।।

It is an old story caused by the association of weapon. Association of a weapon, so said, is the cause for (violence) like that of fire.

kva ca śastraṁ kva ca vanaṁ kva ca kṣātraṁ tapaḥ kva ca ।
vyāviddham idam asmābhir deśadharmas tu pūjyatāṁ
।। 4 ।।

On one hand weaponry, on the other, the forest, (What is the relationship between them?) On one side the kṣatriya and on the other, the ascetics; both are opposites. Our duty is to respect the rules of the place.

kadaryakaluṣā buddhir jāyate śastrasevanāt ।
punar gatvā tv ayodhyāyāṁ kṣatradharme cariṣyasi ।। 5 ।।

Dirty mindedness is caused by the use of arms in the minds of (individuals); you will follow the warriors' path on going back to Ayodhyā.

akṣayā tu bhavet prītiḥ śvaśrūśvaśurayor mama ।
yadi rājyaṁ hi saṁnyāsya bhaves tvam nirato muniḥ ।। 6 ।।

That you will become a joy of my mother-in-law and my father-in-law when you will hand over the kingdom (to an eligible successor) and with pleasure become an ascetic.

dharmād arthaḥ prabhavati dharmāt prabhavate sukhaṁ ।
dharmeṇa labhate sarvaṁ dharmasāram idaṁ jagat ।। 7 ।।

With *dharma* grows prosperity; by *dharma* one acquires happiness; everything is obtainable through *dharma*; the world has for support the quintessence *dharma*.

ātmānaṁ niyamais tais taiḥ karṣayitvā prayatnataḥ ।
prāpyate nipuṇair dharmo na sukhāl labhate sukham ।। 8 ।।

By mastering with efforts, by imposing (on one's own self) such and such a restriction the sages obtain *dharma*; bliss is not obtained by enjoyment.

nityaṁ śucimatiḥ saumya cara dharmaṁ tapovane ।
sarvaṁ tu viditaṁ tubhyaṁ trailokyam api tattvataḥ ।। 9 ।।

O! Ye Gentleman, always pure minded, practise *dharma* in the hermitages; everything is known to thee, even the three worlds.

strīcāpalād etad upāhṛtam me dharmam ca vaktum tava kaḥ samarthaḥ ।
vicārya buddhyā tu sahānujena yad rocate tat kuru mā cireṇa ॥ 10 ॥

Owing to the feminine anxiety, I have uttered all this. Who can speak to you about the *dharma*? But even then, think over it with your brother and act as it pleases you.

Sītā ends her discourse on *dharma* by giving the example of a sage who was so much absorbed in asceticism that even Indra got scared. So the God comes, in disguise, gives a weapon and requests the sage to keep it till his return. By the fear of losing it, the sage begins to carry it with him wherever he went. Once, by fun he used it to cut the grass. Surprised by the sharpness and the rapidity of the weapon, gradually, the sage begins to make use of it often. In the beginning he was using it for small purposes but progressively his actions become more and more cruel. These veal actions make him to fall in worst of hells.

Rāma understood the quintessence of her speech and took a vow that he will not touch weapons without reason. When Indra's army approaches Rāma to kill the animals that trouble them most, his answer makes the reader understand that he is impressed by Sītā's discourse. He gives a negative answer by reminding them the vow that he has made: "not to touch the weapons to kill the animals in the forest without reason"

In Sanskrit and also in other Indian languages the *dharma* has a wider meaning. It is difficult to render its exact translation in European languages. So we have maintained the same term *dharma* in our translation. The most important point that is mentioned here is that the world is based on *dharma*. It stands good even today. Vālmīki's ideas about the protection of the nature are also of the actuality.

These passages prove that already the Sage Vālmīki was worried about the ecology at his time. Since the times of *Rāmāyaṇa*, human nature has not changed. Even today one speaks of ecology but the actions are not coherent.

7

Theodor Stcherbatsky and His Followers on Translation of Sanskrit Philosophical Texts

Victoria Lysenko

THE contribution of Sanskrit to the development of world thought could not take place without the work of translation of texts in different domains of traditional knowledge. That is why it is important to be aware of the translation enterprise, its problems and challenges. In every translation there is a different amount or degree of what is properly being translated. It depends upon a distance between the "input" and the "output" languages, which may be defined by the difference between their appropriate cultural and civilizational perspectives. Within the frames uniting languages of one family, there may be many common structures, words, expressions, which can simply be transposed from one language to another, for example, Latin words in Roman languages.

If we take the so-called East–West civilizational and cultural opposition, the most important distance is that between Western civilization and China. We may not even call it an opposition in the proper sense of the word, because these civilizations are simply incommensurable as different systems of reference. Within the frame of the hieroglyphic system quite another style of reasoning had been developed, many problems, formulated on the basis of

Indo-European languages, did not arise for this very reason as the French scholar François Julien brilliantly showed. For instance, China had no ontology, no such concepts as substance, quality, time, subject, object, etc. Instead, there evolved an interesting concept of becoming as the unfolding of a self-regulation – Dao – of Nature.[1]

What unites Indian and Western thought is the Indo-European linguistic matrix which allows a certain kind of meaning-making. Sanskrit is in no way less apt to express philosophical meanings than ancient Greek or Latin. It distinguishes between being and non-being, being as presence and being as becoming – verbal roots *AS* and *BHU*, substrates and attributes, and more concretely substance (*dravya*) and quality (*guṇa*), subsistence (*sthāna*) and motion (*karman*), time (*kāla*) and space (*dik*), subject as such (*Ātman*), object (*artha*), knowing subject (*jñātṛ*), and agent (*kartṛ*). In Sanskrit, it is possible to form abstract substantives and, hence, to operate abstractions and general terms. The kinship can be traced not only in the domain of thought-structuring categories but also in related problematizations and conceptualizations as, for instance, the relationship between substance and quality, essence and phenomenon, part and whole, between universals and particulars, and cause and effect. One may call this fundamental structural affinity a common Indo-European horizon of meanings.

As Russian is even closer to Sanskrit by its grammatical structure than many of modern European languages, it allows a more literal translation.[2]

---

1 François Julien, *Le Détour et l'accès, Stratégies du sens en Chine, en Grèce*, Grasset, 1995; Un Sage est sans idée, ou l'autre de la philosophie, « L'ordre philosophique », Seuil, 1998; Du « Temps », *Éléments d'une philosophie du vivre*, Paris, réed. Le Livre de Poche, 2012.

2 We have six cases, three genders, no articles.

In this paper, I will dwell on the methodological problems pertaining to the translation of Sanskrit philosophical texts raised by famous Russian Buddhologist and Indologist Theodor Stcherbatsky (1866–1942) and developed by his brilliant disciple Otto Rosenberg (1888–1919). Then, I will address myself to the problems of translation as discussed by some modern Russian Sanskritologists.

In the translation of Sanskrit philosophical texts Stcherbatsky followed what he had called the philosophical method as against the philological method of literal, or word-to-word translation. He was one of the first European scholars to single out Sanskrit philosophical texts as a special gender of Sanskrit literature.

> These texts are written in a distinctive style that has little to do with the style of poetic and narrative literature. They also have special technical terms, the value of which is not always easy to guess. For a long time European scholarship, engaged in the development of other branches of Indian literature, did not pay enough attention to these works. They were considered as obscure and full of barren scholastic subtleties, which were of no evident or hidden value. This view led to the fact that the ancient Indians were declared to be generally incapable of exact thinking and clear presentation. These merits were attributed exclusively to the ancient Greek and modern science. If such an opinion has been circulated even among Sanskritologists what one might expect from scholars to whom the original Indian writings were completely inaccessible.[3]

Stcherbatsky, further, explained that this state of affairs subsisted until the return from India of Georg Bühler, who

[3] Here and further on I quote from the first famous Stcherbatsky's philosophical work entitled *Theory of Knowledge and Logic According the Teaching of the Late Buddhist*, vol. 1, Sanct-Peterburg, 1903, pp. 53-54 (modern re-edition, 1995, pp. 56-58) (in Russian).

during his prolonged stay in this country had established close relations with the native Indian scholars and worked with them on the translation of some Śāstric texts. Wrote Stcherbatsky:

> With the help of local tradition, the rich content of the Sanskrit scholarly literature has become evident, and one has to replace the charge against Indians that they are incapable of exact thinking with the charge against European scholars that they are incapable to understand them.

After publication of Jacobi's translation of one of the best Indian works on the theory of poetry "no one will doubt that in the depth of analysis, in the power of thought and precision of expression Indian scholars had no equal in ancient times".[4]

As far as philosophical texts proper are concerned Stcherbatsky remarks:

> . . . the difficulty of their translation has increased by the fact that philosophy hasn't language of its own and expresses the concepts it has to operate with, using metaphors. The translator now and then has to deal with the words, well known to him, but referred to some concepts that clearly have nothing in common with the ordinary meanings of these words. Only through a hypothetical reconstruction of the philosophical system in question, one can at the beginning only approximately define the concept, which is metaphorically denoted by such a term. A literal translation would be completely useless as it does not express a thought of the author.[5]

In other words, a word-to-word translation will present the translation of the metaphor, rather than of a term.

Stcherbatsky continues:

---

4 *Theory of Knowledge and Logic*, p. 54.

5 Ibid., p. 55.

> The difficulties in translating technical terms had lead some scholars to the practice of leaving technical terms without translation.

Russian scholar is against this practice. He said that in his own work:

> We did not leave a word untranslated. We generally tried where possible to penetrate into the thought of the author in its entirety and to express it in Russian as it could be expressed by the author himself, if he would have to write in that language. In those cases when we had to deviate considerably from the Sanskrit text or to introduce insertions and supplements which were needed to make the text more understandable, we add a note with a literal translation. But it should be remarked that the literal translation may be relevant only for those who are familiar with the Sanskrit language. Those who are not familiar with it, if they would like to compare the literal translation of some particular place with the statement of its meaning and by doing so to check the adequacy of translation, they can easily fall into mistake, since the translation of each element of Sanskrit proposition is rather an explanation of its construction than the rendering of the thought it contains.[6]

In conclusion, Stcherbatsky refers to the requirements for translation formulated by the famous Russian philosopher Vladimir Soloviev with regard to the Greek classics, especially Plato:

> After having mastered the ideas of the original text in their fullness and accuracy of expression, in any particular case, representing some difficulty for the literal translation, it is necessary to put yourself a question: How does this author – say Plato (one easily can replace Plato by Dharmakīrti or Śaṅkara) – with all the peculiarities of his mind, character,

[6] *Theory of Knowledge and Logic*, p. 55.

> style and way of thinking as we know them from historical sources – express this thought in all its shades of meaning had he knew Russian, and had he wrote in that language?[7]

A good translation, according to Soloviev, is a translation in which a translator so to say platonize himself, while making Plato to think like a Russian thinker, so a good translation of Plato must draw upon two sources – Greek and Russian languages. If we replace Plato by Dharmakīrti, the situation of the good translation will be as follows: Russian translator must make himself Dharmakīrti and make Dharmakīrti to think in the spirit of Russian language. Is such a situation possible?

Let us note, first, that neither philological nor interpretive methods of translation outlined by Stcherbatsky do not purport to hermeneutical reflection. Stcherbatsky implicitly believes in the absolute transparency of the input original language, and the language of the translator, or output language, Sanskrit and Russian for each other. The main guideline was to him a certain idea, which is one, whereas languages expressing it may be different and interchangeable. This approach is based on the conception of so-called *philosophia perennis*, eternal philosophy – quite widespread in his time. Historical and cultural dimension is something secondary as compared with a number of eternal philosophical ideas that may be expressed in different languages, in different cultures and historical periods.

Those European thinkers who believed in *philosophia perennis* profess a certain understanding of language: according to them, language is merely a docile instrument of expressing thought. So the main task is to identify this or that idea, considered to be perennis, the question of its formulating in different languages – is of the secondary order. If Dharmakīrti had come

---

[7] *Theory of Knowledge and Logic*, p. 56.

to the same ideas as Kant (time and cultural distance are of no importance), we commit no error in rendering his thoughts in Kantian categories.

Let us turn to Otto Rosenberg. For him, some overlap or similarity of thought between India and Europe does not make the task of translation easier. On the contrary, it makes it more difficult:

> The original point of departure and the main problems are the same in Europe and in India, differences within their traditions, too, because the laws of thought are the same for all, but taking in account that the development of these streams of thought in Europe and India were quite independent from each other, the way taken by either tradition, were different, there were another formulations of the issues, another methodology, and terminology, many of the concept have a different meaning. That's why sometimes it is so hard to find a suitable translation. Difficulties are in words but not in the thoughts.[8]

If Stcherbatsky said about his research that in it: ". . . the language of Buddhist philosophers is rendered as far as possible by the language of modern philosophy",[9] Rosenberg wrote:

> Whenever possible, the exposition [of the Buddhist philosophy – V.L.] should be carried out in a simple language, avoiding technical terms and refraining from underlining the parallels [with Western philosophy – V.L.]. Insertion of the European philosophy into the Buddhist scheme of ideas is extremely dangerous, it can easily lead to a false understanding of Buddhism: each [Buddhist] technical term has its own relation

---

[8] Publication of the manuscript note of Rosenberg in my paper in Russian: "Stcherbasky and Rosenberg: Double Portrait against the Background of the Époque", *Works of Russian Anthropological School*, Moscow, 2007.

[9] Ibid., p. 6.

> to a number of other terms which unwittingly come up by association. Therefore, even if the two terms – one European and one Buddhist – correspond to each other, their related associations may be quite different. That is why the translation of Buddhist terms, and, in general philosophical terms of other cultural systems is so difficult. The difficulty lies not in the peculiarities of language, but in the heterogeneity of the series of associations related in each case, with this or that concept. Therefore it is necessary for the translation of some technical terms by our (Russian) words, for example, "object", "sensuality", "mental", etc., to make a reservation, pointing out to the ideas which are arising in the person brought up with the help of these foreign terms. *Artha* and *viṣaya* correspond to the term "object", but they have nothing in common with the idea of objectum. "Salvation" and *nirvāṇa* are the same, since both are the ultimate religious goal, but the association of the word *nirvāṇa* with the concept like "salvation" is impossible.[10]

It is hard to escape the impression that by these words Rosenberg implicitly criticized his teacher, his interpretive method, because all he had mentioned here: the use of the special Western terminology, of the parallels, or "the insertion of European philosophy into the Buddhist scheme of ideas", may have a direct relation to the works of Th. I. Stcherbatsky. Rosenberg, unlike Stcherbatsky, dealed with what we now call the hermeneutical reflection. He problematized the translation not as a rendering of senses pertaining to one language by the means of another language, but in a much more fundamental way – as a tool for understanding of the other cultural tradition. If we translate any philosophical term relying only on its "purely linguistic" value as a word, the concept rendered by it may remain inaccessible,

---

[10] Rosenberg, "Problems of Buddhist Philosophy", re-edited in: O.O. Rosenberg, *Works on Buddhist Philosophy*, Moscow, 1991, pp. 81-82.

but the concepts are not necessarily transmitted even in the case of the so-called philosophical translation. Sanskrit philosophical terms are loaded with their specific associations, the same with terms of the European philosophical vocabulary, which are, too, embedded in their net of associations. The associative character of terminology is a serious problem for the translator noticed by Rosenberg but completely ignored by Stcherbatsky.

Rosenberg continues:

> As far as literal translations – in the etymological sense – are concerned, one can run across a new threat: the translated term may coincide with the proposed translation only in one of its meanings, in which case there may arise a misunderstanding and the inability to properly understand the translation. Equivalents such as the notorious "«law», «loi» instead of «*dharma*», «name and form» instead of «*nāmarūpa*»", etc. are translations of this category. . . .[11]

Elsewhere, Rosenberg puts forward the following argument:

> As the special terms are borrowed from the ordinary language, their etymological meanings contribute little or nothing to the understanding of their philosophical significance in the system, in exactly the same way we pay relatively little attention to the basic etymological meanings of philosophical terms and abstract words in general.[12]

According to Rosenberg,

> The question concerning the method of translation of the Buddhist terms is still far from resolved, it is necessary, according to need, to apply one or the other mode of translation.[13]

---

11 *Works on Buddhist Philosophy*, p. 82.

12 Ibid., p. 105.

13 Ibid., p. 82.

Thus, the translation strategy of Rosenberg consists not in a commitment to one or to another method of translation – literal or interpretive, for him the use of the method depends on the situation in question. Elsewhere, he adds one more important feature:

> We should not seek to establish the same meaning for all the cases, we should not, after making sure that this is impossible, prematurely conclude, that the Buddhist authors are illogical and not systematic. The works on Buddhism are suffering from this tendency to render a term always by the same equivalent.[14]

Rosenberg concludes his reflections with the words:

> The difficulty indicated above is of the utmost importance: it constantly reminds us that, although almost all ideas are evidently common, however they are expressed differently. We can meet in the Buddhists texts the same solutions of the same issues as in the European systems, however, their methods are different, and the issues are explored in a different manner. The value of systematic Indian philosophy as well as Indian philosophy in general lies in the fact that in it the problems which are known to us are analysed differently. Therefore it is particularly important to keep to the original Buddhist schema, not transposing the Indian ideas into the frame of our systems.[15]

Thus the gap, the discrepancy between the Buddhist and Western systems, is, according to Rosenberg, an important stimulator for our hermeneutical reflection. Why the otherness of Buddhism and Indian philosophy in general was so precious to him, why it was so important not to lose, not to dissolve it in a universality of *philosophia perennis*? And how should we understand this

---

[14] *Works on Buddhist Philosophy*, p. 149.

[15] Ibid., p. 82.

otherness, if we have no other means then those forged within the European culture?

In modern Russian Indological studies, Vladimir Shokhin, an admirer and follower of Stcherbatsky[16] calls his method of interpretive translation an "hermeneutic extreme".[17] He definitely opts for a literal translation:

> The task we set before ourselves in the translation of classical Sāṁkhya texts was to reveal their literal meaning – hence the frequent use of square brackets and an attempt to avoid what may be called interpretive, or modernizing translation, as well as transliteration of the terms without translation.[18]

According to him the translated texts have to speak "with a European in his language and not soliloquizing in their own".[19]

But, as we know, the European philosophical language is the language forged by European philosophers like Plato, Descartes, Kant and Hegel. What is then the difference between the literal translation in Shokhin's and the interpretative translation of Stcherbatsky?

In my opinion, the old dispute about literal and interpretative translation of the Sanskrit texts is actually a dispute about the different levels of interpretation. Strictly speaking, a literal translation, that is, translation of the word, not of the concept, when dealing with philosophical texts is counter-productive

---

[16] He wrote an excellent book about him *Stcherbatsky and His Comparative Philosophy*, Moscow: Institute of Philosophy, 1998.

[17] Ibid., p. 187.

[18] *Moonlight of Sāṁkhya («Sāṁkhya-kārikā» « Sāṁkhya–kārikā-bhāṣya» «Tattva-kaumudī»)*. Introduction, Translation from Sanskrit into Russian, and Notes by V.K. Shokhin, Moscow, 1995, p. 8.

[19] Ibid.

(in that respect I agree with Stcherbatsky), but Stcherbatsky's intention to transpose the Sanskrit text into the European system of reference in order to make life easier for the reader is also open to criticism.

The desire to translate the Sanskrit text in such a way that it would talk with the European reader in his or her own language (which was a purpose of both Stcherbatsky and Shokhin) creates an illusion of the absolute transparency of Indian tradition, its complete and thorough expressibility in the horizon of European categories and concepts. It seems to me that the modern reader is quite prepared to discover the resistance of the material pertaining to other culture, to be aware of the dockings and discordings between European and Indian systems of thought. Modern reader of philosophical literature is quite capable to understand that there are untranslatable terms, and problematic translations. A modern translation from my point of view must not only explain but also problematize, highlight the cultural otherness of the other as against one's own cultural identity. In other words, a translation is a dialogue between two languages, two cultural systems. A good translation, in my view – is a translation which takes in account the situation of the translator in-between two cultures, which embraces not only the immediate meaning of this or that word or sentence, but also the general self-images and self-description of both Indian and European traditions.

Let us return to Vladimir Soloviev example referred to by Stcherbatsky. In my opinion, it is important to preserve a cultural distance between Plato, or Dharmakīrti, and Russian, or European philosophical discourse. Before translating the Sanskrit term *manas* by the word "mind", the translator must put the following question – can mind be insentient according to the

European philosophical sense of this word? As we know, it is not possible, so *manas* which in some Indian philosophical schools is understood as an instrument of conscious Self (*ātman*), deprived of its own consciousness, cannot be translated as "mind".

For Andrew Paribok, our famous Sanskrit and Pāli scholar, as well as for Vladimir Shokhin, the translation of every word – is a victory of translator, while the Sanskrit term in the Russian transcription or transliteration without translation – is his or her defeat. In this respect they follow Stcherbatsky's ideas. However, it seems to me that any principle of translation, even if by itself it is reasonable, has its limits. Well, the translation will speak with the reader in his own language, but the cultural flavour of the original text will completely evaporate. Hence, a disappointment and even mistrust of the readers towards some translations that look like habitual Western philosophical discourse.

A translator should not be afraid of Sanskrit terminology. Introducing Sanskrit terms, which do not have analogues in Russian or in other languages, could be a contribution to their development. Such Sanskrit words, like *karma* and *saṁsāra* are already firmly established in our everyday language. The Russian language is full of all sorts of loans and open to innovation. It is good to gradually accustom the reader to the Sanskrit terminology, simplifying its assimilation by transliteration in Cyrillic and breaking compound words into their constituent parts.

For the Russian translation of the Sanskrit philosophical texts a problem of the loaned foreign philosophical terminology suggests itself. Andrew Paribok believes that since the original Sanskrit or Pāli text does not contain any loaned foreign terminology, it is necessary to ensure that the translated terms remained Russian, not foreign words.[20] However, in practice it is impossible to implement such a principle, especially with regard to the specific logical or philosophical terminology, basically, borrowed from Roman languages. You can certainly say "love of wisdom", "liubomudriye" instead of "philosophy", but this Russian word does not cease to be a translation of the relevant Greek term. It seems to me that the "linguistic patriotism", understood as a desire to remain within the Russian language – is an absolute Utopia, especially when dealing with philosophical texts. After all, our cultural heritage is not limited to "autochthonous" Russian philosophy (whether such a philosophy ever existed is still a question?). It would therefore be wrong to somehow restrict the use of European philosophical terminology in the translation of Sanskrit texts. What is important is to explain what kind of meaning this or that European term has in relation to India. For example, one can use the expression "Indian syllogism", but the restrictions of application of this term to the Nyāya or Buddhist logic should be elucidated. The main thing is to keep the balance between the typological similarity of our traditions of thought, which makes them constituent elements of the common Indo-European horizon of meanings, on the one hand, and the distance separating their cultural and civilizational frames, on the other. In this sense, my point of view is closer to that of Rosenberg who made an accent on the otherness, than to that of Stcherbatsky who put forward the idea of *philosophia perennis*.

---

[20] *Questions of King Milinda*, Introduction, Translation from Pāli into Russian, and Notes by A.V. Paribok, Moscow: Oriental Literature,1989, pp. 15-16.

8

Contribution of Sanskrit to World Thought
The Case of Consciousness studies

Anindita Niyogi Balslev

THE subject matter of discussion in the course of these three days is "Contribution of Sanskrit to World Thought". This important topic that has a wide spectrum is worth reflecting upon especially under the present socio-political circumstances when much needs to be done in order to remove the imbalances between knowledge and power through institutional mechanisms. It is therefore laudable that educational institutions like Rashtriya Sanskrit Sansthan are created and which in turn seek to draw our attention to this matter urgently.

I am personally deeply thankful for the invitation that Kulapati Kutumba Shastry has extended to me. I see this, first, as an occasion to share some of my own concerns especially with reference to teaching of philosophy in a global context. Second, since Sanskrit has been a medium of several disciplines over the centuries, this also provides an opportunity to listen to and learn from other scholars who will address the general theme of this meeting from various perspectives.

As a student of philosophy I am especially pleased that the event is taking place in Śṛṅgerī – an adored place of pilgrimage associated with the name of one of the greatest philosophers that has ever lived. As we know, Ācārya Śaṅkara's philosophical exposition of Advaita Vedānta centres on a bold formulation of the idea of consciousness as absolute and foundational. His rendition of this view is a piece of philosophical marvel, even when one seeks to disagree with that reading. Ancient critics deservedly described his style (*śailī*) as one that combines clarity with depth (*prasanna-gambhīra*). One learns from it that when abstruse vocabulary is deliberately coined as an explanatory tool, it does not necessarily make the issues more comprehensible. Moreover, his discourse has not only enriched and empowered the practice of rigorous and abstract philosophical thinking, it has also shown how profound its impact can be when it is integrated into a philosophy of life and not viewed just as a figment of ivory-tower speculation. Indeed, while thinking aloud about the contribution of Sanskrit as a medium of expression in the context of the ongoing philosophical enterprise in the domain of consciousness-studies today, it is tempting to observe that some acquaintance with his impeccable style of expression and mode of argumentation can provide inspiration to anyone engaged in reflective thinking, be that in India or elsewhere.

Let us note that in our time the importance of humanities in general is being played down in educational offerings – this phenomenon is visible worldwide. Under these circumstances, the concern for the propagation of Sanskrit as a language is certainly of crucial importance. However, it seems to me that more attention also needs to be focused on how to make accessible ideas from various fields of enquiry that have been expressed through the medium of Sanskrit (as in Darśana Śāstra, Arthaśāstra, Dharmaśāstra, etc.) over the centuries. For figuring out how best to serve the cause of teaching Sanskrit as a language there are scholars present here, many of them actually belong to the Rashtriya Sanskrit Sansthan created in many parts of India with this in view, who are well equipped to address this question.

My concern, however, is how to address the latter task especially with reference to teaching of philosophy. The question is what further needs to be done that can in some way enhance curiosity and eventually appreciation of these remarkably rich thought traditions that are still being marginalized at present. Do we need able translators who can translate those original texts, commentaries, glosses, etc. that have not been translated before or have not been adequately done so? Do we also need along with these lucid and critical renditions of the network of ideas discussed in such works? If these philosophical renditions in Sanskrit are made available into other languages in a way that can ably highlight their conceptual significance, the latter may eventually attract attention of readers to the translated texts and from thereon gradually to the sources in the original language – that is in Sanskrit. Perhaps, some may even become keen to specialize in that area of investigation. It sounds like a colossal work but was it not the case that such projects were actually undertaken when the Indian Sanskritic civilization was at its peak inside India and was spreading itself outside of India? In any case it seems important to figure out some ways and means for a wider appreciation of the kind of contributions for which Sanskrit has been the vehicle in different fields and make these accessible to a larger audience – that is to those who cannot be expected to go to the original sources straightaway. There are those who are open to ideas and are not votaries of the thesis of untranslatability or of any radical form of cultural otherness, as advocated by certain proponents of extreme form of cultural relativism.

Surely, inability to read a certain language cannot stop one from appreciating ideas made accessible through translations.

Had that been so, how have they propagated, for example, French or German philosophical traditions in UK, USA, Australia or in India for that matter? One does not have to be an Indologist in order to appreciate the conceptual world of India but one may choose to become one when a steady acquaintance with the profundity of the Indian conceptual world pushes one toward it. Today an open "cross-cultural conversation" in various areas of human enquiry is crucial with the view of creating some balance between knowledge and power and for that appropriate tools need to be found.

In order to exemplify this point, I would like to make a few observations, based on some aspects of my own study of the large topic of consciousness in which I have been engaged over the years. (Apart from a number of published papers, there is my monograph entitled *The Enigma of I-consciousness*, Oxford University Press, New Delhi, 2013.) This ongoing research has, on the one hand, made me keenly aware of the invaluable resources that the Sanskritic philosophical literature contains on this subject – much of which still remains to be mastered in an adequate and exhaustive manner. Consciousness-studies that occupied Indian philosophers from ancient days have finally acquired a dominant place also in the West – in fact now for quite some time and especially since the demise of behaviourism. In such philosophical circles, references to ideas and theories from the Indic sources are still rare for various reasons.

It is evident that in order to assess what really is the nature of the contribution that the philosophical discourse in Sanskrit has made to world thought, one has to be first aware of the fact that among many other different field of queries, Sanskrit has been the vehicle of major and variegated philosophical traditions of thought. Think of the limited number of students of philosophy worldwide who at all get a chance to be made aware of that fact through their regular syllabus.

In other words, the intention of arriving at any consensus with regard to what these traditions have given to world-thought – which is the important concern of this meeting – one needs to situate these ideas for which Sanskrit has been the career in a larger setting where similar concerns are studied and have been recorded in other languages. A cross-cultural context is needed if we are to evaluate and adequately appreciate the manner in which the Sanskritic philosophical tradition has actually anticipated, formulated and responded to queries in specific domains of investigations. However, have we as yet really succeeded in bringing together the philosophical traditions in a global context even for the sake of obtaining an over-all view at least with regard to recorded reflections on specific themes?

Interestingly, we all know that those who are engaged in studying the thought traditions of India belong not only to the Indian soil but are from different parts of the globe, as the present gathering reflects. Still these endeavours have remained restricted to a handful of scholars. Certainly, an open and interesting question that needs to be asked today pertains not only to the kind of institutional setting and mechanisms that are put in place for teaching Sanskrit as a language but also those that are needed for propagating the legacy of philosophical knowledge for which Sanskrit has been the vehicle in the present day departmental structures of higher education.

Speaking of philosophy, it is pertinent to ask whether the educational offerings of departments of philosophy adequately reflect the importance of handing over to the young generations these resources. The situation in India with regard to the curriculum of philosophy in universities has lately made some improvements but still so far no drastic effort has been noticed to annul the Macaulian programme of colonial time.

Let me also mention here that apart from a few exceptional cases, the Indian philosophical tradition is practically ignored in the curricular of the philosophy departments in the West. It is studied occasionally in those departments that deal with area studies or language or religion. As a result, very few mainstream philosophers in the West take the pains to look elsewhere for conceptual resources outside of their own cultural horizon or enjoy the benefit of encountering other alternative modes of thinking. Reluctancy to incorporate these ideas, as I have said in various meetings held in the Western soil – some of which are also available in print – leads to the perpetuation of the image of a "mythical, mysterious and non-rational East". We need to become aware of the forces, as I said earlier, which seek to control and influence what is called politics of knowledge. What subjects and languages are allowed to flourish and which must keep struggling for survival are closely interlinked with the forces that shape the over-all history of a culture in specific regions.

Today those of us who are present here – no matter where we may be from – are all inheritors of the resources of the Sanskritic tradition, even if in visibly different ways. Apart from sharing the bit of research-based knowledge from the specific fields that we are working in, such occasions are opportunities to join forces in order to explore venues for correcting these asymmetries in the impartation of knowledge to the young and to the generations to come. If not anything else, let us at least break the silence in appropriate places where some action can be provoked with regard to this rich legacy of knowledge for which Sanskrit is the medium.

Leaving aside other domains, to perceive the enormity of philosophical literature alone has been for me an overwhelming experience. Here too we can focus only on some selected texts and works of particular authors as we pursue the specific areas of our interest. During the remaining time available to me, let me restrict my comments to a specific topic that has been acknowledged by philosophers across cultures to be a matter of central importance, viz. the theme of consciousness. Even a broad survey of the alternative conceptual strategies that were employed by these ancient thinkers and the kind of issues they have struggled within their theory-making effort is awe-inspiring. Their contribution in the domain of consciousness studies alone is stupendous. A perusal of the distinct conceptual scenarios lays bare the fact that these thinkers had anticipated many of the alternative theoretical courses in their own reflections that emerged later on in the history of philosophy elsewhere.

It is equally humbling to note how when serving their preferred viewpoints, these Masters make no claim of originality. Their brilliance is often hidden in their professed roles as *bhāṣyakāra, ṭīkākāra,* etc., i.e. as composers of commentaries, sub-commentaries, glosses as they proceeded to strengthen and enrich their traditions of thinking while at the same time answering various queries and rebutting objections that were raised. In brief, they did not seek to avoid polemics, rather, they openly engaged themselves in debates with the view either to arriving at a consensus or winning an argument or even admitting defeat. In other words, the ratiocination process could continue vigorously helping the building of a robust and a lasting intellectual tradition that is manifold and variegated. As an engaged observer of this process of exchange and exposition of ideas, it is almost a bit of a shock to come across the remarks made by philosophers of such high calibre as Husserl, Heidegger or Hegel, just to mention a few names, with regard to the complex philosophical enterprise in the Indian cultural soil. Although my detailed comments on this matter are available in print, I will briefly refer to this here in order to make a point. Note that some of these remarks that I will read out to you shortly, do not seem to me to be expressions of any mischievous design that led them to project the "otherness" of the Indian intellectual tradition in this way but are rather indicative of their lack of knowledge that prevented them from making a correct assessment with regard to the contributions of the Sanskritic philosophical tradition to world thought – a topic which is of direct relevance for this conference.

Hegel said that the Indians did not "raise their intuitions to the level of concepts". Husserl thought that among the Indians and the Chinese were not to be found those who through "interpersonally-bound communal work strive for and bring about theoria and nothing but theoria". Heidegger claimed that the phrase "Western-European philosophy" was nothing but "a tautology", since philosophy was in essence Greek.

However, as we know, in course of time history of Indian philosophy written both by Westerners and Indians became gradually available. It is obvious that it is not through a priori reasoning but via actual first-hand knowledge of the intellectual tradition alone that one could confidently ascertain that "today there is no need for speculation about whether there is philosophy in India or not" – as was observed by the Indologist-cum-philosopher W. Halbfass. Given the possibility of present-day organization of educational programme, it is indeed regrettable that philosophers like Śaṅkara, Nāgārjuna, Diṅnāga and Uddyotakara – just to mention a few names at random from the Indian thought traditions – are not taught in the same department where Hegel, Husserl or Hume and so forth are venerated. The point I am seeking to make is that if we really intend to correct the asymmetries in cross-cultural philosophical exchanges, it is hightime to re-organize our educational offerings, even if that calls for a plural understanding about what philosophical enterprise is all about. Surely an absence of this effort can only obstruct a true meeting of cultures and an authentic encounter among the world religions. Consequently, stereotypical readings and clichés in cross-cultural context are bound to prevail. These latter are not easy to dismantle unless those in control of the educational channels become more alert everywhere.

Now let me use the last few minutes by focusing on the story of the intellectual struggle that is amply reflected in the Sanskritic philosophical literature that has relevance for what is now designated as the area of consciousness-studies. As I mention some of the issues that have been raised and over which centuries of debates and discussions took place, it will hopefully become evident why I so strongly feel that these records need to be known by all those engaged in the study of the large theme of consciousness: It seems to me that despite variations and differences in the global traditions of enquiry, there is discernible a common pool of concerns and questions that cannot be simply ignored or underplayed. Consider, for example, the following issues. Is the egological structure integral to consciousness or not? No matter on which side of the debate one is, a philosophical enquiry has to offer an account of I-consciousness, explain its status and constitution. There are questions that are asked in all philosophical circles regarding whether all consciousness is intentional, i.e. "consciousness of something", or is consciousness in essence non-intentional? How to account for consciousness of consciousness? Is a state of consciousness self-revealing or must it be revealed by a subsequent state? Is consciousness a substance, a quality, or a function?

Records are available showing that all these questions have been elaborately discussed by ancient Indian philosophers. The process of intellection has brought forth alternative answers to various queries, some of which got crystallized into full-fledged theories.

It is also worth mentioning here that the documents of the controversies between the Indian naturalists and the mainstream philosophers who opposed naturalism are simply fascinating. A reconstruction of the naturalistic movement in India that provoked controversies representing is worth attempting. The contents of these discussions that are readily available do reflect the issues poignantly and these are also pertinent for the present-day battle of ideas between the exponents of naturalism and its opponents. On the basis of the analogies used by the *dehātmavādin, indriyātmavādin* and *manātmavādin* of the Cārvāka camp in support of their respective versions of Svabhāvavāda, one sees the trends anticipating various versions of physicalism, reductionism, epiphenomenalism, etc. of which we know many sophisticated formulations today. On the other hand, there are plenty of documents showing how the schools that emerged within the Upaniṣadic, the Buddhist and the Jaina traditions – while championing the cause of Ātmavāda, Ānātmavāda and Anekāntavāda – systematically took up the challenges and offered various forms of non-naturalistic theories. I am inclined to think that knowledge of these exchanges could be of crucial importance today when naturalistic thinkers are playing a dominant role in the West in the domain of consciousness-studies. Indeed, a common frame of enquiry with regard to these crucial issues is needed for the benefit of all.

In conclusion, I have tried to draw your attention to the kind of contributions that the Sanskritic philosophical traditions have made in the domain of philosophy by referring to the area of consciousness-studies, while emphasizing the need for restoring balance between knowledge and power in a larger setting as well as in our educational offerings.

9

Donation as a Value
Concept and Expansion

Satya Pal Narang

THE synonyms of *dāna* are collected in SKD (see: *Dāna*) including those found in *Amarakośa* (2.7.29), *Trikāṇḍaśeṣa* and *Śabdaratnāvalī*.[1] They are collected in their widest sense. According to *Śuddhitattva*, the donation is profoundly successful and fruitful at the pilgrimages and becomes infinite there.[2] The items of donation become fruitful to the maximum extent in the places and times where they are not available. Its result multiplies when given in *yugādi* and *manvantarādi*.[3] It is based mainly on the concept of Dharmaśāstra and not historical development. It should be given in the name of the deities and will bring the maximum fruit. Heaven and hell are the objectives of the donation.[4]

Removal of the diseases through various types of donations is also available in Hārīta.[5] Vaiśyas have been listed as *dānavajras* (whose weapon is liberality) to whom all the activities of

---

1 For other dictionaries, etc. See synonyms: quoted in SKD; *Dāna*, pp. 700-01.

2 *Śabdakalpadruma* = SKD; *Dāna*, pp. 699ff.

3 Ibid., p. 700.

4 Objective: *Svarga* and *naraka*, quoted in SKD, p. 700.

5 Hārīta II.1 is quoted in SKD; *Dāna*, p. 700.

donation are attributed.[6] The income arising out of interest, agriculture, business and the income of the kṣatriyas come in the scope of donation.[7] It is particularly given at the time of *saṅkrānti* (equinoctial passage) of the Sun and Moon and at the pilgrimages like Prayāga and Gayā. The Āgamas give stress on the worship of *guru* at the time of donation.[8]

Donation: Definition

Dāna has been defined as: to relinquish one's rights and to transfer to another person.[9] *Dāna* is defined as the giving up one's property where a donor, a recipient and the faith with *dharma* are the ingredients. *Deśa* and *kāla* are also the constituents of the donation.[10] It has been categorized as *kāma-dāna, krīḍā-dāna* and *harṣa-dāna* also. It means that its wider scope is the physical and psychological.[11]

Objective

The attainment of the heaven and avoid hell are the objectives that are described through donation.[12] It bestows the fruit of *bhukti* and *mukti*.[13] The concept, procedure and the items are available in *Vahni Purāṇa* which is quoted in SKD.[14] *Dāna* wins both *svarga*

---

6 Quoted in SKD; *dānavajra*, p. 701, quoted in the *Mahābhārata.*

7 Quoted in SKD, p. 700.

8 *Dāna*: quoted in SKD.

~*lakṣaṇa*: quoted in SKD; Also: *pātra, śraddhā, dharma, deśa, kāla*, quoted in SKD

9 *Dharma-śāstra-śabda-koṣa*, p. 349.

10 Quoted in *Śuddhitattva*: SKD; *Dāna*, p. 699.

11 *Dharma-śāstra-śabda-koṣa*, p. 349.

12 *Svarga* and *naraka*, quoted in SKD, p. 700.

13 Quoted in SKD, p. 700; also see: *Dānadharma*: quoted in SKD, p. 700.

14 Ibid., p. 701; ibid.

and *naraka* (*ubhayaloka*).[15] There is nothing that does not come in the control through *dāna*. According to *Mahābhārata*, there is no better *dharma* than donation. It pacifies all the sins.[16] With *dāna* even the deities and the warriors on the earth come in the control. According to *Durgāsapataśatī*, if appropriated with devotion through flowers, incent, etc. she gives, money, sons, intelligence and the religion.[17] The sacrificial form of *dāna* is called *dakṣiṇā*.[18]

Types

On the basis of *Gītā*, three types of donations, viz. *sattva*, *rajas*, *tamas* are available.[19] *Kūrma Purāṇa* has given the four classes: *nitya*, *naimittika*, *kāmya* and *vimala*.[20]

Vedas

ṚGVEDA (ṚV)

The act of donation is frequently alluded to in ṚV.[21] The

---

15 Quoted in SKD, p. 700; *Dharma-śāstra-śabda-koṣa*, p. 349.

16 *Mahābhārata*: quoted in SKD, p. 700 – Śāntiparvan.

17 *Durgāsapataśatī: stutā sampūjitā puṣpairdhūpagandhādibhistathā* I *dadāti vittaṁ putrāṁśca matiṁ. dharma gatiṁ śubhām* II 12.41 II

18 quoted in *Matsya Purāṇa*: quoted in SKD; *Dharma-śāstra-śabda-koṣa*, p. 349.

19 *Dānapati*: quoted in BRSW *sattva*, *rajas*, *tamas* quoted in *Gītā*: quoted in SKD also.

20 *Kūrma Purāṇa* quoted in SKD; *Dāna*, p. 700.

21 ṚV = *Ṛgveda*: ed. Paropakariṇī Sabhā, Ajmer, or used by BRSW = Böhtlingk and Roth: Sanskrit Wörterbuch/MWD.

MWD = (Monier Williams, *Sanskrit-English Dictionary* (2008 revision) Also MWD: Electronic version through Internet: The system adopted is not generally replaced here according to standard diacritical marks system. Here meanings given are: donor: giving, a giver, donor, liberal îṚV. &c.; His predecessor: BRSW; Schmidt: Nachtrage: (successor); APTE and Pune Encyclopaedic →

importance of donation is found from antiquity in India to the extent that there is a hymn which praises the act of donation.[22] A subject value is found, viz. the liking for donation.[23] It includes the donations to the authors of the praise and *dakṣiṇā* to the performers of the sacrifice. It is not a development in Indian soil but have the parallel words in cognate languages.[24] There is a

→ Dictionary: generally give the same meaning and enter the same words with difference in format or citations or sources.

MWD: Offer: dAna}2{dAna4}1 ún. the act of giving îRV. îS3Br. îMBh. &c.The offer of oblations in the sacrifices is Havya. MWD: Havya: .{dAti}3{dAti} ¯ {havya4-}.

22 Dānastuti: : work: quoted in BRSW; MWD: R̥V: {dAnastuti}3{dAna4 – stuti} úf. "praise of liberality", N. of a kind of hymn.: See: Macdonell and Keith: *Vedic Index* – I – *Dāna*: pp. 350-51; Winternitz: HIL. (index) *dānastutis* and *dānadharmas*: its relation to the epics and the divergent interpretations of.; For citations in the Vedic literature: See: Bloomfield: *Vedic Concordance*: *dātā*; for different interpretation and other words: Upadhyaya, *Vaidikakośa*, pp. 683ff.

23 MWD: Mbh: .{dAnavat}3{dAna4 – vat} ({dA4ø}), úmfn. having or bestowing gifts, liberal î R̥V. viii, 32, 12.

MWD: dAna}2{dAna4}1 ún. the act of giving î R̥V. îS3Br. îMBh. &c.

Liking: ; {-vAra} ({dA4tø}), úmfn. liking to give îRV. i, 167, 8 ; iii, 51, 9 ; v, 58, 2. _

24 Offer: donation, gift Lat. ¶{donum}] îRV. îS3Br. &c. ({ønaMdA}, ÷to offer.

IE: Indo-European Lexicon: Pokorny Master PIE Etyma. These Indo-European materials are intended to provide background information . . . 223-26, dō- : də-, also dō-u- : dəu- : du-, IE, to give, donate . . . http: //www.utexas.edu/cola/centers/lrc/ielex/PokornyMaster-X.html223-26 (through internet – 24 August 2011).

Shambhala: Giving: Generosity is very important in Buddhism. In Sanskrit there is a word, *dāna*, which at its Indo-European root is related to "donation". *Dāna* is generosity, or giving in. *Dāna* is also connected with devotion and the appreciation of sacredness. Sacredness is not purely a religious concept alone, →

reference to the persons abounding in gifts.[25] Precious gifts are also referred to in R̥V: given and distributed by the kings or by

→ but it is an expression of general openness – how to be open, how to kiss somebody, how to express the emotion of giving. You are giving yourself, not just a gift alone. So real generosity comes from developing a general sense of kindness. – Chogyam Trungpa Rinpoche (Internet)

The Northern California Ziji Initiative: donate – Dictionary Definition : Vocabulary.com : The verb donate has always meant "to give", all the way back to the Latin verb *donāre*, "to give as a gift". Trace it back even further, to the ancient Indo-European

Monosyllabic Prefixes, Cases & Conjugation in Indo-European Languages by Gaurang Bhatt (From Internet: unedited)

Table 2 From The Loom of Language

Sanskrit	*Old Persian*	*Greek*	*Old Slav*	*Latin English*	*Biblical*
Dadami	Dadami	Didomi	Dami	Do	I give
Dadasi	Dadahi	Didos	Dasi	Das	Thou givest
Dadati	Dadaiti	Didoti	Dasti	Dat	He giveth
Dadmas	Dademahi	Didomes	Damu	Damus	We give
Datta	Dasta	Didote	Daste	Datis	Ye give
Dadati	Dadenti	Didonti	Dadanti	Dant	They give
Italian	*French*	*Icelandic*	*Dutch*	*AmerEng*	*Danish*
Io do	Je donne	Eg gef	Ik geef	I give	Jeg giver
Tu dai	Tu donnes	Thu gefur	Jij geeft	You give	Du giver
Egli da	Il donne	Hann gefur	Hij geeft	He gives	Han giver
Noi diamo donnons	Nous	Vjer gefum	Wij geven	We give	Vi giver
Voi date donnez	Vous	Thjer gefith geven	Jullie	You give	De giver
Esi danno	Ils donnent	Their gefa	Zij geven	They give	De giver

[25] MWD: Bound: ARV: dAnApnas}3{dAnA7pnas} úmfn. abounding in gifts, R̥V X.22.11.

MWD: {atidAz}1{ati-ûdAz} to favour with a gift, present îRV.

the deities.. . .[26] It is quite possible that the presents were offered by the parties won by their superior warriors in the battlefield. It was not a donation in its ethical sense but in its political sense. Later it has developed to the *dāna* in the *rājanīti* along with *sāma, daṇḍa* and *bheda*. Its ethical side is found from the side of the deities which may be due to the praise for them or gifts to the persons won.[27] The huge payments are alluded to with the words *atidā* and *bhūri*.[28] Perhaps, it had a relation to giving the medicines.[29] To Savitṛ, the division of the wealth is attributed.[30] For their *inter se* relationship and supremacy, there are divergent concepts.[31] Yāska has given the etymology of *deva* from the root *dā*[32] also which is preserved in local languages also. For example,

---

26 Magha: Agni: MWD: ṚV 3.13.3 *dātā yo vanitā magham . . .*

ṚV: . . . . Magha: *hantā yo vṛtraṁ sanitota vājaṁ/dātā maghāni maghavā surādhāḥ* ||

(It is a gift and the food to Vṛtra, a strong enemy of Indra.)

Ṛṣabho Vaiśvāmitraḥ/agni/. . . . *sa yantā vipra eṣāṁ sa yajñānathā hi vaḥ* |

ṚV 4.17.8 . . . *vāmadeva* /Indra . . . *satrāhaṇaṁ dādhrṣiṁ tumramindraṁ mahāmapāraṁ vṛṣabhaṁ suvajram* |

27 MWD: .{anudeya}2{anu-de4ya} ún. a present î ṚV. vi, 20, 11

MWD: .; ({anu-de4yI}), úf. a bride's maid (îGmn. and îSa1y.) î ṚV. x, 85, 6 ; 135, 5 and 6.

28 MWD: atidA}1{ati-dA} û1. to surpass in giving îRV. viii, i, 38, to pass over in giving îKa1tyS3r. _

29 2.33.12 . . . gṛtsamada/Rudra . . . *kumāraśitpitraṁ vandamānaṁ prati nānāma rudropayantam* |
bhūrerdātāraṁ *satpatiṁ gṛṇīṣe stutastvaṁ* ***bheṣajā*** *rāsyasme* ||

30 ṚV 1.22.7 . . . Medhātithiḥ kāṇvaḥ/savitā . . . *vibhaktāraṁ havāmahe . . . vasościtrasya rādhasa . . . savitāraṁ nṛcakṣasam.*

31 Macdonell: *Vedic mythology*: tr. Hindi: Suryakanta, pp. 28-33.

32 The *Nighaṇṭu* and the *Nirukta*, ed. Lakshman Sarup: *Daivatakāṇḍa:* 7.16: *devo danādvā . . .* besides the other etymologies.

in a few spoken languages of Punjab, the word *devanā* is used for giving which has a direct relation to *deva* (deity). SKD has derived Dānu from the root √*dā* and has been quoted in the R̥V.[33]

Deities represented by Agni are the giver to a liberal person or a hero.[34] The allotment of a portion (*aṁśa*) may be in its legal sense in R̥V.[35] A few persons go out of the system and are not interested in giving anything.[36] It is quite possible that the snatching of the horses or sale thereof was known in R̥V. Money is not paid by a number of people from public.[37] A few people

---

33 SKD.; *Dāna*, p. 701.

34 *Hero:* . R̥V.3.24.5 . . . . Viśvāmintra/Agni . . . . . *agni dā dāśuṣe rayiṁ vīravantaṁ parīṇasam* ।

śiśīhi naḥ sūnumataḥ

Vasu: . . . . Vasiṣṭha/Indra: . . . . R̥V 7.20.2: *dātā vasu:*

hantā vr̥tramindraḥ śūśuvānaḥ prāvīnnu vīro jaritāramūtī ।

kartā sudāse aha vā u lokaṁ dātā vasu muhurā dāśuṣe 'bhūt ।।

35 MWD: {aMzapradAna}3{a4Mza - pradAna} ún. allotment of a portion.

36 MWD: {aditsat}1{a4-ditsat} [îRV. vi, 53, 3, &c.] or {a-ditsu} úmfn. (úDesid. fr. û1. {dA}), not inclined to give. _ MWD: .{adAman}2{a-dAma4n} úmfn. not liberal, miserly î R̥V. _

37 MWD: {anazvadA}3{an-azva4 - dA} ({a4n-a4zva-}), úmfn. one who does not give horses îRV. v, 54, 5.

Teutonic Mythology: *Compare O. Schrader, *Sprachvergleichung und Urgeschichte* (1883) . . . of Hindooic antiquities, gave new reasons for the theory that the Aryan Hindoos were. . . . The Aryan folk-streams, which in pre-historic times deluged Europe, were in this. . . . The horse was also known, but it is uncertain whether it was used for riding or . . . http: //www.boudicca.de/teut.htm;

http: //www.jcu.edu/faculty/nietupski/rl251/projects/n_silk_road/trade/main.htm

Many other items were also part of the exchange on the Silk Roads. Domestic animals such as horses from the West were imported →

may be with ego are not interested in giving even the blessings.[38] The relation of Aditi to the root *dā* is doubtful.[39] There had been people in the society who were not interested in giving to any

→ particularly in China. China had its own breed of horses since antiquity, but these foreign purebreds, sometimes known as the heavenly horses, were in demand.

http: //www.iranchamber.com/history/articles/persian_gulf_trade_late_antiquity.php

Persians in East Asia

By the late Sasanian period, we know that the Persians controlled the seas and came into conflict with the Romans. The question here is whether the state was actively involved in the control of the waterways or simply that the Persian merchants dominated the trade without heavy state intervention. The Sasanians were competing with the Romans and disputing trade concessions as far as Sri Lanka, and it appears there was even a Sasanian colony in Malaysia, but again they do not appear to be military colonies. Persian horses were shipped to Ceylon, and a colony was established on that island where ships came from Persia.

For a hymn of horse and its interpretation in R̥V. See S.P. Narang, "On the word Aśva in the R̥gveda", *PAIOC*, 1982, pp. 215-21; *R̥gveda men aśva-śabda para vicāra*: (Hindi version) Śodha Prabhā, Delhi.

38 MWD: {anAzirdA}3{a4n-Azir-dA} úmfn. not giving a blessing îRV. x, 27, 1.

39 MWD:..; for 1. {a4-diti}, ¯ above), not tied, free îRV. vii, 52, 1, boundless, unbroken, entire, unimpaired, happy îRV. îVS., ({is}), úf. freedom, security, safety.; boundlessness, immensity inexhaustible abundance, unimpaired condition, perfection, creative power, N. of one of the most ancient of the Indian goddesses ("Infinity" or the "Eternal and Infinite Expanse", often mentioned in îR̥V., daughter of Dakṣa and wife of {aditija}3{a4-diti – ja} úm. a son of Aditi, an Āditya, a divine being..{adititva}3{a4-diti – tva4} ún. The condition of Aditi, or of freedom. It shows the arbitrariness of payment and reluctance to pay. unbrokenness îRV. vii, 51, 1 .{aditinandana}3{a4-diti – nandana} m.= {-ja}, ¯q.v. _

person or were miser in nature.[40] But there are a few who will give even without demand.[41]

Giving the daughter in marriage is known in the R̥V.[42] Besides the meaning a present, it was the bride's maids who accompanied the bride which is an inseparable part of the family in the epics who advised the bride and made decisions in the structure of the family, e.g. Mantharā in *Rāmāyaṇa* or *dhātrī* elsewhere. The custom continued later also.

ATHARVAVEDA (AV)

A negative approach to donation is profusely found in the *Atharvaveda*. Perhaps, the followers of the *Atharvaveda* were less associated with *yajña* cult and hence *dakṣiṇā* is equally followed less.[43] It is corroborated by Tibet Cāṇakya-Rajanīti-śāstra

---

40 MWD: Not giving: {adAtR}1{a-dAtR} úmfn. not giving; Miser: .; not liberal, miserly {adAman}2{a-dAma4n} úmfn. not liberal, miserly îRV. _; .{aditsat}1{a4-ditsat} [îRV. vi, 53, 3, &c.] or {a-ditsu} úmfn. (úDesid. fr. û1. {dA}), not inclined to give.

41 : MWD: {abhikSadA}1{a-bhikSa-dA4} [îPadap. {abhi-kSa-dA4}], úmfn. Giving;

without being asked î R̥V. vi, 50, 1; .{abhikSita}2{a4-bhikSita} úmfn. not asked for alms îS3Br. _

42 (cf. {kanyA-}): King Svanaya's *kanyādāna* to Kakṣivān R̥V 1.126.3. Cf. Śivasaṅkara Kāvyatīrtha: *Vaidika itihāsārthanirṇaya* (reprinted: Brahmadeva Vidyālaṅkāra, Kurukshetra, 2009) for anti-historical view and refutation.

43 MWD: .{adAna}1{a4-dAna} ún. (û1. {dA}), not giving, act of withholding îAV. &c.

MWD: .{adAnya}2{a-dAnya4} úmfn. not giving, miserly îAV. _

MWD: {adAtR}1{a-dAtR} úmfn. not giving .; not liberal, miserly

Cf: through Google:

Hymns of the Atharvaveda, tr. Maurice Bloomfield . . . VII.70. Frustration of the sacrifice of an enemy – 42. II.7. Charm . . .

→

which belongs to the adjacent area of Kashmir (particularly the Paippalāda recension) and which depicts Vedic *yajña* differently and with conflict *vis-à-vis* Cāṇakya-Rajanīti-śāstra.[44]

Vājasaneyī Saṁhitā (VS)

A person giving safety is found in VS.[45]

Taittirīya Saṁhitā (TS)

In TS, the concept of fond of giving donations or a liberal person which is found in *Taittirīya Brāhmaṇa* (TB) as well.[46] Yājñyavalkya not only generated a new recension of the *Yajurveda* (YV), i.e. *Śukla YV* but also forcibly took half of the share of *dakṣiṇā* from Vaiśampāyana.[47]

Brāhmaṇas

In the Brāhmaṇa literature, generally, without donation, nothing is successful. So *bhūridakṣiṇaḥ* is associated with sacrifices.

AITAREYA BRĀHMAṆA (AIT. BR.)

In Ait. Br. it is related to be given which has become a value and

---

→ îAV. &c. .; (úmfn.), not giving. _MWD: . {adAnya}2{a-dAnya4} úmfn. not giving, miserly îAV. _.; not giving (a daughter) in marriage.; not paying, not liable to payment.

MWD: .{adAna}1{a4-dAna} ún. (û1. {dA}), not giving, act of withholding.

44 See: S.P. Narang, *Satya Vrat Śāstrī Fel. Vol.: Some Observations on the Expansion of Values in Cāṇakya Tradition to Tibet.*

45 MWD: . . .; for 1. {a4-diti}, ¯ above), not tied, free îRV. vii, 52, 1, ; {abhayasani}3 {a4-bhaya – sa4ni} úmfn. giving safety îVS. xix, 48.

46 MWD: {{dAnakAma}3{dAna4 – kAma} ({dA4ø}), úmfn. fond of giving, liberal îTS. îTBr.

47 C.V. Vaidya, *Mahābhārata-Mīmāṁsā* (Hindi), p. 435.

found in Manu as well.[48]

TAITTIRĪYA BRĀHMAṆA (TB)

In TB a person fond of donation is alluded to in the Taittirīya tradition.[49] It means that donation had become a habit and the donor got the pleasure in this activity.

ŚATAPATHA BRĀHMAṆA (ŚB)

The act of giving and donation is available in ŚB along with the tradition beginning from R̥V.[50]

Upaniṣads

MUṆḌAKA UPANIṢAD

This concept is found in the provinces where *Muṇḍaka Upaniṣad* flourished (the place unknown). *Muṇḍaka Upaniṣad* thinks that the sacrificial activities are superfluous (*plavā hyete adr̥ḍāḥ yajñarūpāḥ* . . . 1.2.7). Elsewhere it is found to be an instrument to cross the bondages of the birth and death.

KAṬHOPANIṢAD

The donation of the elderly cows is mentioned in *Kaṭhopaniṣad.* Those who donate them go *asurya loka* which is equal to hell in later literature. The theme like giving off a son to the god of death (*mr̥tyu*) which might have developed in the complicated system like Triṇāciketas fire is found in this Upaniṣad.

---

48 MWD: {dAtavya}3{dAótavya} úmfn. to be given îAitBr. îMn. &c.

49 *Dānakāma*: quoted in BRSW

MWD: {dAnakAma}3{dAna4 – kAma} ({dA4ø}), úmfn. fond of giving, liberal îTS. îTBr.

50 MWD: ; donation, gift Lat. ¶{donum}] î R̥V. îS3Br. &c. ({ønaMdA}, ÷to offer-Gift: MWD: dAna}2{dAna4}1 ún. the act of giving î R̥V. îS3Br. îMBh. &c.: , donor, liberal î R̥V. &c.

BṚHADĀRAṆYAKA

Cow-*dāna* is found elaborately in this Upaniṣad. It continued in the *Mahābhārata.*[51]

Meaning and Etymology

NIGHAṆṬU

The *Nighaṇṭu* has enlisted the following meanings in the context of the root √*dā.*[52]

DEVA-NIGHAṆṬU

SKD has quoted *Deva-Nighaṇṭu* for the synonyms of *dāna-karma.*[53]

NIRUKTA

Nirukta uses the word *adāyin* in the sense of a person who does not give.[54]

Lexicography: Synonyms

Besides *Nighaṇṭu* and explanations of Yāska, *Amarakośa* has frequently been quoted. It has been quoted for the synonym of *dāna.* Trikāṇḍaśeṣa has also been quoted in this context along with *Śabdaratnāvalī.*[55] At *dānaśīla,* the synonyms from Hemacandra are also quoted.[56] Medinī has been quoted for Dānu

---

[51] C.V. Vaidya, *Mahābhārata-Mīmāṁsā* (Hindi), p. 457.

[52] MWD: .; ({I}), úf. údu. heaven and earth îNaigh..; a cow, milk î R̥V..; speech îNaigh. (cf. î R̥V. viii, 101, 15).; the earth îNaigh.{aditi}1{a4-diti}3 úmfn. (û4. {dA} or {do}, {dyati} Nigh: .{dAnapara}3{dAna4 – para} úmfn. devoted to liberality; {-tA} úf. liberality îNa1g. v, 29. the earth îNaigh.

[53] Quoted in SKD; *Dāna,* p. 700.

[54] MWD: .{adAyin}2{a-dAyin} úmfn. not giving îNir.

[55] Quoted in SKD; *Dāna,* p. 699.

[56] Quoted in SKD; *Dānaśīla,* p. 701.

and its synonyms.[57] *Mahābhārata* and *Bhāgavata* have also been quoted for *dānava*.[58]

MAHĀBHĀRATA

In *Mahābhārata*, it is available in the senses (in the footnotes) as per MWD.[59] *Ijyā, adhyayana* and *dāna* are the dominant values in *Mahābhārata* from which *dāna* is essential for everyone. Amongst various types of donations, the donation of cow is the most important which continues from the allusions of the

---

57 Quoted in SKD; *Dānu*, p. 701.

58 Quoted in SKD; *Dānava*, p. 701.

59 Pay

MWD: ; ÷to pay one out (?) îMBh. vii, 9499. _

MWD: .{dAda}2{dAda} úm. (û {dad}) gift, donation îMBh. ix, 2117; 2269

MWD: MBH: .{dAnavat}3{dAna4 – vat} ({dA4ø}), úmfn. having or bestowing gifts, liberal î R̥V. viii, 32, 12 îMBh. xiii, 55.

MWD: dAna}2{dAna4}1 ún. the act of giving î R̥V. îS3Br. îMBh. &c.

MWD: {dAnazIla}3{dAna4 – zIla} úmfn. liberally disposed îYa1jn5. îMBh..; úm. N. of a translator of îLalit.

MWD: MBH: .{dAnapati}3{dAna4 – pati} úm. `" liberality-lord "', munificent man îMBh. îR..; N. of A-kru1ra îMBh. îHariv..; of a Daitya îHariv. [474, 2]

MWD: {agradAtR}3{a4gra – dAtR} úmfn. offering the best bits (to the gods)-îMBh.

MWD: {agrapradAyin}3{a4gra – pradAyin} úmfn. offering first îMBh..; ÷to pay one out (?) îMBh. vii, 9499. _

MWD: {arthadAna}3{a4rtha – dAna} ún. donation of money, present îMBh.

MWD: {abhyAdA}1{abhy-A-dA} û1. úA1. (rarely úP. îHariv.) to seize, snatch

MWD: away, (úPot. {-dadIta}) îMBh. i, 3558= xii, 10999= xiii, 4985: úA1.

Upaniṣads.[60] Two cows are referred to as *guru-dakṣiṇā*.[61] In the daily routine of the king, worship of and donation to brāhmaṇas including *dakṣiṇā* of the cows with gold on their horns is found in *Mahābhārata*.[62] Cow-*dāna* is found elaborately. Donation of various items is available for *prāyaścitta* which is available in different later Smṛtis.[63] The person giving donations attains the heaven.[64]

Puṇya-phala of various types of *dāna* is available in the Anuśāsana-parvan.[65] Acceptance of *dakṣiṇā* by the teacher has been depicted in *Mahābhārata*. It is thought to be a bestower of *svarga* and *apavarga*.[66]

In most of the types of marriage, the donation is an essential ingredient. There are a number of questions on *śulka* for *kanyādāna*. For Brāhma type of marriage, the donation is also essential. But only with *śulka-dāna* the marriage does not become final.[67] The gift of precious jewels to other kings is known in *Mahābhārata*.

---

[60] C.V. Vaidya, *Mahābhārata-Mīmāṁsā* (Hindi), p. 457.

[61] Ibid., p. 209.

[62] C.V. Vaidya, *Mahābhārata-Mīmāṁsā* (Hindi), p. 209.

[63] Ibid., See: Prāyaścitta.

[64] *Garuḍa Purāṇa*: Dānavidhi: quoted in SKD, p. 701.

[65] C.V. Vaidya, *Mahābhārata-Mīmāṁsā* (Hindi) : *svarga aura naraka kī kalpanā*.

[66] Ibid.

[67] Ibid., p. 235; cf. *Ṛgveda*: . Also: A.S. Altekar, *The Position of Women in Hindu Civilization*, pp. 42-43; for the groups of thought for *śulka* in the Smṛtis and the history of development of thought including *Mahābhārata*, Ādi and other places: see Sternbach: JSAIL: *Types of Marriage*, pp. 38ff, giving in marriage (cf. {kanyA-}): King Svanaya's *kanyādāna* to Kakṣivān ṚV 1.126.3.

Cf. Śivasaṅkara Kāvyatīrtha: *Vaidika itihāsārthanirṇaya* for anti-historical view and refutation.

The forcible taking of the *dakṣiṇā* for the sacrificial purpose is alluded to in the *Mahābhārata*.[68] Items like gold, *tila*, cow and food besides *bhūmi*, *kanyā*, and cloth (*vastra*, etc.) is available in the *Mahābhārata*.[69]

Donation: Prohibitions

The donation is prohibited at the time of taking the food, sex, sleep and in the evening.[70] A person who promises to donate and does not give, is called a *brahma-ghātaka*. The recipient interprets it in his own favour and thinks it a serious offence. It is because the person is killing the expectations of the recipient.[71] The defence is given to a person who takes away from bad persons and gives to good persons. For *dānaśīla*, *Mahābhārata* has been quoted.[72] According to *Brahma Purāṇa*, generally a donation is not to be accepted from a śūdra. The items previously offered to the dead are not to be accepted as donation.[73] Donation for *yajña* is not found in the Tibet-Cāṇakya-Rājanīti-Śāstra because they were not in favour of the *yajña*.

Āgamas

The Āgamas give stress on the worship of *guru* at the time of donation. The donation of *vṛṣotsarga* and *homa* is also prescribed.[74]

---

68 C.V. Vaidya, *Mahābhārata-Mīmāṁsā* (Hindi).

69 Ibid., pp. 457-58.

70 SKD quoted in *Śuddhitattva*, p. 70.

71 Ibid., p. 700.

72 Quoted in SKD; *Dāna*, p. 701.

yat phalaṁ dānaśīlasya kṣamāśīlasya yat phalam ।
yacca me phalamādhane tena saṁyujyatāṁ bhavān ॥

73 Quoted in SKD.

74 *Dānasāgara*: quoted in *Kāmadhenutantra: jñānatarpaṇa*: quoted in SKD, p. 701.

Kalpa

KĀTYĀYANA-ŚRAUTASŪTRA

It appears that the works on rituals are giving stress on the excess donation because the performers of *yajñas* are the beneficiaries. There may be a competition of the donors and a recipient of the donations.[75]

Classical Sanskrit Literature

KĀLIDĀSA: KUMĀRASAMBHAVA

The giving a daughter in marriage is found in *Kumārasambhava.*[76] The donation according to Kālidāsa is not unilateral but bilateral in the context of the deities in the heaven and men on the earth who perform the sacrifice. With the exchange of the property on the ground and the heaven, they preserve both *lokas.*[77] *Kanyādāna* is described best in one of the verses of *Śākuntalam* (*artho hi kanyā . . .*). A few natural items as dowry were given to Śakuntalā. Donation of one's own life by Dilīpa for the protection of the cow is another ideal depicted by Kālidāsa.

Māgha: Giving of the gifts is found in the Śiśupālavadha. Dānaśauṇḍa is also found in it.[78] Mallinātha has given both the meanings of donation and rut of the elephants on the word *dāna.*[79]

---

75 MWD: Excess: {atidA}1{ati-dA} û1. to surpass in giving îRV. viii, i, 38, to pass over in giving îKa1tyS3r. _

76 One who gives a daughter úgen.) in marriage (cf. {kanyA-}) îKum. vi

.{dAtRtva}3{dA4tR - tva} ún. úid. îHariv. 14414 îRagh. îCa1n2. A number of other details: B.S. Upadhyaya, *India in Kālidāsa: Presents and Decoration.* Also Hindi version.

77 Cf. Raghu0 I.*dudoha gāṁ sa yajñāya . . .* : See: Apte's Dictionary also.

78 Quoted in SKD, p. 701; Dānaśauṇḍa: quoted in SKD; *Dāna,* p. 701, quoted in Māgha: 14.46.

79 Māgha: 5.37; Mallinātha quoted in SKD, p. 699; MWD: (úB. {dAya}) →

Naiṣadha: Śrīharṣa uses the word *dānapāramitā* in the sense of perfection of liberality which is used in Bauddha literature as well according to MWD.[80]

Daśakumāracarita: The person worthy of a gift is depicted by Daṇḍin.[81]

Rājaraṅgiṇī: Liberal giver is mentioned by Kalhaṇa.[82]

Subhāṣita: As depicted in the *Mahābhārata*, it was a routine to give donations everyday. A hall for donation is described in the *subhāṣitas*.[83]

Folk literature

PAÑCATANTRA

Pañcatantra has used *abhayapradāna* in the political sense of provision of fearlessness.[84] Manu has also used it in the similar sense.[85]

→ îSis3, pp. xix, 114.

MWD: .{dAdada}3{dAda - da} úmfn. gift-giving îS3is3. x îib. _

80 {dAnapAramitA}3{dAna4 - pAramitA} úf. perfection of liberality îKa1ran2d2. îNaish.

MWD: .{dAdada}3{dAda - da} úmfn. gift-giving îS3is3. x îib. _

81 MWD: .Dasa: {dAnayogya}3{dAna4 - yogya} úmfn. worthy of a gift îDas3.

82 MWD: {dAtRtA}3{dA4tR - tA} úf. the being a giver, liberality îRa1jat.

83 MWD: Subh: .{dAnazalA}3{dAna4 - zalA} úf. hall for almsgiving îSubh. 127.

84 MWD: . {abhayavacana}3{a4-bhaya - vacana} ún. [îPan5cat.] orð [îHit.] assurance.

MWD: . {abhayapradAna}3{a4-bhaya - pradAna} ún. = {-dAna} îPan5cat. ; MWD: .{abhayavacana}3{a4-bhaya - vacana} ún. [îPan5cat.] orð [îHit.] assurance of safety.

85 MWD:.{abhayadakSiNA}3{a4-bhaya-dakSiNA} úf. promise or present or protection from danger îMn. iv, 247, .{abhayadAna}3{a4-bhaya →

HITOPADEŚA

Provision of assurance of safety is found here[86] like that of *Pañcatantra*.

KATHĀSARITSĀGARA

To be given in marriage;[87] giving of *argha*[88] and proper names with donation[89] are found in *Kathāsaritsāgara*.

Purāṇas

BHĀGAVATA PURĀṆA

A habit of donation is found in the word *dānavrata*. This concept might have been borrowed from Śākadvīpa. *Bhāgavata Purāṇa* may have a connection with Śākadvīpa. That is why the inhabitants of Śākadvīpa are named as *dānavrata*.[90]

BRAHMA PURĀṆA

According to *Brahma Purāṇa*, generally a donation is not to be accepted from a śūdra. The items previously offered to the dead

---

→ – dAna} ún. giving assurance of safety.; MWD: .{abhayaprada}3{a4-bhaya – prada} úmfn. giving safety îMn. iv, 232, &c.

86 MWD: {abhayavacana}3{a4-bhaya – vacana} ún. [îPan5cat.] orð [îHit.] assurance of safety.

87 MWD: ; ÷to be given in marriage îDa1yabh. (Pait2h.) îKatha1s.

88 MWD: {arghadAna}3{argha – dAna} ún. presentation of a respectful offering.

89 MWD: .{dAnavarman}3{dAna4 – varman} úm. "whose armour is liberality", N. of a merchant îKatha1s.

MWD: .{dAnavIra}3{dAna4 – vIra} úm. "liberality-hero", munificent man îKatha1s.

90 *dānavrata*: quoted in BRSW; MWD: Bhag: {dAnavrata}3{dAna4 – vrata} Wfn. devoted to liberality.; úm. úpl. N. of inhabitants of S3a1ka-dvipa, Bh. v, 20, 28.

are not to be accepted as donation.[91]

Procedure of Donation

Matsya Purāṇa has propounded the procedure of donation (*dānavidhi*) chapter 98 which is entered in SKD.[92] In the Sūtras like Pāraskara, Purāṇas, Smr̥tis, *Śuddhitattva* quoted in SKD., *Smr̥ticandrikā*, etc. the procedure of *dāna* and *dakṣiṇā* for the rituals of *pitr̥s* is described. After taking bath and wearing good clothes, the donation should be given according to one's desire. The money to be donated should be self-earned. It may be abundant or less is immaterial. Whatsoever donation is given, it should be with the worship of the deity. It should be given in the name of all those for whom the donation is being given.[93]

According to *Vahni Purāṇa*, the donation should not be given with a negative instinct, i.e. fear, anger and ego, etc. The donation given against the spirit of the Veda or to a person who is the killer of an embryo; to a thief, to a person engaged in bad activities; to a person jealous of a brāhmaṇa; to the husband of a *vr̥ṣalī* (a woman of low caste) and to a crooked person is useless.[94]

Relation of Donation to Objects Donated

The donor of the water attains satisfaction; the donor of the food (*anna*) gets infinite pleasure which shall not decay. The donor of *tila* gets desirable progeny and the donor of the lamp gets nice

---

91 MWD: {agradAnin}3{a4gra - dAnin} úm. a degraded brāhmaṇa who receives presents from *śūdras*, or takes things previously offered to the dead *BrahmaP*.

92 Quoted in *Matsya Purāṇa*: in SKD.

93 *Śuddhitattva* quoted in SKD: Procedure of: p. 699.

94 *Vahni Purāṇa*: quoted in SKD p. 701. Perhaps, it is different from *Agni Purāṇa* available these days.

eyes. The donor of the earth gets everything. The donor of gold gets long life. The donor of the house gets high palacial houses. The donor of the silver gets beautiful face. The donor of the cloth gets assimilation to or conformity with the moon. The donor of the horse gets conformity with the deity Aśvins. The donor of the ox gets prosperity *par excellence*. The donor of a conveyance and bed gets a wife and the donor of *abhaya* gets prosperity. The donor of the corn gets pleasure and the donor of the Veda (Brahma) gets *Brahman*. The donor to the knowers of the Veda gets greatness in the *svargaloka*. By giving the grass to the cows, one is relieved of all the sins. By the donation of fuel, one gets the light in the body. By giving the medicine, and greasy food to a patient, one becomes diseaseless and gets long life. The donor of an umbrella crosses the tortures of the strong heat.[95]

Besides various types of gifts, an illegal gift is also mentioned. A person who is not entitled for a gift is also mentioned in the dictionaries.[96] *Kanyādāna* is another item which is frequently alluded to in the books on law and Dharmaśāstra.[97]

MĀNAVA GR̥HYASŪTRA

A father or brother who gives a daughter or sister in marriage is mentioned[98] (see: *Kanyādāna*).

MANU

Manu has referred to *dānadharma* or duty of liberality. A general

---

95 *Mahābhārata*: quoted in SKD. p. 700, Śāntiparvan.

96 MWD: {adeyadAna}3{a-deya – dAna} ún. an illegal gift.

MWD: {adAyAda}1{a-dAyAda4} úmf({I4}, in later texts {A}) ún. not entitled to be an heir.; destitute of heirs.

97 MWD: giving in marriage (cf. {kanyA-}

98 MWD: îMa1nGr2. i, 8 îMn. in, 172 îPait2h. îR.

gift is also mentioned.[99] Restoring or paying back is also referred to.[100] *Abhayadāna* is also known, i.e. giving assurance of safety which is found in Bauddha texts and *Pañcatantra* as well.[101]

---

[99] MWD: Manu: .{dAnadharma}3{dAna4 - *dharma*} úm. duty of liberality îMn. îHit.

MWD: Manu: .; bribery îMn.vii, 198 (cf. {upA7ya}).

MWD: a gñgift îMn. îYa1jn5. îHit. &c.

MWD: Manu: ; ÷to bestow a gñgift îMn. iv, 234).

[100] MWD: .; a creditor îMn. viii, 161 the arranger of a meal, iii, 236.

MWD: .; paying back, restoring îMn. îYa1jn5.

MWD: .; a father or brother who gives a daughter or sister in marriage.

MWD: .; one who gives a daughter úgen.) in marriage (cf. {kanyA-}) îKum. vi.

MWD: .{abhayadakSiNA}3{a4-bhaya - dakSiNA} úf. promise or present or

MWD: {dAtavya}3{dAótavya} úmfn. to be given îAitBr. îMn. &c.

MWD: .; ÷to be paid or restored îMn. viii îPa1n2. 3-3, 171 îKa1s3.

[101] MWD: {abhayaprada}3{a4-bhaya - prada} úmfn. giving safety îMn. iv, 232, &c.

MWD: {abhayapradAna}3{a4-bhaya - pradAna} ún. = {-dAna} îPan5cat.

MWD: {abhayayAcanA}3{a4-bhaya - yAcanA} úf. asking for safety îRagh. xi, 78.

MWD: {abhayavacana}3{a4-bhaya - vacana} ún. [îPan5cat.] orð [îHit.] assurance.

MWD: protection from danger îMn. iv, 247, &c.

MWD: .{abhayadAna}3{a4-bhaya - dAna} ún. giving assurance of safety.

MWD: .{abhayaMdada}3{a4-bhaya - M-dada} úm. N. of Avalokiteśvara îBuddh.

MWD: {abhayavAc}3{a4-bhaya - vAc} úf. [îHit.] assurance of safety.

YĀJÑAVALKYA

Like Manu, Yājñavalkya has also used *dāna* for paying back, liberal and a gift.[102]

Dakṣiṇā

In the Brāhmaṇa literature, generally, without donation or *dakṣiṇā*, nothing is successful. So *bhūridakṣiṇaḥ* is associated with sacrifices. *Dakṣiṇā* has two types: religious and salary. Generally religious *dakṣiṇā* is known in the books of law which is accepted by Kullūka, etc.[103] Generally cows and calves are given as *dakṣiṇā.*

Donation: Items

Smr̥ticandrikā has quoted the opinion of Vyāsa for the items of donation. They are: cow, land, gold, new clothes and beds for the satisfaction of *pitr̥*s and one's own. The opinion of Pāraskara and *Vāyu Purāṇa* is also quoted.[104] According to Pāraskara quoted in *Smr̥ticandrikā*, the food should be given at parity whereas *dakṣiṇā* may be given without parity. In the opinion of Devala, the priority should be fixed and the preference should be given to *vipras* of *pitr̥s*.[105] According to Br̥haspati, the priority should be fixed as per the donor including those of *jñāti* and *bāndhavas*. It has been explained that the relative from the side of father are *jñāti*s and the relatives from the side of the mother are *bāndhavas*. There is a discussion on the pronunciation

---

102 MWD: paying back, restoring îMn. îYa1jn5.; MWD: {dAnazIla}3{dAna4 - zIla} úmfn. liberally disposed îYa1jn5. îMBh..; úm. N. of a translator of îLalit.; MWD: a gñgift îMn. îYa1jn5. îHit. &c.

103 *Dharmaśāstraśabdakoṣa*: quotes: Pāraskara, Manu, Kullūka, and Dāyabhāga. Also See: *Dāna.*

104 *Smr̥ticandrikā*, III.392ff.

105 *Smr̥ticandrikā* III, pp. 393-95: quoted in the opinion of Pāraskara and Devala.

of *svadhā*, its procedure and time.[106] A number of items in donations are mentioned in *Mahābhārata* for various occasions and diseases which are generally enlisted in the following works.[107] In *Śuddhitattva*, the donation of clothes and ornaments is mentioned which is continued from the very beginning of the concept of donation. Vyāsa has been quoted in *Smṛticandrikā*[108] for the items to be given, viz. cow, land, gold, clothes, beds, or whatsoever is desirable to the *vipras* or to the self or to the *pitṛs*. It should be given without any fraud and for the pleasure of the *pitṛs*. In the opinion of Jamadagni, it should be given to the family-brāmaṇas.[109] According to Vṛddhaśātātapa, the donor should accept the blessings on his head. The opinion of various *ācāryas* has been summed up in *Smṛticandrikā*. In *Matsya Purāṇa*, elephant, horse, cow, oxen, jewels and gold are enumerated as items of donation.[110] A few of these items are enlisted in *Garuḍa Purāṇa* as well.[111] Cows with gold on their horns and silver on their hooves; peaceful in nature; milk-giving – *kṣīriṇī gauḥ* (it is against the concept in *Kaṭhopaniṣad* where the old cows were given in donation – *pītodakāḥ, jagdhatṛṇā*) covered with cloth and with a utensil of *kāṁsya* should be given. Moreover, it should not have any disease or any other physical problem. The quantity of the gold and silver is not identified.[112] Hārīta

---

106 *Smṛticandrikā* III, pp. 395ff where the opinion of *saṅgrahakāra* and Yājñavalkya with others is quoted.The definition of *Svadhā* and its Vedic *mantras* are also quoted.

107 SKD.; *Dāna*, pp. 700-01.

108 *Smṛticandrikā* III, p. 392

109 Ibid., p. 393.

110 SKD.; *Dāna*, p. 700.

111 *Garuḍa Purāṇa*, Dānavidhi: quoted in SKD, p. 701.

112 *Garuḍa Purāṇa*, Dānavidhi, quoted in SKD, p. 701; also see: *Dānadharma*: quoted in SKD, p. 700.

II.1 is quoted in SKD., *Dāna*, p. 700. He has enumerated the items besides enumerated above for the removal of various diseases. They are: earth, sweet food, food, *śāstra-dāna*, *kanyādāna*, salt, *ghṛta*, honey, silver, tin, iron, serpant, scents, oil and mercury. The lamp, house, umbrella, garland, conveyance and tree may be added in the list.[113] Another interesting item is added, i.e. the donation of the books on the meaning of the Veda and the Śāstra of *yajña*. They should be written and donated. Alternately, the cost of their writing should be donated.[114] The books on Itihāsa and Purāṇa may also be donated in written form.[115]

Smṛticandrikā[116] has quoted *Vāyu Purāṇa* for the donation for the infinity of *pitṛs*. Whatsoever is the best in this world and whatsoever is delightful to one's ownself should be given to *pitṛs*. The most desired objects to oneself should be donated to *pitṛs* (see: Items). Gift of the food is also frequently alluded.[117] The food is supposed to be a divinity also.[118]

Psychological

According to Pāṇinian system, the action of donation begins with the thought that I shall give and not with the actual transfer of the item, e.g. *brāhmaṇāya gāṁ dāsyāmi.* According to another thought quoted in SKD, one has to think of the person to whom wealth or donation is to be given.[119]

---

113 *Garuḍa Purāṇa*: Dānavidhi: quoted in SKD, p. 701.

114 Ibid.

115 *Garuḍa Purāṇa*: Dānavidhi: quoted in SKD p. 701.

116 *Smṛticandrikā* III, p. 398.

117 .{annadAna}3{anna – dAna} ún. the giving of food.
.{annadAyin}3{anna – dAyin} úmfn. = {-da} above.

118 {annadevatA}3{anna – devatA} úf. the divinity supposed to preside over.

119 Quoted in SKD.

Works

A number of works are quoted in BRSW and also taken by MWD.[120] Other works are available in manuscripts detailed in

---

120 *Dānapaddhati*: work quoted in BRSW.

Dānakusumāñjalī: work: quoted in BRSW.

Dānāsura: : work: quoted in BRSW.

Dānahemādri: : work: quoted in BRSW.

Dānādhikāra: : work: quoted in BRSW.

Works mentioned in MWD

Work: .{dAnamaJjarI}3{dAna4 - maJjarI} úf.

Work: {dAnahemAdri}3{dAna4 - hemA7dri} úm. = {-khaNDa}.

Work: {dAnasAgara}3{dAna4 - sAgara} úm. "gift-ocean",

Work: {dAnoddyota}3{dAno7ddyota} úm. N. of úwk. _

work: {dAnadinakara}3{dAna4 - dinakara} úm. N. of úwks.

Work: .{dAnakamalAkara}3{dAna4 - kamalA7kara} úm.

Work: .{dAnadarpaNa}3{dAna4 - darpaNa} úm.

Work: .{dAnakalpataru}3{dAna4 - kalpa-taru} m.N. of úwks.

Work: .{dAnamanohara}3{dAna4 - manohara} úm. N. of úwks.

Work: .{dAnamayUkha}3{dAna4 - mayUkha} úm. N. of úwk.

Work: .{dAnapaddhati}3{dAna4 - paddhati} úf. N. of úwk. on the 16 offerings îRTL. 415.

Work: .{dAnaparibhASA}3{dAna4 - paribhASA} úf. N. of úwk.

Work: .{dAnapArijAta}3{dAna4 - pArijAta} úm.

Work: .{dAnapradIpa}3{dAna4 - pradIpa} úm. N. of úwks.

Work: .{dAnaprakaraNa}3{dAna4 - prakaraNa} ún.

Work: .{dAnaprakAza}3{dAna4 - prakAza} úm.

Work: .{dAnavidhi}3{dAna4 - vidhi} m. N. of úwk.

Work: ~{-kathana} ún. {-vidhji} úm. {ømA7dhyA7ya} úm. N. of úwks. On alms-giving.

Work: {dAnabhAgavata}3{dAna4 - bhAgavata} ún. N. of úwk.

→

CC (*Catalogus Catalogorum*) Aufrecht and NCC (*New Catalogus Catalogorum*) ed. Raghavan etc.

Tantra

BILATERAL

In Śākta Tantra, bilateral donation from the side of the deities and the devotees is mentioned.[121]

Compassion

Compassion is at the root of the donation which is an all-pervasive entity in the form of *dayā*.[122] Her form as a mother bestows all the ingredients that a mother can offer to the children.[123]

Child Donation

The theme like giving off a son to the god of death (*mr̥tyu*) which might have developed in the complicated system like

---

→ Work: .{dAnakusumAJjali}3{deAna4 – kusumA7Jjali} úm.

Work: .{kelikaumudI}3{keli-kaumudI} úf.

Work: .{dAnakaumudI}3{dAna4 – kaumudI} úf.

Work: .{dAnakaustubha}3{dAna4 – kaustubha} úm. orn.,

Work: .{dAnakriyAkaumudI}3{dAna4 – kriyA-kaumudI} úf. N. of úwks.

Work: .{dAnakhaNDa}3{dAna4 – khaNDa} ún. N. of part 1 of Hema7dri's úwk.

Work: .{dAnacandrikA}3{dAna4 – candrikA} úf. N. of úwk.

121 *dāna:* > bilateral: Tantra: *dadāti, prati+gr̥h*

Durgāsaptaśatī: Kīlaka:

dadāti pratigr̥hṇāti nānyathaiṣ ā prasīdati ।
ittham-rūpeṇa kīlena mahādevena kīlitam ॥ 8 ॥

122 *Durgāsaptaśatī : yā devī sarvabhūteṣu dayā-rūpeṇa saṁsthitā* ।

123 *Durgāsaptaśatī: yā devī sarvabhūteṣu mātr̥-rūpeṇa saṁsthitā* ॥ 25 ॥

Triṇāciketas fire, might have been uprooted by Jainas and Bauddhas. It did not go to Tibet and China where *yajña* was thought to be like a fight of the rams (*huḍu*) in Tibet-Cāṇakya-Rājanīti-Śāstra. The uprooting of the bad customs like abduction by the royal power was known in Kālakācārya story of the Jainas[124] later in the twelfth century CE. Other social reforms are noted in the works of Hemacandra and others. Hemacandra got abolished the profession like-selling and meat-selling and provided the substitute professions to them in Gujarat.[125]

Yajña

Donation for *yajña* is not found in the Tibet-Cāṇakya-Rājanīti-Śāstra because they were not in favour of *yajña*. This concept is found in the provinces like Kaṭha (Himachal Pradesha) in *Kaṭhopaniṣad* which thinks that the sacrificial activities are superfluous (*plavā hyete yajñarūpaḥ*). Elsewhere it is found to be an instrument to cross the bondages of the birth and death.

Political Science

With regards to political science *dāna* (to give off money to the opponent king) is available in Tibet-Cāṇakya-Rājanīti-Śāstra also.

Cause of Mokṣa

Donation for *yajña* is not found in the Tibet-Cāṇakya-Rājanīti-Śāstra because the text is not in favour of *yajña*. Elsewhere it is found to be an instrument to cross the bondages of the birth and death.

---

[124] See: Winternitz: HIL.2.

[125] S.P. Narang, *Hemacandra's Dvyāśrayakāvya: A Literary and Cultural Study*, Delhi: Munshiram Manoharlal, 1972.

Buddhism

The donation in names through the names of *dānaśīla*, *dānādhikāra* and *dānaśūra* can be inferred in Buddhism.[126] The perfection of liberality is *dānapāramitā*.[127] Giving the assurance is one of the features of Buddhism.[128]

No Donation

Against the donation tradition, there are a few people who are not liberal or miser or philosophically not in favour of donation including a daughter in marriage.[129] The miserly people are known from R̥V. itself including those who are not interested even giving a blessing.[130] It continues even in

---

126 MWD: {dAnazIla}3{dAna4 – zIla} úmfn. liberally disposed îYa1jn5. îMBh..; úm. N. of a translator of îLalit.

MWD: . budd: {dAnAdhikAra}3{dAnA7dhikAra} úm. N. of a îBuddh. úwk.

MWD: Budd: {dAnazura}3{dAna4 – zura} úm. = {-vIra} îKatha1s..; N. of a *bodhisattva* (v. l. {sUra}) îBuddh.

MWD: Budd: .{dAnaMdadA}3{dAna4 – M-dadA} úf. N. of an *apsaras* or of a female *gandharva* îKa1ran2d2.

MWD: {anupradAna}2{anu-pradAna} ún. a gift, donation îBuddh.

Dānaśīla: in *Lalitavistara* in Tibet quoted in BRSW.

Dānavīra: quoted in BRSW.

127 MWD: {Nais: .{dAnapAramitA}3{dAna4 – pAramitA} úf. perfection of liberality Ka1ran2d2. îNaish.

128 MWD: .{abhayaMdada}3{a4-bhaya – M-dada} úm. N. of Avalokites3vara îBuddh.

129 MWD: {adAtR}1{a-dAtR} úmfn. not giving.; not liberal, miserly; .; not giving (a daughter) in marriage.

130 MWD: .{adAman}2{a-dAma4n} úmfn. not liberal, miserly îRV. _

MWD: {anAzirdA}3{a4n-Azir-dA} úmfn. not giving a blessing îRV. x, 27, 1.

AV[131] and the tradition of etymology, i.e. the *Nirukta*.[132]

No Acceptance

There might be a tradition of detached people in the society or saints who do not accept anything from any person.[133] It is very rare but even in the modern times, a few sects do not accept anything from anyone in theory, but in practice it is different. The scattered similar thoughts may be searched in the Upaniṣads. Samatā-founded by saint Maṅgata is one of such living sects. Such thoughts might have entered the Buddhism of Tibet and China in theory through the routes of expansion of Buddhism in earlier period. In the Afghanistan Bauddha manuscripts, there are manuscripts which lay down the importance of *dāna*. Even in modern ages donation is not denied in Buddhism .

Saint Tradition

Śaṅkarācārya is a follower of *mokṣa* tradition which is different from Dharmaśāstra tradition. Perhaps, Śaṅkarācārya does not encourage the donation tradition.[134] It is because they do not collect money and instantly fulfil their minimum needs. Moreover, it is a hindrance in the way of *mukti* of the others,

---

131 MWD: .{adAna}1{a4-dAna} ún. (û1. {dA}), not giving, act of withholding îAV. &c..; (úmfn.), not giving. _

MWD: .{adAnya}2{a-dAnya4} úmfn. not giving, miserly îAV. _

132 MWD: .{adAyin}2{a-dAyin} úmfn. not giving îNir. _

133 MWD: {anAdadAna}1{an-AdadAna} úmfn. not accepting.

134 S.P. Narang, "Ethical Values in Śaṅkarācārya's Writings", in *Ādi Śaṅkarācārya* (*12th Centenary Commemoration Volume*), Gandhinagar, 1992, pp. 49-56, Gujarati Version: Adi Śaṅkarācāryanī kṛtionmān naitika mūlya,

in *Ādi Śaṅkarācārya: dvadaśa śatābdī smṛtigrantha*, Ahmedabad, 1995, pp. 188-95, tr. Shuchita Mehta.

i.e. donees who are moving according to their own wish. But nowadays this tradition is lost and most of *maṭhas* are collecting money through various sources and agencies.

God Is Giver

According to saint Malūka (a saint of the medieval ages),[135] God gives everything to the birds and beasts even when they do not do any work. It may have resemblances to the Maskarī cult which propounds that do not do any work (*mā+√kṛ* – as per explanation of Patañjali on Pāṇini: *maskaramaskariṇau . . .*).

There is another tradition of saints who opines: Nothing to take: Nothing to give: only remain happy.[136]

There is another sect Samatā in Haryana at Jagadhari near Yamunā and having so many branches in Haryana and Punjab founded by the saint Maṅgata Ram who wants poverty instead of prosperity from God.[137] The concept might have migrated to mountains from Jagadhari and might have developed a blended thought with Buddhism and other saint traditions.

Donation Excess

Excess of donation is alluded to through the word *pāramitā* with *dāna*.[138] According to a *sūkti*, there is an end to an ocean but there

---

135 God is the giver to all: = Malūka: *ajagara kare na cākarī pañchī kare nā kāma dāsa malūkā kaha gaye sab ke dātā rāma* || – Malūkadāsa says: A huge serpant (swallower of a goat) does not do any service; a bird does not do any work. Rāma is the donor to all.

136 *Kuccha lenā nā denā magana rahanā*: folk song.

137 *Maṅgata māṅge dīnatā* (Samatā sect): *Samatā-vilāsa*.

138 *Dānapāramitā*: quoted in BRSW; MWD: pAramita}3{pAra4 - m-ita} úmfn. gone to the opposite shore.; crossed, traversed; transcendent (as spiritual knowledge) îW.

is no end to *dāna*.[139] The concept is an old one with *atidā* in R̥V and has a nexus in the ritual works.[140] In Buddhist literature, the excess donations are indicated with the words *dānaśīla*, *danādhikāra*, *dānaśūra*, etc. The words like *bhūridakṣiṇā* indicate to the excess donation. The words are found in R̥V, *Taittirīya Brāhmaṇa*, *Mahābhārata*, etc. which are generally associated with the sacrifices.[141] In the Brāhmaṇa literature, generally, without donation, nothing is successful. So *bhūridakṣiṇaḥ* is associated with sacrifices.[142]

---

139 No end to *dāna*: *vidyate sāgarasyānto dānasyānto na vidyate* Q.SKD.

140 MWD: See: Ati: {atidA}1{ati-dA} û1. to surpass in giving îRV. viii, i, 38, to pass; over in giving îKa1tyS3r. _

141 { MWD: bhUrida}3{bhU4ri - da} úmfn. " much-giving ", liberal, munificent îBhP.

MWD: {bhUridakSiNa}3{bhU4ri - dakSiNa} úmfn. attended with rich presents or rewards îMBh.

MWD: .; bestowing rich presents (esp. on brāhmaṇas at a sacrifice), liberal îib.

MWD: ; ({am}), úind. with rich offerings or presents îib.

MWD: .{bhUridA}3{bhU4ri - dA4} úmfn. = {-da} îRV. îTBr.

MWD: .{bhUridAtra}3{bhU4ri - dAtra} ({bhU4ri-}), úmfn. rich in gifts îRV.

MWD: .{bhUridAvat}3{bhU4ri - dA4vat} úmfn. "much-giving", munificent îRV.

.; {-tara} úmfn. úid. îib. (cf. îPa1n2. 8-2, 17 îVa1rtt. 2 îPat.)

.{bhUridAvan}3{bhU4ri - dA4van} úmf({arI}) ún. úid. îib.

142 {atidAtR}3{a4ti - dAtR} úm. a very or too liberal man.

.{atidAna}3{a4ti - dAna} ún. munificence

.; excessive munificence.

{atyAdAna}3{aty-AdAna} ún. taking away too much.

Cause of Bandha

Excess donation leads to bondage. The example of Bali is quoted generally.[143]

Root of Donation

The root of the donation is compassion and prayer in Śākta tradition (DSS 12.41); Salvation in Saint tradition; It is Kripā śaraṇa in Maṅgata traditon. It is *sevā*, *bhakti* and *sukhdhāma* in Ānandapur sect besides Balipradāna.

Time of Donation

Its time is just now before our own eyes and not beyond (*parokṣa*).[144] According to *Garuḍa Purāṇa*, the donation should be given everyday particularly on the festive occasions.[145] Both *deśa* and *kāla* for donations are also defined. *Pātra, śraddhā* and *dharma* are also to be considered.[146] It should be given at the time of the eclipse of the Sun and the Moon and at the time of *saṅkrānti*.[147] The places of donations are the pilgrimages like Prayāga and Gayā.[148]

Donation: How Much

The quantity of the donation depends upon the wealth and intention to give. A person with ten cows should give one;

---

143 Cause of *bandha*: *atidāne balirbaddhaḥ*: *Cāṇakyaśataka*: 50.3 and its variants in *Śārṅgadharapaddhati*, 76.26.1.

144 ~quoted in SKD; *Dāna*, p. 699: *parokṣe kalpitaṁ dānaṁ pātrābhāve kathaṁ bhavet.*

145 *Garuḍa Purāṇa*: *Dāna*: quoted in SKD, p. 701.

146 *Dāna*: quoted in SKD: ~*Lakṣaṇa*: quoted in SKD; *pātra, śraddhā, dharma, deśa, kāla*

147 *Mahābhārata*: quoted in SKD, p. 700.

148 Ibid.

person with 100 should give ten; person with 1,000 should give 100 and a person with many should give 1,000 or according to his intention to give. It hardly matters whether you are giving small or large in number. Wives and sons become a part of one's own self and can be sold if needed in emergency.[149]

Donation: To Whom

According to *Mahābhārata*, the donations should be given to a virtuous person.[150] According to *Vāyu Purāṇa* quoted in *Smṛticandrikā* it should be given to a virtuous person (*guṇavat*). It should be given with faith to a person who deserves it. *Garuḍa Purāṇa*[151] has propounded that the donation should be given to brāhmaṇas. More than that it should be given to the persons engaged in activity (*kriyā*). It is not certain that *kriyā* here should mean the action or ritual. Superior to them is the knower of Brahmā (*brahmavettā*). It means: spirituality is the most superior and better than caste and action. Moreover, it has laid emphasis on the persons who are educated (*vidyā*) and having austerity (*tapas*).

Elsewhere, it should be given to the persons born in the *gotra*. In their absence, it should be given to their relatives (*bandhu*). If there is no *sakulya* or their relatives, it should be given to one's own students belong to the same caste. If no one is available, it should be thrown in the water.[152]

149 Quoted in *Śuddhitattva*: SKD.; *Dāna*: pp. 699ff.

150 *Mahābhārata*: quoted in SKD, p. 700, Śāntiparvan.

151 *Garuḍa Purāṇa* = Gāruḍa : Dānavidhi: quoted in SKD, p. 701, MWD: .{dAnapAtra}3{dAna4 - pAtra} ún. "object of charity", N. of a ch. ofîPSarv.

152 Quoted in SKD; *Dāna*, p. 699, Gotraja: *gotrajebhyastathā dadyāt tadabhāve'sya bandhuṣu* ।

yadā tu na sakulyaḥ syānna ca sambandhibāndhavāḥ ।
dadyāt svajātiśiṣyebhyastadabhāve 'psu niḥkṣipet ॥

Jainism

In Jainism it has a relation to *antarāyakarma*. *Antarāyakarma* depends on the mental status of the donor.[153]

Expansion: Tibet

TIBETAN TRADE

The development of international trade in Eurasia had its beginning in the Early Medieval ages (*c.* CE 600–840) during the time when the Tibetan Empire was the major power in Central Asia.[154]

The Tibetan empire up to the present is surrounded by Indo-European speakers on the south and west; by Turkic and Mongolic speakers on the north and north-east; by Chinese on the east; and by Burmese speakers on the south-east.[155]

The main road to China goes from Lhasa to Tachienlu via Gyam-do, the capital of Kong-po, and then on through Cham-do. From the latter village there are two routes to Tachienlu one going to the east through Kan-ze, the other south-east through Ba-tang and Li-tang. Tachienlu is on the border between Tibet and China.[156]

Bauddha scholars carried the texts of poetics, lexicography (*Amara*), *Abhidhāna*, *Nītiśāstra* which included donation, grammar, poetics, metrics, drama, Vajrayāna songs, Caryāgīti

---

[153] See: *Jainendra-Siddhānta-Kośa.*

[154] The eastern route via Tachienlu to China. quoted in Chapter III. Tibetan Trade: Internet.

[155] The north-eastern route via Koko to China, the Turks and Siberia: ibid; The trans-Himalayan routes: to Ladakh, Kashmir, Indian States, Nepal, Sikkim, Cooch Behar, Bhutan, Assam: Internet.

[156] Sir Charles Bell, *The People of Tibet*, Oxford (reprint) 1965, pp. 120-21; quoted in from Internet: secondary source.

and Vajragīti to Tibet through various routes. It is possible that the texts containing the concept of donation were also carried as a value. Donation for *yajña* is not found in the Tibet-Cāṇakya-Rājanīti-Śāstra because they were not in favour of *yajña*. But *yajña* and donation are found in Tibet in a different form in medical science. *Yajña* for preparation of *suvarṇabhasma* was seen by me at Dharmaśālā which means it transferred its field from religion to medical science.

Expansion: China

In the north and north-west of India there were great centres of learning, such as the universities of Nālandā and Takṣaśilā (Taxila) where for hundreds of years not only all branches of secular knowledge, especially medicine, but also the philosophical and theological literature of the Buddhists were cultivated with great zeal. Indian *paṇḍitas* went thence to Tibet and China, learned Tibetan and Chinese, and translated Sanskrit works into these languages. Chinese pilgrims like Hsuan Tsang learned Sanskrit at Nālandā.[157]

As mentioned earlier, Bauddha scholars carried the texts of poetics, lexicography (*Amara*), *Abhidhāna*, *Nītiśāstra* which included donation.[158] They are being searched and restored by modern scholars.

---

157 Winternitz: HIL, II, pp. 226-27.

158 Manuscripts.

Published: Manuscripts in the *Schøyen Collection* I, Jens Braarvig, ed., *Buddhist Manuscripts*, vols. 1 and 2; Oslo 2000 and 2002.

Foremost is a collection of manuscripts found in caves in Bamiyan, in Afghanistan, in 1993-95. They comprise around 5,000 leaves and fragments, with around 7,000 micro-fragments, from a library of originally up to 1,000 manuscripts . . . the following classification is based on the information of *Schøyen Collection* available through Internet: →

The migration of manuscripts from India to Afghanistan and to Tibet and China is to be investigated with authority. But Bauddha scholars were carrying the texts including the theme of donation to various regions. It was a part of the religion.

→ Buddhism: The religion of these manuscripts is : Buddhism:

22.1. Āgama sūtras: MS 2179/44 India, 2nd-3rd c. MS 2376/1 India, 4th c. 22.2.

Mahāyna particularly *Prajñāpāramitā-sūtras*; see also MS 2169, China, 620-756, MS 2450 Japan, eighth-century. MS 2342 Japan, tenth-eleventh-century. MS 2371 Tibet, *c.*1400 22.3. *Mahāyāna-sūtras*; MS 2378/1 India, *fifth-century*. MS 2385 Bamiyan, Afghanistan, sixth century. See also MS 2152, and China. . . .

Mahāsāṅghika: The Buddhist Monastery of Mahāsāṅghika Bamiyan, Afghanistan (seventh century CE contains the manuscripts of the same *sūtra*.

A few fragments with Kharoṣṭhī script from the same library are in a private collection in Japan. Further 60 birch-bark scrolls and fragments in Kharoṣṭhī script in British Library, which according to Richard Salomon are "The Dead Sea Scrolls of Buddhism". Similar fragments were in the Hackin collection in Kabul Museum, which was destroyed during the recent Afghan civil war. There are 725 leaves and fragments with similar scripts from this period found in Chinese Turkistan, now in Berlin.

2. Cave in Hindu Kush, Bamiyan. Commentary: Three version of the *sūtra* are now available, and, exceptionally, all of them are preserved only in Indian languages. No translations into Chinese, Tibetan or any of the Central Asian languages formerly used for the transmission of Buddhist literature are known. Only the Pāli version of the Theravāda school. The Cankisūtra of *Majjhima-Nikāya* is preserved in its entirety.

. MS 23851. Bhaiṣajyagur-sūtra 2. Vajracchedika-sūtra; Diamond-Sūtra MS in Sanskrit on birch-bark, Bamiyan, Afghanistan, sixth century, 46ff., 6 x 18 cm, single column (5 x 17 cm), 5-6 lines in Gilgit/Bamiyan ornate type book script.

Mahāsāṅghika-lokottaravādins: prātimokṣa-vibhaṅga of the →

The North-Western Routes

The trade routes pass through Kashmir and across the Karakorum and thence to Kashgar, Khotan, Yarkand and other markets in Chinese Turkestan.[159]

Taking Lhasa as the centre, one of the routes to India is that which runs west and north throughout the length of southern Tibet to Leh, the capital of Ladakh; another goes westward to Almoṛā.

The Trans-Himalayan Routes

The trade between Tibet and its southern neighbours has been carried out since ancient times. The lure of trans-Himalayan trade was Lhasa: India and Tibet were the principal partners

→ mahāsāṅghika-lokottaravādins MS in Sanskrit on palm leaf, India, sixth century, 1f. + 2 partial ff., originally ca. 4 x 38 cm, single column (ca. 3, 5 x 36 cm), 6 lines in a calligraphic Gilgit/Bamiyan type I script, with 1 string hole dividing the leaf *c*. 75-25 per cent. Binding: India, sixth century, poti with 1 string hole dividing the leaf ca. 75-25 per cent. Context: MANUSCRIPTS: 2179, 2372-2386 and 2416 come from a Library that must have been of considerable size originally, maybe 1,400 MANUSCRIPTS: or more.The original numbers of this MS was MANUSCRIPTS: 2382/269, 2382/270, 2381/7, 2382/uf6/4f, 2382/uf6/2c, 2381/67, 2381/109. Provenance: 1. Buddhist monastery of Mahāsāṅghika, Bamiyan, Afghanistan (seventh century); 2. Cave in Hindu Kush, Bamiyan. Commentary: The text is a part of a commentary on a *pacattika* offence.

Material gift : *amisadāna/dharmadāna* -2. Cave in Hindu Kush, Bamiyan. Commentary: One section of the text obviously deals with the concepts of "material gift" (*amisadāna*) and "gift of the Law/Doctrine" (*dharmadāna*). The hoard contains a great number of hitherto unknown Buddhist texts, as well as the oldest surviving MS testimony to some of the most important texts of Mahāyāna Buddhism.

[159] A. Lamb, *Britain and Chinese Central Asia*, London: Routledge and Kegan Paul, 1960, p. 143.

while Nepal formed the principal venue through which this trade was conducted. It was in the seventh century CE that the emergence of powerful Tibetan kingdom with its capital at Lhasa transformed Kathmandu Valley into the intellectual and commercial entrêpot between India and central Asia. It appears that only limited trade was carried out during the next several centuries.[160]

The expansion of the thought and the Indian impact beyond doubt with small points with their influence should be investigated. The impact and movement of thought is from *Bāṣkala Saṁhitā* to Sialkot. The concept migrated to Afghanistan and to China on the one side and from Tibet to China on the other. The concept must have moved from various routes to Tibet and China. The changed routes and geographical data are to be restored for the movement of the thought. The manuscripts are the evidence to this hypothesis including the works like *Ratnāvalī*, an anthology which is lost in Sanskrit and is restored back from Chinese to Sanskrit. The geographical data from *Mahābhārata* and the Bauddha texts is to be interpreted afresh for the definite conclusion. The regional data and proverbs may help in this connection from the local languages. It is only a small conceptual collection and investigation where the author does not claim the impact exercised in various centuries beyond doubt.

---

[160] L.E. Rose, *Nepal-Strategy for Survival*, Berkeley: University of California, 1971, p. 10.

10

Sarvaṁ Sarvātmakam
Abhinavagupta's Interpretation of the Maxim

Bettina Bäumer 'Sharada'

THE theory that "everything is connected to everything", "every part contains the whole",[1] "all is in all" or *sarvātmakatvāvāda* has early origins. Albrecht Wezler has dedicated a series of articles to this *vāda*, tracing it back to the Upaniṣads,[2] and to the grammarian Patañjali in the second century BCE, besides the early Sāṁkhya and the Jaina author Mallavādin and his *Dvādaśāranayacakra* (as preserved in the *Nyāyāgamānusāriṇī* commentary by Siṁhasūri). A theistic version of the doctrine is found in Rāmānuja.[3] Various theories are connected with it, depending on the philosophical system, and I will not go into these different interpretations, ranging from the cosmological to the ontological, Advaitavāda and Īśvaravāda.

Although Wezler has gone into great detail regarding the origins and development of this theory in early Indian thought,

---

1 And other translations. Cf. R. Torella, *Examples of the Influence of Sanskrit Grammar on Indian Philosophy*, p. 155.

2 Cf. *Chāndogya* 6.2.1, Uddālaka Āruṇi.

3 Cf. A. Wezler, Remarks on *Sarvasarvātmakatvavāda*, p. 174: "One feels induced to assume that it originated in theistic circles, perhaps influenced by tenets of early Sāṁkhya."

he has not mentioned its application and transformation in Abhinavagupta, where it has reached its culmination. This genial author, who has brought to completion many earlier ideas in a grand synthesis, has inherited both, the cosmological and theological implications of the *sarvasarvātmakatvavāda*, without falling into the dangers of a naturalistic view, as in Sāṁkhya,[4] or an ontological theistic view.

Abhinavagupta does not treat *Sarvaṁ sarvātmakam* as a philosophical theorem requiring argumentation and proof, he rather accepts it as a given truth, something like *prasiddhi* in the context of Āgamic revelation.[5] The maxim is therefore, as far as I could see, not developed in his philosophical works, but in his tāntric exegetical works, most extensively in his *Vivaraṇa* on *Parātrīśikā Tantra* (PTV). Accepting it as a universal theory he applies it in many fields.

The most obvious source for an Advaita Śaiva would be the Bhairavāgamas, the scriptural basis of their tradition. There the context is theological, as it belongs to the description of Śiva's characteristics, but since theology and cosmology are closely linked in the Āgamas, it does not remain confined to the Divine aspect.

In the *Netra Tantra* (NT) Śiva is praised as:

prathamo hyeṣa deveśaḥ sarvajñaḥ sarvagaḥ śivaḥ ||

---

[4] Cf. the summary by Wezler, op. cit., p. 176: "Starting from the observation that the sentence *Sarvaṁ sarvātmakam* is paraphrased in the texts by the sentences *sarvaṁ ekam ekaṁ ca sarvam* and *sarvaṁ sarvatra* [*vidyate/asti*], this ontological statement can be shown to mean that every – necessarily material – phenomenon contains in itself at least one representative of each and every species of things."

[5] Cf. *Tantrāloka* 36.35, etc.

sarvasarvātmako deva ādisṛṣṭi pravartakaḥ ।

– NT 4.5-6[6]

The Lord of gods is first, he is all-knowing and all-present, Śiva. This God is of the nature of being all-in-all; he is the initiator of the original creation.

Kṣemarāja, in his Udyota commentary, explains *sarvasarvātmaka thus*:

sarvaṁ sarvaṁ yasya sa sarvasarvaḥ ātmā svarūpam yasya tādṛk . . .

He who is the all of all, the self or the essential nature of everything. . . .

It means that it is Śiva who pervades everything by his essence (*svarūpa*).

Further on Kṣemarāja explains *sarvasarvātmaka* by *parādvayavyāptiḥ*, i.e. "pervasion by supreme non-duality", Śiva's all-encompassing non-duality with everything in the universe.

In PTV, Abhinavagupta expands on another early source of the idea (not noticed by Wezler), namely the *Mahābhārata*. He comments on the following *śloka* of the Śānti-Parvan by taking it bit by bit:

yasmin sarvaṁ yataḥ sarvaṁ yaḥ sarvaṁ sarvataśca yaḥ ।
yaśca sarvamayo nityaṁ tasmai sarvātmane namaḥ ।।

– MBh XII.54

In whom everything is, from whom everything proceeds,
Who is everything and everywhere,
Who is immanent in all things, eternal,
To him, the self of all, I pay homage.

The subject matter of PTV being *anuttara*, the Unsurpassable,

---

[6] Cf. also NT 4.7: *deveśaḥ sarvasarvātmakaḥ*

Absolute, *sarvātmane namaḥ* is applied to it, and every phrase of the verse is connected with *anuttara* – not with any manifest divine form like Śiva or Bhairava. However, *Sarva* being one of the names of Śiva, the theorem *sarvaṁ sarvātmakaṁ* may still be called theistic, as it can be connected with *sarvaṁ śivātmakam* and similar expressions in the Āgamas.

However, given Abhinavagupta's all-embracing vision of reality, the theorem is a fit expression that he can apply in all areas. In this paper I can only give a few examples.

First of all, the commentary on *yataḥ sarvam* (from whom everything proceeds) gives him the occasion to state the outline of his entire theory.

> Now *anuttara* is that from which proceeds this "great manifestation" (*mahāsr̥ṣṭi*) which enfolds within itself hundreds of crores of unlimited *māyīya* (phenomenal) creations. As has been said, "That from which proceeds everything". So, this universe consisting of *cit, citta, prāṇa, deha* (i.e. four kinds of subjects), pleasure and pain, senses, the five elements and (objects like) jar, etc. abide without difference in one, supreme, divine Consciousness as simply forms of consciousness (*bodhātmakena rūpeṇa*). Though the divine universal consciousness never ceases to exist, for it ceasing, there will be the contingency of universal darkness, yet there does not exist difference consisting of reciprocal absence (of objects), for all objects are omnifarious in that state (*viśvātmāna eva bhāvāḥ*). If all things were not situated in that universal Bhairava consciousness, then even the initial indeterminate perception which is of use in urging the senses towards their objects would not be there. Therefore, the entire multitude of existents exists there, without the appearance of appropriate objectivity (lit. thisness), identically with I-conciousness only, void of all differentiation. There is absolutely no difference there whatsoever. In that universal

> Bhairava consciousness, the entire manifestation lies clearly at rest. – PTV, p. 77[7]

At the end of this lengthy commentary he states: "This very *anuttara* contains all in its womb" (*tadevānuttarametadsarvaṁ garbhīkṛtya . . .* p. 32).

Being based on *anuttara* and on universal consciousness, Abhinavagupta proceeds to all kinds of applications.

For example, in the field of grammar he states that the verse commented upon contains all the cases of *yat*, and hence it exhausts all possible relationships. He applies it in the case of the grammatical persons, where there seems to be a separation between the third person, indicating insentiency (*jaḍatā*) and the first person, indicating sentiency (*cidrūpa*). But

> since everything is an epitome of everything (*sarvaṁ hi sarvātmakam iti*, or "since everything consists in everything"), according to this universal principle, even the insentient third persons, shedding their insentiency, become able to share in the quality of the second and first person, just as (in expressions like) "listen, o mountains!", or (in the saying of Kṛṣṇa in the *Gītā*), "of mountains I am Meru"
> – (tr. p. 72, modified).

What these examples imply is that there is a fluid relationship between the three persons, flowing into each other. These examples also show one of the aims Abhinavagupta has in mind while using this principle, namely to overcome separation and difference (*bheda*) at all levels.

The principle of *sarvaṁ sarvātmakaṁ* also offers Abhinavagupta a basis for showing that his *advaita* does not exclude multiplicity and variety.

---

[7] Page numbers refer to the translation of Jaideva Singh (see References).

> In the nature of consciousness, the omnifariousness of everything (*sarvasarvātmakatā*) is always present. That highest Divinity, viz. *parā*, though consisting of the highest stage of non-differentiation is teeming with endless variety, containing within Herself as she does the *parāparā* expansion of *paśyantī*, etc. – PTV, p. 91

It is the all-pervasive consciousness, which in Abhinavagupta's system is never disconnected from language, which makes for the interconnectedness of the elements of language and the levels of the *Word* (*Vāk*).

> Therefore, though the condensation of the phonemes becomes distinct only in the *vaikharī* or gross aspect, yet it abides primarily in the supreme verbum (*parāvāk*) which is all inclusive (*sarvasarvātmaka*). . . .
>
> Therefore one and the same venerable supreme verbum (*ekaiva parābhaṭṭārikā*), being all inclusive, abides as the highest Lord in all, whether stone, tree, animal, man, god, Rudra, *pralayākala* or *vijñānākala* (*kevalī*), *mantra*, *mantreśvara*, *mantramaheśvara* and others. Therefore, *mātṛkā* whose body consists of letters (and sounds) which reside in various stations as their very soul either in indistinct (*asphuṭa*) or imperceptible (*avyakta*) way as in *madhyamā* or in distinct (*sphuṭa*) or perceptible (*vyakta*) way as in *vaikharī* is declared as the efficacious potency of *mantra* (*mantravīrya*).
>
> – PTV, pp. 176-77

He explains the background of this connectedness:

> The plane of the supreme word (*parāvāgbhūmiḥ*) of these phonemes is the one described (here), where these (phonemes) exist in the form of pure consciousness, uncreated, eternal. In such a condition of pure consciousness there are no separate forms of existence (*sarvasarvātmakatā*): all is perpetually and actually produced (*satatodita*). – PTV, p. 145

André Padoux, in his excellent study on *Vāc*, gives a concise summary of the theory:

> Thus we can see that, from the standpoint of the Trika, where "all is in all" (*sarvasarvātmaka* – that is, where there are no separate forms of existence since consciousness is all-pervasive), where the empiric arises from the Absolute, is rooted in it and can never move away from it, the lower one goes through the levels of the word, the less is there is to be said, since everything is there, seminally, right from the beginning. It is the source, the supreme word, Consciousness, which alone is of true import. – Padoux, *Vāc*, p. 222

Even all the complexity of language can be reduced to the first phoneme, *a*, the "symbol" of *Anuttara* and *Akula*:

> *A* is the stage of the Supreme Word (*parāvāgbhūmi*) in which alone of these phonemes there is the non-conventional, eternal, natural form consisting of nothing but Consciousness. In the "body" (*vapus*) made of Consciousness the interconnectedness of everything is ever present (*sarvasarvātmakatā satatoditaiva*).
>
> – PTV, p. 91

The most encompassing field of application of the theory is the total vision of reality in the thirthy-six *tattvas* of the Āgamas, comprising the cosmic elements, the human and the divine levels (hence not only cosmology but cosmotheandric reality). Abhinavagupta demonstrates the inherence of the *tattvas* in each other according to the same principle that "every part reflects the whole", or "every element is contained in every other element" (alternative translations).

> Thus that very last *tattva*, viz. *pr̥thivī* (earth) while maintaining its character as earth and holding within itself all the innumerable earlier *tattvas* (e.g. water – *jala*, fire – *agni*, etc.) as inseparable from itself, appearing in that form (*bhāsamāno*) and viewed in that aspect (*vimr̥śyamānaḥ*) is complete in

> itself. Its precedent *tattva* also (i.e. *jala* or water) having the posterior *tattva* (i.e. *pṛthivī* or earth) as its background, being identical with the appearance and perceptibility present in the earth category and not renouncing the completeness of its posterior *tattva* (i.e. the *pṛthivī tattva*) inevitably brings within its compass the fullness of all the preceding *tattvas* also and appearing and being carefully considered in that way is integral in the same way. Thus one by one, all the preceding *tattvas* (*agni* – fire, etc.), not being separated from their posterior two or three ones, including within themselves the delightful existence of their antecedent *tattvas* in accordance with the non-divergence from the nature of Bhairava which has accrued to them, are perfectly integral. Thus that category becomes a form very proximate to its chosen self-luminous Bhairava and that form becoming a self-chosen abode of rest is designated Bhairava. – PTV, p. 113

This is not just speculation, but it has to be experienced in spiritual practice, for which Abhinavagupta gives examples from *Vijñāna-Bhairava* (v. 60, etc.).

In a powerful statement he even applies this consciousness to limited space:

> *pradeśamātramapi brahmaṇaḥ sarvarūpam*
>
> Even in a limited portion of space the entire form of *Brahman* is present. – p. 47

Moving from the areas of language and cosmology to psychology Abhinavagupta comes to the realm of emotions. Emotional experiences are interconnected due to the intimate relation of vital energy with divine consciousness.

> Of the form, sound, etc. even a single one, because of its being made powerful by the augmented vigour referred to previously, can bring about the excitement of the senses pertaining to all other objects also. Since everything is an epitome of all things for all people, even memory or idea

> of a thing can surely bring about agitation because of the excitement of innumerable kinds of experiences like sound, etc. lying subconsciously in the omnifarious mind. . . .
>
> When the vital energy that has been lying within and identical with one's Self in a placid state (*svamayatvena abhinnasyāpi*) is agitated (*vikṣobha*), i.e. when it is in an active state, then the source of its pleasure is the Supreme I-consciousness full of creative pulsation, beyond the range of space and time (*adeśakālakalitaspandamayamahāvimarśa-rūpameva*), of the nature of perfect Bhairava-consciousness, the absolute sovereignty, full of the power of bliss. – PTV, pp. 42-43

Not only joyful emotions, but painful experiences are equally connected with the centre of consciousness, and lead to an "expansion of the essential nature" (Somānanda, *Śivadṛṣti* V.5). The locus for this experience in the yogic body is the central vein (*madhyanāḍī*, p. 44 tr.).

Similarly, the limbs of the body are symbolically (and ritually) interconnected:

> Though the limbs, head, mouth, etc. have been indicated separately, yet each one of them is specifying the other. This fact has already been established by the principle: "Everything is the epitome of all' (*sarvaṁ sarvātmakaṁ*). – PTV, p. 252

The principle that "everything is connected to the totality", "every part contains the whole of reality", and a variety of other translations, is closely associated with other central themes of Trika:[8] one is the concept of fullness (*pūrṇatā*), implying equally the pervasion of divine consciousness in everything. *Sarvaṁ sarvātmakam* provides the idea of *pūrṇatā* with a "method"

---

[8] It could also be shown in Abhinavagupta's disciple, Kṣemarāja, e.g. his *Pratyabhijñāhṛdayam*, *sūtra* 4 and auto-commentary, where he uses the metaphor of the universal body of the Divine: *viśvaśarīra* (ed. and tr. Jaideva Singh, pp. 55-57).

to demonstrate in various cases and fields of experience and reality. The other is the theory of reflection or *bimba-pratibimba*, which Abhinavagupta applies in the *Parātrīśikā Vivaraṇa* to the relation between *tattvas* and phonemes (*varṇa*). It is because of the principle of the presence of everything in everything that reflection is possible; and vice versa, things and states are interconnected because there is a Divine reflection in the whole of reality.

Each one of these central principles of understanding Reality ultimately points to an all-inclusive *paramādvaita*. As Abhinavagupta himself sums it up in his *Mālinīvijaya Vārttika* (MVV):

> *tatra pūrṇaikarūpatvāt sarvaṁ sarvatra cāpi tat* ।
> *anyathā khaṇḍanāyogān na pūrṇā pūrṇatā bhavet* ॥
> – MVV I.132

> And in this (highest reality)[9] because it is always replete, everything is also in everything. Otherwise this fullness would not be complete, since division would be possible.[10]

Although both the connected "theories" *Sarvaṁ sarvātmakam* and *bimba-pratibimbavāda*, tend towards oneness, yet they allow for differentiation and the beauty of manifestation. As Abhinavagupta says in *Parātrīśikā Vivaraṇa*:

> In the supreme consciousness, however, as is the light, so is the reflection, even in the outer activity. Therefore, all things appear as non-different (from consciousness), just as water is in water, or flame in flame, not just like a reflected image.
> – PTV, p. 111

---

[9] *Paratattve* from the previous verse, 131.

[10] Tr. J. Hanneder (modified), p. 81, Abhinavagupta's *Philosophy of Revelation; Mālinīślokavārttika* I.1-399, Groningen 1998.

R. Torella sums up the vision of the totality of Kashmir Śaivism in the following way:

> One of these themes, which runs through the whole of Kashmir Śaivism, may be condensed in the formula *Sarvaṁ sarvātmakam,* "all is in all", "all is made of all". No reality may be said to be separate and self-contained, since everything is pervaded by a single nature, *śivatā* (as Somānanda insistently repeats in the *Śivadr̥ṣṭi*) or the Power. Thus there do not really exist separations or confines of any kind, there is nothing that remains definitively excluded from this circulation of the dynamism of Consciousness, which comes about precisely through this infinite melting and coagulating. Thus from everything it is possible to make the leap or immerse oneself in the heart of the absolute, precisely because this absolute, in a certain sense, does not have any centre (except the I) or because its centre is everywhere.
>
> – R. Torella, op. cit., p. 155

The theme of our seminar is the "Contribution of Sanskrit to World Thought". What the world needs most urgently today is a vision which makes possible the integration of our fragmented and divisive attitudes, at every level. We are in search of a wholistic understanding and practice which could heal our divisions. We cannot and need not invent such a view, we have only to revive what has been there in this great tradition, interpret it in terms of our present-day problems and situations, and apply it in life, individually (spiritually), socially, politically, and, last but not least, in ecology. To my mind, the great intuition of the interrelatedness of all things, in a way comparable to the Buddhist *pratītyasamutpāda,*[11] could serve as a bridge between the

[11] This is not the place for a comparison, but one important difference may be noted. The Buddhist *pratītyasamutpāda* (interdependent origination) is more concerned with causality, whereas *sarvasarvātmakatva* is not formulated in relation to time or cause.

ancient Indian thought and the present-day situation. However, it needs a deep understanding of both, and a bridge-building in order to make these ideas fruitful for the world.

References

Parātriṁśikātattvavivaraṇa of Abhinavagupta: *The Parātriṁśhikā with Conmmentary. The latter by Abhinavagupta*, ed. Mukunda Rāma Shāstrī, KSTS 18, Bombay, 1918.

Abhinavagupta, *Parātrīshikā-Vivaraṇa: The Secret of Tantric Mysticism*, English translation, with notes and running exposition, by Jaideva Singh. Sanskrit text corrected, notes on technical points and charts dictated by Swami Lakshmanjee, ed. Bettina Bäumer, Delhi: Motilal Banarsidass, 1988 ff.

Netra Tantra (NT): *The Netra Tantram with Commentary by Kṣemarāja*, ed. Madhusudan Kaul Shastri, 2 vols. Bombay: KSTS, 1926, 1939.

Kṣēmarāja, *Pratyabhijñāhṛdayam: The Secret of Self-recognition*, ed. and tr. Jaideva Singh, Delhi: Motilal Banarsidass, 1963 ff.

Hanneder, Jürgen, 1998, *Abhinavagupta's Philosophy of Revelation: An Edition and Annotated Translation of Mālinīślokavārttika* I.1-39, Groningen Oriental Series Volume XIV, Groningen: Egbert Forsten.

Padoux, André, 1990, *Vāc: The Concept of the Word in Selected Hindu Tantras*, Albany: State University of New York Press.

Wezler, Albrecht, 1981, "Studien zum Dvādaśāracakra des Śvetāmbara Mallavādin. I. Der *sarvātmakatvavāda*", in: *Studien zum Jainismus und Buddhismus*, Wiesbaden (Franz Steiner), pp. 359-408.

——, 1982, "Paralipomena zum Sarvātmakatvavāda (I)", in *WZKS*, **XXVI**: 149-66.

——, 1987, "Remarks on the *sarvātmakatvavāda*", in *Philosophical Essays: Anantlal Thakur Felicitation Volume*, Calcutta: Sanskrit Pustak Bhandar, pp. 166-81.

——, 1992, "Paralipomena zum Sarvasarvātmakatvavāda II", in *Studien zur Indologie und Iranistik*, Band 16/17, Reinbek, pp. 287-314.

11

Wisdom from the Sanskrit Texts for Management

S. Ram Mohan

Management and Value Foundation

THE concept of effective management is often presented as the contribution of Western thinkers and is considered as the competitive edge of the developed countries. This paper presents the facts that management concepts, even though not classified as a separate subject in ancient Hindu Śāstras, have been dealt with in great depth in ancient Sanskrit texts. *Bhagavad-Gītā* has several valuable points in this direction. The concept of systemic thinking, presented much later by thinkers like Peter Senge, has been esoterically brought out in *Bṛhadāraṇyaka Upaniṣad.*

Ethical and moral dimensions are also given great importance. Business schools, after the tell-tale scandals of Enron, AT&T and the replete storms of unethical behaviour of high officials in Capitol Hill have woken up to the need for re-engineering the management ideas and behaviour to factor in ethical values and the need to not merely raise student's awareness of the problem but also to provide the criteria for determining ethical business behaviour in situations with conflicting values.

Management and re-engineering concepts are not new to Indian ethos. The Vedāntic wisdom is cherished through the insight and experience of our sages in the *manas-budhi-ahaṅkāra* interface. The value foundation for the Indian system is based on the three principal values or ultimate realities – goodness, beauty and truth, as enshrined in *Ṛgveda*.

> विश्वानि देव सवितुः दुरितानि परा सुव। यद्भद्रं तन्न आ सुव।
>
> *viśvāni deva savituḥ duritāni parā suva* ।
> *yadbhadraṁ tann ā suva* ।। – *ṚV* V.82.5
>
> Savitā! God! Send far away all evil; Send us what is good.

The *ṛṣi* in *Ṛgveda* says:

> Sinless for noble power under the influence of Savitā-God. We contemplate all that is beautiful.

Thus the management deliberately makes the choice of goodness, beauty and truth. The value system is so lofty that Veda states that truth, not even God, is the one which upholds the earth.

> अनागसो अदितये देवस्य सवितुः सवे। विश्वा वामानि धीमहि।।
>
> *anāgaso aditaye devasya savituḥ save* ।
> *viśvā vāmāni dhīmahi* ।। – *ṚV* V.82.6

Indian texts delineate the link between management and values which provides the base for the organizational or societal function. It is very different from the skewed principles of corporate governance, with emphasis on profit orientation to the exclusion of ethics, environmental needs, quality needs, etc. *Hitopadeśa* says:

> Getting a deserved object from an undesirable source is not a satisfying practice. But at the same time, adventure and risk-taking are positive values.

The Western thinkers treated the people-oriented values, work-oriented values and spiritual values in separate compartments. The managerial value areas like achievement, efficiency responsibilities, responsiveness, etc. have been treated as means to establish competitive edge over the competitor. In the beginning, the impact of the spiritual values in managerial cultures had not been properly appreciated in the West in the beginning. Only the phenomenal success of Japanese industry made the West to look at the Zen values that shaped the holistic cultural milieu of Japanese industry and society. These aspects have been dealt with at length in our heritage texts much earlier.

The wise executives follow the codes and rules with implicit faith and do not deviate from it, like a cart proceeding in the nominated and treaded path.

रेखामात्रमपि क्षुण्णात् आ मनोर्वर्त्मनः परम्।
न व्यतीयुः प्रजास्तस्य नियन्तुर्नेमिवृत्तयः।।

rekhāmātramapi kṣuṇṇāt ā manorvartamanaḥ param ।
na vyatīyuḥ prajāstasya niyanturnemivṛttayaḥ ।।

– Kālidāsa, *Raghuvaṁśa* 1.17

The Sanskrit ethos emphasizes values rooted on the tripod of reason feeling and deeds. Even while the need for a professional to make money is recognized, *nyāya*, *dayā* and *karma* are given the highest place. For instance, for a doctor whether he gets paid or not, the treatment of patients never goes without fruit.

चिकित्सा नास्ति निष्फला।

cikitsā nāsti niṣphalā ।

But the fruit may vary from situation to situation – it could be *puṇya*, friendship, fame, knowledge and experience. This is also highlighted in verse 769 of *Viśvaguṇādarśa Campū* in the reply of Viśvāvasu to the cynical comments of Kṛṣanu. Later Viśvāvasu also explains the appropriate place given by the government servants in properly executing their public duties while maintaining their private and religious life properly tuned.

अशुभपुषि कलावप्यप्रमत्ताः स्वधर्मादनुदिनमुपकारानाचरन्तो बुधानाम्।
बहुजनपरिपुष्टौ बद्धदीक्षास्त एते तनुसुखमपि हित्वा तन्वते राजसेवाम्।।

aśubhapuṣi kalāvapyapramattāḥ svadharmādanudinam-
upakārānācaranto budhānām ।
bahujanaparipuṣṭau baddhadīkṣāsta ete tanusukhamapi
hitvā tanvate rājnasevām ।।

– *Vis* 530

The value plays an important role in shaping the quality of leadership and the power of influencing others. Leadership means setting the right example – A good example is given in *Hitopadeśa* where Cītragrīva, the king of pigeons, refuses to allow his friend Hiraṇyaka, the mice king, to sever his bonds first, but insists on the release of his subjects first.

> They bear an equality to me as regards kind, substance and qualities, say, then when and what will be the fruit of my being their Lord?

The role of ethics in corporate life has been vividly explained by Abraham Zaleznik and Konosuke Matsushita in *The Managerial Mystique Restoring Leadership in Business.*

Synergy in Heritage Texts

Chester Barnard, in his seminal work, *The Functions of the Executive,* attempts to provide a comprehensive theory of co-operative behaviour in formal organizations. The spirit of co-operative endeavour is delineated in the 10th Maṇḍala of *R̥gveda* in the Puruṣa-Sūktam. It was a great co-operative endeavour undertaken with profound devotion by the entire community. Here a symbolic *yajña* was performed, out of which the created beings and natural beings took their form. Thus the purpose of the endeavour was attaining totally their individual minds with the total mind or cosmic consciousness. This represents what

Zaleznik later termed as "spontaneous co-operation". This is achieved by reducing the proportion of *pravṛtti* and increasing *nivṛtti*. Thus the process of realizing unity in the midst of differences and *ekātmānubhūti* is achieved. This is the basis for what later managerial scripts call synergy or Stephen Covey's "win–win" attitude.

The greatest political thinker of Indian heritage Kauṭilya himself, in the concluding portion of *Arthaśāstra,* observes that the purpose of his work is to bring together spiritual good, material well-being and happiness. Thus, spiritual good is the foundation upon which material goodness and happiness are based. The purpose of state must be the welfare of the people. This is exemplified in *Śākuntalam.*

प्रवर्ततां प्रकृतिहिताय पार्थिवः सरस्वती श्रुतिमहती महीयताम्।।

pravartatāṁ prakṛtihitāya pārthivaḥ sarasvatī śrutimahatī mahīyatām ||

– *Śākuntalam* 7.35

Peter Senge makes a clear distinction between espoused theories and theories-in-practice. Often blind adherence to theories or rituals leads to considerable loss. A dynamic change consciousness is essential. This is exemplified in *Śrīmad Bhāgavatam.* When young cow-herds sent by Kṛṣṇa to get food approached the brāhmaṇas performing "Āṅgirasa Yajña" for accession to heaven, they were refused food by the brāhmaṇas. But the wives of the brāhmaṇas, intuitively realizing the divinity of Kṛṣṇa, came rushing to him with offerings. Eventually the brāhmaṇas, realizing that they had lost due to this dyed-in-the-wool adherence to rituals, cursed themselves – their threefold birth, learning, vows of continence, pedigree, etc. which made them impervious the touch of Divinity.

धिग् जन्म नस्त्रिवृद् विद्यां धिग् व्रतं धिग् बहुज्ञताम्।
धिक् कुलं धिग् क्रियादाक्ष्यं विमुखा ये त्वधोक्षजे।।

dhig janma nastrivṛd vidyāṁ dhig vrataṁ dhig bahujñatām ।
dhik kulaṁ dhig kriyādākṣyaṁ vimukhā ye tvadhokṣaje ।।

– *Bhāgavatam* 10.23.39

A very interesting scene is witnessed when the espoused theory takes a back seat in the Vāli–Rāma debate. While Vāli is asking pointed questions, Rāma is defensive. The child-ego of Rāma is pleading to Vāli's parent ego in the Transaction Analysis route when Rāma mouths defences like:

प्रतिज्ञा च मया दत्ता तदा वानरसंनिधौ

pratijñā ca mayā dattā tadā vānarasaṁnidhau

I have promised Sugrīva.

न वयं स्ववशे स्थिता:

na vayaṁ svavaśe sthitāḥ

I was not in control of myself.

The solution is found in *Bhagavad-Gītā*'s work ethics approach. Work well done is verily *yoga* (BG II.50). "Let not results of your actions become your motive. You shall not also be attached to inaction". The theme unfolds with greater clarity in the subsequent chapter. A clear-cut differentiation is made between the action to be done (*karma*), the work to be avoided (*vikarma*) and finally the absence of both, i.e. inactivity (*akarma*); from a holistic perspective. Kṛṣṇa declares that he alone can accomplish everything who distinguishes between inactivity in activity and activity in inactivity.

The second part of *Gītā* verse quoted "know activity in inactivity" is also very significant. Inaction represents the absence of visible or physical actions. At the same time the mind is engaged in deep analysis and thought process. This is the Stephen Covey's Quadrant II stage where the conceptual and intellectual activities take predominant role. This drives the organization in the fast lanes of growth in a competitive environment. *Śrī Bhāṣyam* of Rāmānuja distinguishes *karma* as routine activities (*sthūla*) and *akarma* as *sūkṣma* (latent power). Thus the physical and intellectual activities have their respective roles.

From a managerial angle, inactivity-in-activity is the basis for ideas like Total Quality Management, where the elimination of non-value adding activities has been identified as the main cost-reducing agents. The essence of all these theories is locating the inactivity (unproductive actions) amidst productive activities (*karmaṇya karma yaḥ paścet*). This is the basis for many modern management theories, right from F.W. Taylor to Peter Drucker. Drucker packages this differently when he says "Be prepared to abandon everything, lest we have to abandon the ship". This is also the basis for core-competence analysis.

Excellence is achieved by concentrating only on core-competence areas and outsourcing others. Defining this re-engineering approach, *Taittirīya Upaniṣad* says:

> Your present package of *prajā*, *karma* and *dharma* cannot bring in success. Only by *tyāga*, unlimited success can be attained.

The very first verse of *Īśa Upaniṣad* also emphasis this:

> तेन त्यक्तेन भुञ्जीथाः
>
> *tena tyaktena bhuñjīthāḥ*
>
> Enjoy through renunciation.

Thus, the concept of giving up something for a more favourable alternative has been repeatedly stressed in the Upaniṣads. Both the pairs of negation and affirmation are stressed. This is the essence of modern theory of re-engineering where sets of activities or process are abandoned for a more profitable alternative system.

Taittirīya Upaniṣad thus puts to an end that theory that abundance of resources like workforce (*praja*), skills (*karma*) and finance (*dhana*) would assure success by themselves. It is imperative to introduce necessary process-changes by giving up irrelevant actions.

The co-ordination of the managerial activities is depicted in *Kaṭhopaniṣad*'s Charioteer Matrix

ātmā - Charioteer

śarīra - Chariot

buddhi - Driver

manas - Rein holder

Indriyas - Horses

A perfect fusion of the above takes the chariot to the desired destination. If co-ordination fails, the chariot will go astray. This is later brought out in Mckinsey's *7S.Matrix*.

The ideal mindset for a manager to be efficient and effective provided by *Gītā*'s paradigm.

समत्वं योग उच्यते

samatvaṁ yoga ucyate

Antaḥkaraṇa and Problem-solving

Normally the decision-making process is done through the three tiers of *manas–buddhi–ahaṅkāra* interface dealing with ordinary, complicated and complex situations. The better type of managers develop their *antaḥkaraṇa* (intuitive capacities) transcending the *jñānendriyas*. Emerson calls it as the "inner gleam" which is the right instrument to advice on complex decisions. Normally the "*vr̥tti* and *saṁskāra*" act at conscious and subconscious levels to influence the final decision. In a person who has developed the inner gleam and inner knowledge, *antaḥkaraṇa* helps him to arrive at the right decisions. This inner gleam is developed through following the right path. Buddha discribes them as right faith, right aspiration, right speech, right conduct, right livelihood, right effort, right mindfulness and right contemplation (Noble Eightfold Path).

Indian heritage advises the practitioners not to have a short-sighted adherence to the past and not to be led by other's opinions, however numerous they are. It emphasizes on a no-hold-barred enquiry method. Such an enquirer is known as *jijñāsu* – like Naciketas. Such person will surely embrace success. Kālidāsa says in *Mālavikāgnimitram*:

> Nothing is superior because it is not old nor some Kāvya is ridiculed because it is new. The noble souls examine in detail and accept that which is good. The fool is led by other's thought.
>
> मूढः परप्रत्ययनेयबुद्धिः।
>
> *mūḍhaḥ parapratyayaneyabuddhiḥ* ।

Svadharma: The Route to Success

The concept of *svadharma* finds repeated expression in *Gītā* (II.31, 33, XVIII.47, 42). With multinational corporations from various parts of the globe entering India at an alarming pace, each ushering their own work culture, this statement on *svadharma* merits a careful analysis.

The standing example is Japan. The war-ravaged economy was written off by the West. But the Samurai traditions of Japan helped Japan to re-emerge as a mighty economic power on a very short time making it as a super economy next only to that of US. The management practices of Japan, once ridiculed by the

West, are now being followed avidly by them – Ringi System of decision-making, respect for elders and systems, quality circles, etc. The company song and code of values developed a sense of commitment there.

This exemplifies the importance of *svadharma*. Many ideas which have worked successfully in USA, when transplanted in UK, did not find success there even though the cultures were similar, like empowerment, informal relationship with the boss, etc. One of the reasons for opposition to WTO, even in developed countries, is this fear of cultural fallout from USA.

Gītā says:

स्वधर्मे निधनं श्रेय: परधर्मो भयावह:।

svadharme nidhanaṁ śreyaḥ paradharmo bhayāvahaḥ ।

Understand and perform your *svadharma* – an elegant understanding of one's ethos in the context of a rapidly changing society. This is the core teaching in value management in our heritage texts. These concepts have stood the test of time – ever fresh and ever effective.

12

Yoga in America: Twists and Turns

T.S. Rukmani

TODAY in America it is claimed that one out of four or five Americans practise *yoga*. Meditation is becoming popular in medical schools and educational television programmes regularly feature lectures by doctors trained in allopathic medicine advocating *yoga* and meditation for good health. Disillusionment with allopathic treatments and a desire to go back to natural living has also kindled interest in *yoga* and the technique of meditation taught by *yoga*. Even prisoners are being taught *yoga* and meditation and it is reported that they are less aggressive after they start *yoga* practice. Of course, most people practise mainly *haṭha-yoga* and the philosophical underpinnings of *yoga* as described in Patañjali's *Yoga-Sūtras* is not their concern at all. It is more a body culture and is a muti-billion industry today. Its large popularity in all walks of life has allowed it to come under the gaze of religious practitioners and recently one of the pastors of a Christian church condemned Christians who follow this path as according to him the popular discipline of meditation and stretching is so interwoven with Eastern mysticism that it is at odds with the Christian understanding. He says:

---

* I have used material from Louise Bardach's write up on Vivekananda in *The New York Times*, Sunday Review, the opinion pages, 1 October 2011, in preparation of this paper.

> Christians who practise *yoga* are embracing, or at a minimum flirting with a spiritual practice that threatens to transform their own spiritual lives into a "post-Christian, spiritually polyglot" reality.

The Southern Baptist Theological Seminary President Albert Mohler further wrote on his blog:

> Christians are not called to empty the mind or to see the human body as a means of connecting to and coming to know the divine.

He adds:

> Believers are called to meditate upon the Word of God, an external Word that comes to us by divine revelation not to meditate by means of incomprehensible syllables.

Mohler drew a lot of criticism both from Christians who practise *yoga* as well as Hindus who took umbrage at the way *yoga* was described. Defending the practice of *yoga* in many churches many people saw that *yoga* was unrelated to its ancient roots in India and was equally present in other cultures as well. A number of Hindus and especially the Hindu American Foundation (HAF) joined the fray and the debate ranged for a few months. Now the debate turned to whether *yoga* can be separated from its Hindu roots. It even got into the main papers and David Waters wrote in the *Washington Post*:

> Some Hindus are concerned that *yoga* has been confiscated. Some Muslims are concerned that Hindus are using *yoga* as a tool of conversion. Buddhists remain detached from the issue. But some Christians are concerned that practising *yoga* will lead to theological confusion.

This gradually became more of a political debate as participants viewed each other as having different agendas and were using *yoga* as a prop to further their own interests. The HAF ran a series of articles titled "Take Back Yoga" emphasizing its roots in Hinduism. "The Hindu American Foundation concludes from its research that *yoga*, as an integral part of Hindu philosophy, is not simply a physical exercise . . . but is in fact a Hindu way of life" and following that there was a bitter exchange between members of HAF and Deepak Chopra, the new age *guru*. In general this controversy arose as some Hindus were concerned that *yoga* has been confiscated and removed from its roots in Hinduism.

The purpose of the "Take Back Yoga", campaign was not to ask *yoga* devotees to become Hindu, or instructors to teach more about Hinduism. "Its purpose was to make people become more aware of *yoga*'s debt to the faith's ancient traditions". Thus as Paul Vitello wrote in the *New York Times,* 27 November 2010:

> The question at the core of the debate – as to who owns *yoga*? – has become an enduring topic of chatter in *yoga* web forums, Hindu American newspapers and journals catering to the many consumers of what is now a multibillion-dollar *yoga* industry.

The *New York Times* went on to state that some religious historians as well as Deepak Chopra believed that *yoga* originated in the Vedic culture of Indo-Europeans who settled in India in the third millennium BCE, long before the tradition now called Hinduism emerged. There were other historians who trace *yoga* to *Bhagavad-Gītā* composed anywhere between the fifth and second centuries BCE.

Loriliai Biernacki, a professor of Indian religions at the University of Colorado, weighed in and said the debate had raised important issues about a spectrum of Hindu concepts permeating American culture, including meditation, belief in *karma* and reincarnation, and even cremation. "All these ideas are Hindu in origin, and they are spreading", she said. "But they are doing it in a way that leaves behind the proper name, the box that classifies them as 'Hinduism'. "

I was also asked to address this issue at a recent Hindu–Christian meeting in San Francisco. Being totally "apolitical" the whole debate seemed to me as being way off the mark. I consider such controversies invariably springing up because the arguments are from two different perspectives. In fact, as my friend Rahul Peter Das said:

> The problems begin with the failure to distinguish properly between academia and public life outside this.

People, like those in HAF though professionals, are not academics specialized in the history of religion nor Indian philosophy but those who are in the public life and have a popular understanding of Hinduism albeit in a more sophisticated way than the common man. Their reaction is more from the heart than from the head. As Wendy Doniger remarks:

> Such Hindu Americans, concerned about their image, fear (not without cause) that their religion has been stereotyped in the West as a polytheistic faith of "castes, cows and curry".
>
> They counteract these charges by swinging to the other extreme and arguing that everything in India is, and always has been, spiritual.

When Hindus state that *yoga* has its roots in Hinduism they understand its origins within its history of Vedic origins minus all its metaphysical, ontological and axiological underpinnings. The distinction between Hinduism and *yoga* is not so much an issue for them as in general everything starting with the Vedas and all practices and beliefs are subsumed under the rubric of Hinduism heuristically. One needs to separate this Hindu understanding of *yoga* from the broader global context in which it has got mired these days. Any idea or practice when transferred to a larger context will take on a life of its own and will also imbibe some of the characteristics of the alien atmosphere in which it is adopted.

We all have to concede that the word *yoga* after all is a Sanskrit word and comes with some meanings attached to it which are rooted in Hinduism. One needs to also note that *yoga* underwent a number of changes already in India by the time Patañjali's *Yoga-Sūtras* were composed and more so by the time texts like *Haṭhayoga-Pradīpikā* were written. *Yoga* has a long history and each country and culture also has brought in its own variations and understandings to what was originally imported into their respective soils. This is the nature of ideas and practices which try to find a base in alien soil. In order to appreciate how each culture changes and absorbs an alien concept or idea one needs to only look at the various images of Buddha in the different lands it has moved to. Surely the Gāndhāran Buddha due to Greek influence looks very different from the Mathurā one and so does the Chinese, Japanese and other carvings of Buddha in their lands, each bringing its own distinct version of representation. Nearer home in North America when one sees the way Śrī Kr̥ṣṇa is depicted in the ISKCON pictures one notices that he is not even shown as dark but more like a white man. Thus in all this discussion on *yoga* one tends to gloss over the "complex history of *yoga*. There is an ancient Indian *yoga*, but it is not the source of most of what people do in *yoga* classes today".

In this controversy over *yoga*, unfortunately, people are arguing at cross purposes. There has to be a mutually agreed upon basis for discussion something like *vāda* advocated by Nyāya philosophy. I am reminded of Śrī Harṣa's statement in *Khaṇḍanakhaṇḍakhādya* where he says:

> *tacca vyavahāraniyamasamayabandhādeva dvābhyām api tābhyām saṁbhāvyate iti vyavahāraniyamasamayameva badhnītaḥ* ।
>
> Some rules and conventions of debate, by mutual consent, have to be stipulated at the beginning and those are sufficient for a debate/discussion.

On my part I would say that *yoga*'s roots go back to the muni-sūkta of the *R̥gveda* where the description of a *muni* flying in the air and wearing soiled clothes with flowing hair do indicate some affinity with Patañjali's description of some of the *vibhūti*s in his third *pāda* called the Vibhūtipāda.

In this context it would be good to understand the history of American *yoga*. Today there are a number of *yoga* studios and *āśramas* in North America of many shades and colours. Even in Montreal where I live there are a number of *āśramas*. The ones I personally know are Śivānanda Vedānta Centre/Āśrama, Sattva-Yoga, Mokṣa-Yoga, Transcendental Meditation, Self-Realization, and Aṣṭāṅga-Yoga. I am sure there are many more which I am not acquainted with. Some are just studios concentrating on cultivating a body culture emphasizing *āsanas* (body postures) while others take care to give some instruction in Patañjali's philosophical message of *yoga* along with promoting *āsanas*.

Looking at the widespread presence of *yoga* in North America today one naturally asks oneself the question as to how *yoga* gained so much of interest and popular coverage which is not easy to answer. Maybe it all started with Swami Vivekananda's visit in 1893 when he addressed the Parliament of World Religions. This exotic figure dressed in ochre robes with a turban, addressing the audience as "Sisters and Brothers of America" and which carried the message of tolerance and universality of Hinduism delivered with great oratory, must have created a tremendous impression as we know from writings in that period. He ignited the audience with his personality and as the Honorable Merwin-Marie Snell wrote:

> No religious body made so profound an impression upon the Parliament and the American people at large, as did Hinduism.

He kindled the curiosity and wonder of the delegates to learn more regarding this Eastern tradition. The rest is history as we all know. But Vivekananda's message was more about the aspect of tolerance in Hinduism and the unity concept of Vedānta than an exposition of the *yoga* system in particular. But with his arrival and talks on Hinduism everything that was Hindu "was definitely in". Vivekananda would use both Advaita Vedānta teachings as well as Patañjali's *Yoga-Sūtras* to talk about Eastern spirituality and a sustained interest in Vedānta and *yoga* was generated due to the imposing presence of Vivekananda. It was further nurtured through the Vedānta centres he started in different parts of North America. His was a lasting presence and he made a tremendous impression on many great people at the time.

Writing about Vivekananda, Ann Louise Bardach recounts all the famous people that Swami Vivekananda met during his visit to America in 1893 to attend the World Parliament of Religions.

> The novelist Gertrude Stein, then a student of James's at Radcliffe, reportedly attended Vivekananda's 1896 talk at Harvard – which so wowed the college's graybeards that they offered him (Swami Vivekananda) the chairmanship of Eastern philosophy. He declined, noting his vows as a monk.

Among those who never doubted the messenger during his lifetime was Leo Tolstoy. The restless Russian was especially keen for writings on Ramakrishna, Vivekananda's own *guru*. Two years before his death, Tolstoy wrote, "Since 6 in the morning I have been thinking of Vivekananda," and later, "It is doubtful if in this age man has ever risen above this selfless, spiritual meditation." The Harvard philosopher and psychologist William James was fascinated by the 31-year-old Indian and quoted at length from Vivekananda's writings in his seminal work, *The Varieties of Religious Experience*. "A very nice man! A very nice man!" Vivekananda reported after his first meeting with James, who called his new friend "an honour to humanity". Aldous Huxley was another famous convert to this group. He was formally initiated at the Vedanta Centre in the Hollywood Hills along with his friend Christopher Isherwood, where the two sometimes gave the Sunday lecture, often attended by their friends Igor Stravinsky, Laurence Olivier, Vivien Leigh, Somerset Maugham and Greta Garbo.

Vivekananda's success cannot be solely attributed to his imposing presence and the message he delivered. The groundwork had already been prepared by the transcendentalists like Thoreau, Emerson and others and America was ready to receive wisdom from the East. The transcendentalists rejected all outer forms of ritual and wanted a direct encounter with reality. As Emerson remarked it was seeking "an original relation with the universe". However as Bardach notes:

> The waning of Vivekananda's popularity in America began around the time the baby boomers commandeered the *yoga* business and the ascetic seams between the New Age and the Old Age inevitably frayed.

But *yoga* had come to stay and the trend of *yogī*s travelling to the states and establishing *āśrama*s where instruction in *yoga* and Vedānta were routinely given became a part of American culture in the twentieth century. One such *yogī* is Swami Yogananda of the Self Realization group whose *Autobiography of a Yogi* is still a best seller in America. Like Vivekananda, Yogananda also came to America in 1920, as a delegate to the International Congress of Religious Liberals in Boston but stayed on to establish his Self Realization Fellowship.

Colonial history also had its advantages of exposing India's philosophical and spiritual teachings to Western intellectuals and one of them Ernest Wood travelled in India widely and later went on to write a highly acclaimed book called *The Seven Schools of Yoga*. We cannot forget B.K.S. Iyengar who was introduced to the West by his favourite student, the renowned violinist Yehudi Menuhin. The books published during this time by academics helped in their own way to promote *yoga* in the milieu. Books on Indian philosophy by academics such as S. Radhakrishnan, S.N. Das Gupta, Mircea Eliade and others also put *yoga* on to the academic map. Even today Eliade's *Yoga and Immortality* is a must read for anyone starting on the path of *yoga* studies. Alan W. Watts's *The Way of Zen* was another very important book which drew a lot of praise.

Added to all this was the political circumstances of the period that brought a lot of frustration and disappointment with the Western way of living and which contributed in no small measure to the Westerner moving away from his/her own culture. The Vietnam War also contributed greatly to the disappointment with the Western way of living and a number of people moved away to alternate lifestyles including *yoga* which was viewed as going back to nature. Buddhist meditation also received a fillip in this period with Tibet's occupation by China and the ousting of the Dalai Lama who started travelling regularly to the West and who quickly acquired a number of followers. Thus so many factors coalesced to make *yoga* an enduring presence in North America.

However, like all successful movements there comes a time when opposition and resentment builds up and we see that happening now because of *yoga*'s huge success in the West. But with the evidence of increasing well-being that *yoga* practitioners experience, *yoga* is bound to stay round the globe for a long time to come.

13

Inspirational Leadership
Perspectives from Gītā

B. Mahadevan

Introduction

SPIRITUALITY and ethics are core values that have shaped human life from time immemorial. However, as societies and their institutions progress and go through ebbs and flows, so does the relevance of such core values. Currently business entities are going through challenging times. Post-2000, there has been a wave of scandals related to the information and communications technology (ICT) sector. There were cases such as Enron and WorldCom. In recent times ethical issues were raised in the banking sector (London Interbank Offered Rate (LIBOR) scandal for example). The Satyam episode in India also highlighted the consequences of the fraudulent and unethical practices of business leaders. The several global crises including the banking crisis, the debt crisis and economic recession have brought to light several issues arising out of bad leadership, personal greed and unethical practices. This reminds us of the ancient Indian maxim laid out in *Manu-Smr̥ti*:

> *Dharma* protects those who protect it and destroys those who try to destroy it.[1]

---

[1] This is laid out in Chapter 8 of *Manu-Smr̥ti*. See *Manu-Smr̥ti* 8.15 for details.

Leadership is a powerful enabler that can leverage an organization to great heights, fame and a credible position among the stakeholders. On the other hand, if the quality of leadership is bad, the same organization will experience a downward slide leading to its eventual destruction. Therefore, one of the major issues of great interest as well as concern in business organizations, government and the society is the issue of leadership. There is continuous interest in organizations to understand how great leaders are identified, created and nurtured. Modern research has focused on this issue and several theories have been proposed.

The unfolding business crises and scams have exposed the leadership crunch in organizations. The current practice of leadership seems unable to resolve the major issues facing businesses. Furthermore, this has once again brought to the forefront the role of spirituality and ethical and moral values in all domains of the society including the business. There is a growing interest in recent times among practitioners, educators and researchers on the broad issue of spirituality and its role in business.

A number of scholars mention a paradigm shift in management theory, and practice in the last few years. These changes in management include a shift from an economic focus to quality of life, spirituality and social responsibility (DeFoore and Renesch 1995; Walsh et al. 2003), a shift from self-centredness to interconnectedness (Capra 1996), and a change from a materialistic to a spiritual orientation (Neal 1997). Karakas (2010) reports that Anita Roddick, the founder of the Body Shop, invested a quarter of the company's net profits back to the community to "keep the soul of the company alive". Such traits are exhibited by an individual when she/he is able to imbibe spirituality.

Poole (2009) pointed to several special issues in journals such as the *Journal of Organizational Change Management,* **12**(3) (1999) and **16**(4) (2003), and *The Leadership Quarterly,* **16**(5) (2005). In 2001, the Academy of Management set up a special interest group for management spirituality and religion, with funding to encourage promising dissertations in the field. It has been argued that spirituality is important to employees and that cultivating a spiritually accommodating and supportive environment yields dividends for organizations (Eisler and Montuori 2003).

Styles of Leadership

In the last fifty years, the research and practice in the area of leadership provide two alternative perspectives. One way to understand leadership is from a perspective of responsibility and ownership. In such a perspective leaders believe that they have the freedom to take decisions the way they think is right and have the authority to execute things accordingly. Such a viewpoint is taken because often leaders feel that it is "their" responsibility to get the right performance for the organization. They further feel that it is very important to get the tasks done by monitoring the subordinates in the organization. This model of leadership presents a picture of leaders having position, power and endowment of resources at their disposal. With the power that the leader enjoys in the system, and the endowment of resources at his/her command, the leader feels he/she can deliver the intended results. Unfortunately, such a leadership style creates a climate of what is known as "market contract" for others working in the system. In a market contract people work for the pay and no more. They feel that additional work is not worth unless they are compensated more. This model of leadership is not very promising in bringing the best performance in an organization.

There is a second approach to leadership practised by many today. In this approach, leaders believe that the unique position that they have obtained and the endowment of resources at their command provides them a great opportunity to enable others do their best. Such leaders believe strongly in nourishing leadership talent around by creating space and agenda for others. They derive their joy by becoming irrelevant in many day-to-day matters pertaining to running the institution. This approach will help create a climate of "psychological contract" for others working in the system. In a psychological contract people respond to the call of duty and work beyond the norms if situations demand such a response. They own their place of work much more and feel more involved in many things in their workplace.

It is not too difficult to come to a conclusion that the second approach appears much better than the first and has a greater chance of delivering well. One could also infer that the second approach could help create a sustainable leadership pipeline for an organization. However, the success rate of this has been minimal. According to Collins (2001), failed leadership models predominantly have a pattern. Great leadership in such situations is always associated with an individual who is considered as exceptionally good and perhaps larger than life celebrity. With the result, the leadership model is orchestrated in such a way that the organization which the leader heads is seen as a platform for utilizing the extraordinary talents of the leader. Collins describes such leadership models as "Genius with 1000 helpers" or "Weak General – Strong Lieutenant". Such leaders will be very concerned with their own reputation for personal greatness and will drive the organization with "I" centric style of leadership. In such situations it is expected that others working in the organization are "plastic" and will submit to the dictates of the leader. These competing styles of leadership described above are deeply individualistic.

In modern management theory and research the issue of leadership has been constantly addressed. The emerging perspective is that leaders are responsible for building organizations in which people continuously expand their capacity to learn, to understand complexity and to set the vision for the organization. Toward this end seven new theories of leadership have been proposed in recent times. These include servant leadership, transformational leadership, authentic leadership, ethical leadership, Level 5 leadership, empowering leadership, spiritual leadership, and self-sacrificing leadership.

It is not our intention to dwell into these theories in detail, lest the paper will become longer and may also lose some focus. However, these new theories tend to reorient the perspectives and propose something different from what the older theories are proposing. There appears to be a suggestion that in order to be effective leaders need to blend personal humility with intense professional will. Some of the theories also suggest that the personal traits of good leaders must include unwavering faith, significant life experiences that can spark, a strong inner development and a strong religious belief.

However, if we look at ancient scriptures such as *Bhagavad-Gītā*, *Mahābhārata* and *Rāmāyaṇa*, these ideas are greatly reinforced. Therefore, it is but natural that we get different perspectives of what leadership is and what it can do to an organization by studying these sources.

Inspirational Leadership

If one reads *Gītā* from the perspective of leadership he/she will get a different understanding of what it means than what we know today from modern research and practice. In several chapters in *Gītā*, there are interesting discussions pertaining to the quality of leadership.[2] According to *Gītā*, leadership is at its best only when it becomes inspirational. Inspirational leaders have several attributes. These include:

- Outgrowing their own vision from the narrow perspective of "what is in it for me?" (*Gītā* III.9) to an opportunity to make a difference to the people and the place that they associate with
- Unwavering commitment to lead by example (*Gītā* III.21)
- Developing a high degree of equanimity (*Gītā* II.14). No great leadership is possible without developing a sense of equanimity. Lord Kṛṣṇa drives this point home in *Gītā* in several places (chapters II-XIV)
- Understanding and practising the principle of mutual dependence (*Gītā* III.11)
- Not being afraid of anyone and not generating any sense of fear in others (*Gītā* XII.15)
- An ability to dramatically transform people and entities in a sustained fashion that they come into contact with. It is therefore not surprising that many entities and people in this country and elsewhere have been significantly influenced by a person like Mahatma Gandhi till date. This phenomenon will continue for a long time to come

---

[2] *Bhagavad-Gītā* has been translated and commented upon by a wide array of spiritual leaders, scholars, professionals and other social leaders. Therefore, we do not intend providing detailed references to *Gītā* in this writing. One useful resource could be Swami Ranganathananda's three-part commentary on *Gītā*, *Universal Message of Bhagavad Gita* published by Advaita Ashrama, Calcutta, 2001.

- Leaving behind an impact that guides a large number of people and organizations for a long time to come. Collins (2001) echoes these attributes through his definition of Level 5 leadership, one that transcends self-interest through a paradoxical mix of humility and professional will. In order to achieve such a level of leadership, a strong current of spirituality must run in an individual. Spirituality will broaden the vision of an individual, melt his/her heart, embolden him/her to take steps without fear of failure and significantly increase his/her leadership competence. This seems to be the underlying message in *Gītā* on matters pertaining to leadership.

Three Lessons from Gītā

In several chapters in *Gītā* there are interesting references to the quality of leadership. Of these we focus more on three interesting ideas:

- Strong need to lead by example
- Importance of developing a high degree of equanimity
- Understanding the principle of mutual dependence.

LEADING BY EXAMPLE

Leaders derive their credibility, respect and power from their unwavering commitment to walking the talk. This is because, if the leaders say something and do something else, the followers will not take the leader very seriously. Rather, they will do a similar thing as their leader and nothing else.

यद्यदाचरति श्रेष्ठस्तत्तदेवेतरो जनः।
स यत्प्रमाणं कुरुते लोकस्तदनुवर्तते।। – III.21

yadyadācarati śreṣṭhastattadevetaro janaḥ ।
sa yatpramāṇaṁ kurute lokastadanuvartate ।।

Therefore, Kṛṣṇa warns Arjuna that he needs to lead by example. Viewed from the perspective, leaders hands are tied, they lose the degrees of freedom and the whole world will keenly watch the leaders' action and blindly follow the leaders (मम वर्त्मानुवर्तन्ते मनुष्याः पार्थः सर्वशः। – *mama vartamānuvartante manuṣyāḥ pārthaḥ sarvaśaḥ* – III.23). One of the biggest problems today is that leaders do not practise this value. They think they are above board and in several cases this idea stretches to such a level that they begin to think that they are "above law".

Every individual inevitably plays a leadership role. A child looks upon the parents, elders and the teachers very closely and derives his/her value systems very early in life. These value systems are set at that stage itself and very little change is possible later. Every one of us as responsible parents, head of a family, member of a social or political group needs to understand this issue very seriously.

DEVELOPING A SENSE OF EQUANIMITY

One of the biggest problems that leaders face is their inability to take bad outcomes as it unfolds at times. When everything goes well the leadership is fine. However the moment some unexpected things happen (such as losing something significant, and defeat of one kind or the other) they just lose their balance. This is a problem that requires solution of managing the world "within" the leader and not the "world outside". Modern leadership theories have not even recognized this issue.

No great leadership is possible without developing a sense of equanimity. Lord Kṛṣṇa drives this point in *Gītā* in several places. The first instruction that Arjuna receives from Kṛṣṇa is on this issue, thereby signalling the importance of this aspect. According to Lord Kṛṣṇa, the world is full of dualities, it will blow hot and cold and we will experience joy and happiness as well as some unpleasant moments (मात्रास्पर्शास्तु कौन्तेय शीतोष्ण-सुखदु:खदा – *mātrāsparśāstu kaunteya śītoṣṇasukhaduḥkhadā*). These are the realities of life and they will come and go. If we do not learn to endure them and go through this life as a roller coaster ride, we will never be able to exhibit leadership traits (आगमापायिनोऽनित्यास्तांस्तितिक्षव भारत। – *āgamāpāyino 'nityāstāṁstitikṣiva bhārata* – 2.14.).

If you analyse today's problems, the genesis of them lies in our inability to understand and live through this profound truth. Individuals, young children and the so-called leaders are not able to accept the fact that life has both aspects. They are told that only good things will happen to them and in this manner huge expectations are built. When some bad things happen, they are unable to take it, they get into mental depressions, feel that they are worthless, get into health problems, go to psychological counselling and in some extreme cases commit suicide also. The quality of leadership critically depends on this aspect. Realizing this Lord Kr̥ṣṇa has touched on this aspect in several chapters of *Gītā* (chapters II-XIV).

The issue of developing equanimity is very critical to be a great leader. This is simply because great things are not achieved through excitement. Developing a sense of equanimity enables an individual to master the art of handling the world around us by managing the world within very well. In a way through this Lord Kr̥ṣṇa teaches us how we need to handle ourselves while engaging in the thick of activities.

PRINCIPLE OF MUTUAL DEPENDENCE

Today's era is characterized by dominance of individuality as a value of life. Joint families have given way for nuclear families. Children are constantly taught the virtue of one's own hard work leading to excellence in their studies and other pursuits in life. People with originality (often taken as a good measure for their individuality) are looked at with awe and inspiration. The society also views individual rights as an important element of growth and progress. Asserting individuals right and space in all matters of civil society seems to be the way forward to make a great country. The spirit of questioning everything (as opposed to the spirit of inquiry) and seeking one's own understanding of the issue is another aspect promoted today. In all these matters the common thread is to promote individuality either directly or indirectly. The idea that begins as individuality will soon transform into selfishness as people become very sensitive to their possessions, wants and needs and begin to demand or bargain for these things in life. This will take away the culture of sharing as give and take is simply not easier to practise. Moreover, the way we approach life will be dominated by "what is in it for me?".

If we observe nature carefully we will understand one aspect very clearly. The whole universe is inter-connected. The physical systems such as, rivers, glaciers in the polar regions and mountains have profound effect on us. The plant kingdom and the animal kingdom too exert a considerable influence on us. Lord Kṛṣṇa brings this aspect by advising Arjuna that in order to achieve ultimate prosperity and success in whatever we do we need to honour the principle of mutual dependence. The spirit of sharing and unconditional giving (the virtue of *yajña)* is the basis on which everything in the world sustains. The gods bless the living beings with this virtue and in turn the living beings give back to the gods using this principle. *Paraspara bhāva*, Lord Kṛṣṇa says, is the one that guarantee us ultimate prosperity (*parama sreyas*).

देवान्भावयतानेन ते देवा भावयन्तु वः।
परस्परं भावयन्तः श्रेयः परमवाप्स्यथ।। – IV.11

devānbhāvayatānena te devā bhāvayantu vaḥ ।
parasparaṁ bhāvayantaḥ śreyaḥ paramavāpsyatha ।।

By virtue of the position and the endowment of resources that a leader can command, it blindfolds them to the need to understand importance of mutual dependence. However, the first lesson a leader in an organization need to learn to be successful is the value of mutual dependence. People working with the leader are as important as the leader. A happy and successful married life revolves around the husband and the wife understanding the value of mutual dependence. Particle physicists today have found out that both at the sub-atomic level (*piṇḍa*) and at the cosmos (*aṇḍa*) everything works in perfect harmony because of the universal principle of mutual dependence. Government and society have to honour the principle of mutual dependence. If the elected representatives of the government and the parliament do not honour this principle, some forces will act and remind them of the need for this. We recently witnessed this in the case of Lokapal Bill-related movement by Anna Hazare.

Conclusion

In order to achieve such a level of leadership, a strong current of spirituality must run in an individual. Spirituality will broaden the vision of an individual, melt their heart, embolden them to take great steps without fear of failures and significantly increase their leadership competence. People endowed with modern education, scientific knowledge and wherewithal to perform need to imbibe spirituality to make a winning combination of an inspirational leader. This seems to the underlying message in *Gītā* on matters pertaining to leadership.

References

Capra, F., 1996, *The Web of Life: A New Scientific Understanding of Living Systems*, New York: Anchor Books.

Collins, J., 2001, *Good to Great*, London: Random House Business Books, pp. 17-40.

DeFoore, B. and I. Renesch, 1995, *Rediscovering the Soul of Business*, San Francisco: Leaders Press.

Eisler, R. and A. Montuori, 2003, "The Human Side of Spirituality", in *Handbook of Workplace Spirituality and Organizational Performance*, ed. Robert A. Giacalone; Carole L Jurkiewicz, Armonk, NY.

Karakas, F., 2010, "Spirituality and Performance in Organizations: A Literature Review", *Journal of Business Ethics*, **94**: 89-106.

Neal, J., 1997, "Spirituality in Management Education: A Guide to Resources", *Journal of Management Education,* **21**: 121-40.

Poole, E., 2009, "Organisational Spirituality : A Literature Review", *Journal of Business Ethics,* **84**: 577-88.

Walsh, J.P., K. Weber and J.D. Margolis, 2003, *Social Issues and Management: Our Lost Cause Found*, Ann Arbor, MI: University of Michigan Business School.

14

The Reception of Nāṭya in Europe with Special Reference to Its Reception in Croatia

Klara Gönc Moačanin

THIS is my kind of *prastāvanā* to the words that follow:

> It is difficult to describe and understand the different theatrical forms of past cultures. The richness of sounds, pictures, gestures and atmosphere eludes, our thoughts and words. The echoes of speech, recitation, singing, music have been lost forever. The movements of the actors and the dancers are no longer reflected in the eyes of the long-vanished audiences. Only the preserved theatrical texts and the work of later commentators, very few in comparison with what has been lost, can give us a sense of what the theatre was.[1]

First meeting of Europe with Indian drama was through classical Indian drama (*nāṭya*). It happened in a most propitious way but from this first meeting with sympathy and admiration a long-lasted love did not arise. After first dazzleness, the encounter finished in a self-deception of representatives of Western Orientalism. First there was a sense of wonderment from educated public, later *nāṭya* remained mostly in the hearts and minds of those for whom Orient did not mean just something exotic.

---

[1] Gönc Moačanin 2002: 256.

That first meeting happened when Europe became acquainted with Kālidāsa's *Śakuntalā* which William Jones translated into English in 1789.[2] That *nāṭaka*, an epic drama with love-heroic mythological content in Indian tradition, represented the highest achievement of *nāṭya*. Jones's translation had been republished five times in less than twenty years. Soon after it appeared in 1789, in 1791, followed the German translation from English made by Georg Foster who has sent the book to famous German writer Johann Wilhelm Goethe. *Śakuntalā* made a lifelong lasting artistic impression on Goethe, and after his first astonishment, because Indian *nāṭya* literature was at that time unknown in Europe, he sent his friend F.H. Jacobi verses inspired by Kālidāsa's work:

> *Willst du die Blüte des frühen, die Früchte des späteren Jahres,*
> *Willst du, was reizt und entzückt, willst du, was sättigt und nährt,*
> *Willst du den Himmel, die Erde mit einem Namen begreifen,*
> *Nenn' ich Sakontala, dich, und so ist alles gesagt.*

> *Would you the flowers of early year, the fruits of later year,*
> *would you what gives an inspiration and admiration,*
> *would you what satisfies and feeds,*
> *would you the sky, the earth, with one name describe,*
> *I name you Sakontala you, and with this everything is said.*[3]

In the book on his Italian travels (*Italienische Reise*) which he wrote in his old age he again mentions *Śakuntalā* wrongly that he has read it in 1787.[4] Though Goethe never said that the prologue to his famous Faustus was inspirited by Kālidāsa's *prastāvanā* in

---

[2] Winternitz 1968, vol. 3: 213-17.

[3] Ibid.: 214.

[4] Goethe 2007: 187.

Śakuntalā, Moriz Winternitz[5] first and later Basham[6] thought so. Goethe calls the prologue *Vorspiel auf dem Theater*, he starts with benediction (*nāndī*) and the prologue consists of a dialogue between the director (*sūtradhāra*) and the actress (*naṭī*).[7]

Friedrich Schiller was also filled with wonder while reading *Śakuntalā* and in one of his letters he writes that in whole Greek antiquity there is not such a poetic description of more beautiful femininity or more beautiful love.[8]

Goethe and Schiller even contemplated for some[9] time to stage the piece. They realized that Kālidāsa's drama does not have qualities required by Western theatre, that it has much less action than Western public is used to, because of the feeling that the play pursues a goal of mental peace, of tranquillity.[10]

Schiller, as a great artist, with his intuition sensed what kind of misconceptions will arise in transmission of classical Indian drama on the European stage.[11] After this first wave of romantistic feelings (Goethe, Schiller, Herder, Schlegel) Europeans did not know much about Indian theatre, almost nothing, though in 1827. H.H. Wilson published his book in three volumes *Select Specimens of the Theatre of the Hindus*, with translations of different dramatic pieces. At that time nothing has been known about the *Nāṭyaśāstra* which gives a picture of the existing of a highly-developed theatre in first centuries CE.

---

5 Winternitz 1968, vol. 3: 217.

6 Basham 1959: 433.

7 Goethe 2007: 638, editor's fn. 187, 21.

8 Winternitz 1968: 215, fn. 1.

9 Ibid.: 217.

10 Ibid.

11 Ibid.

Nāṭya combined stylized acting, pantomime, dance, music, with text as the basis. Performance interchanges text in prose and verses, with declamation, recitale, tableau, dance, concert.[12] What we now have of *nāṭya* is only the text because *nāṭya* in its classical form as a performing theatrical art has vanished more than 1,000 years ago despite many efforts to reconstruct it. Music is lost, dance figures without the accompaniment of music are frozen stone sculptures in Chidambaram and in some other south Indian temples.

Plot of *nāṭya* is in Western opinion too static, there always has to be a happy ending.[13] In Indian theatre the characters were stereotypes, in the society imbued with *dharma* where everyone has its own place and role, there is no place for the individual types known in European theatrical culture[14] as in Greek tragedies, Shakespeare's works, in works of French classicists Corneille and Racine and also Moliere. And this was educated European public looked for.

In nineteenth-century Europe *nāṭya* seemed strange to wider public and that took effect on its reception. In staging, only the synopsis of play would be left and the whole rich theatricality of that fascinating theatre was in that way lost. Indologists studied the texts philologically trying in vain to reconstruct the theatre and the way the works of *nāṭya* were performed. And they mostly tried to bring nearer to the public the Indian theatre by comparing it with antique theatres (Greek and Roman).[15] The gap between Indologists and Orientalists and the wider public

---

12 Gönc Moačanin 2002.

13 Gerow 1978: 81.

14 Ibid.: 84.

15 Gönc Moačanin 2014.

became deeper. The time of the so-called Orientalism took hold of arts, so also of theatre. But Orientalism tells more about West than of Orient. Orient is just an impetus for author's artistic vision which is based on superficial knowledge of other culture. And then exoticism is born. M.C. Byrski said:

> In what might be called here exoticism on the European stages we used to mould our rather modest knowledge of India into something which we Europeans could understand and with which we could easily identify ourselves.[16]

In the realm of literature, in this case of theatrical literature, in one way this exoticism can be seen in popularizing Oriental literature from the side of second-rate writers. Idealism of classical Sanskrit literature, and now we are talking about *nāṭya*, with its peculiar world of mythology, fairy tale, tradition was needed to be approached to the wider public that knew nothing of this different, strange and far away world. In this way, one of the most complex and rich theatrical forms in the world, literary and choreographically sophisticated, one of the most lyric theatres – changed its essentiality and became its own antithesis – a melodrama. As Europeans could not understand its multilayered form because of which *nāṭya* eluded definitions, those who tried to understand it compared *nāṭya* pieces with the works of Shakespeare, Elizabethan author like Lyly, with Calderon, with *commedia dell'arte*, etc. Because of misunderstandings that arise when encounter with other cultures of different artistic values, and as West had no real knowledge of them, Indian drama has been called romantic and sentimental. Interpreters did not know anything about the notion of *karman*, nothing about the conventions of classical literature *nāṭya* and its *saṁbhoga-vipralambha-saṁbhoga-śr̥ṅgāra rasa*. They could not

[16] Byrski 1979: 13.

feel sublimity, tranquillity, harmony, spirituality of the dramatic pieces of *nāṭya* which they read in translations not knowing Sanskrit. It is not strange that for average spectator such pieces could just be sentimental melodramas with happy endings, with *deux ex machina* happening all the time.

Why melodramas? Melodrama has associations with characters whose words of love seem like empty phrases, tears, characters as types, pathetic monologues, predetermined happenings and so on. And always a happy ending. These characteristic may remind us of some characteristics of *nāṭya* but it is simplification and can be understood only in the context of what European public experienced while watching Indian pieces. The answer is easy; in nineteenth century they have attended only adapted, re-made, altered, shortened and modified dramas which mostly did not resemble originals. After these kinds of reworkings, *nāṭya* stopped to be an expression of Indian classical theatre and became a European reflection of Indian art.[17]

Theatrical Europe in nineteenth century accepted exoticism from East and the interest of public, as concerning India, was in Kālidāsa's *Śakuntalā* and in Śūdraka's *Mr̥cchakaṭika*. *Śakuntalā* was interesting because of its poetic love and *Mr̥cchakaṭika* with its realism, wittiness and inventiveness. The German adaptation of *Śakuntalā*, made by A. von Wolzogen[18] (performed also in Croatia - later to be explained) does bear no resemblance to the Indian original, it is only a rough synopsis of Kālidāsa's work. Wolzogen's version is a real caricature of the original, real literary bastard - drama was not Indian nor European. The

---

[17] Remark: this part of the text is based on my article "Indian Drama in Croatia", first published in 1990, and republished in Gönc Moačanin 1996: 73-85.

[18] Winternitz 1968, vol. 3: 218.

French adaptation made by G. de Nerval and Mery of Śūdraka's *Mr̥cchakaṭika* was performed in Paris in Odeon in 1850. Though Śūdraka might have been unsatisfied with the performance, it was quite popular. In 1858, Śūdraka has been performed as a ballet in Opera in Paris; music was by Reyer, scenario by Th. Gautier.[19]

German adaptation of Śūdraka's work was made by Emil Pohl under the name of *Vasantasenā*. It was also a caricature of the original but it was better than Wolzogen's *Śakuntalā*. Second French version of *Mr̥cchakaṭika* of Lugne-Poe was performed in the theatre de l'Oeuvre. Lugne-Poe also staged *Śakuntalā* in 1895, and that production was the source of many romantic exotic stagings in different European theatres.[20]

This introduction was needed as a prologue to staging of Indian drama in Croatian National Theatre in Zagreb, the capital of Croatia. Precisely these two works of *nāṭya* – *Abhijñānaśākuntala* and *Mr̥cchakaṭika* were also staged in Zagreb through the merit of theatre's manager Stjepan Miletić (1868–1908). He was an outstanding figure in Croatian theatrical life and culture at the end of nineteenth century Miletić was highly educated, well-read, well versed into the movements of European theatre of his time. He was the author of a valuable book on Croatian theatre (*Hrvatsko glumište*), a good organizer and in only four years of his directorship (1894-98) he managed to give a high artistic status to Croatian National Theatre. He travelled through Europe and visited all the most important theatres – in Vienna famous Burgtheater, theatres in Prague, Munich, Dresden, Lepizig, Berlin; also theatres in Paris and Italy. He witnessed all the main performances staged in the most famous and greatest theatres

19 Kindermann 1970: 85.

20 Ibid.

in Europe of his time. On his theatrical pilgrimages he must have seen in some of these theatres the German adaptations I have mentioned before – Wolzogen's *Śakuntalā* and Pohl's *Vasantasenā*. As unfortunately his correspondence, his diary and the repertoire of German theatres in 1890s is unaccessible to me, it is impossible to say precisely where, in which theatre, in which town, Miletić saw the performances. Whether he visited Wroslaw (then Breslau), in Poland, where at the time Wolzogen's *Śakuntalā* has been staged we do not know because he does not say a word about that in his book. One may ask whether Miletić – as a highly educated intellectual – first found the mention of *Śakuntalā* in Goethe's writings and that it was an impetus for him to look around in Europe for staging Indian dramas. Writing about happenings of Paris theatrical life and performances in famous theatres there, he mentions that *Vasantasenā* was staged again. But we do not know whose translation and staging that was because the forementioned Lugne-Poe's adaptation was staged in 1895, while Miletić wrote his remarks in 1894. And *Vasantasenā* was staged in Zagreb in 1894.

There is an important question why Miletić staged Wolzogen's *Śakuntalā* when in Croatia at that time when there already existed a Croatian translation from Sanskrit by Pero Budmani. Miletić must have had known for the translation because the translator was also teaching the history of world literature in the acting school organized by Miletić. I can find only one answer for this. It was too early to stage Indian dramas at that time as they were because public would not follow them. Even Shakespeare and Greek tragedians were performed in rewritten, adapted and shortened forms.

Śakuntalā and *Vasantasenā* were translated from German into Croatian by August Harambašić, a popular poet of that time.

The translation of *Vasantasenā* is better than that of *Śakuntalā* due to bad Wolzogen's model. But Harambašić also improvised a lot so the public in Zagreb received Indian dramas that were Indian only by name.

Opening night of Śūdraka's *Mṛcchakaṭika* under the title *Vasantasenā* happened on 17 November 1894, and as the translation was published in a literary magazine in 1895, we can easily conclude that Pohl's German translation made a digest of five acts of ten acts in the Sanskrit original. There were altogether fifteen performances till 1908; this shows that *Vasantasenā* was quite popular.

But public was less attracted to *Śakuntalā* when it was first staged on 11 March 1897. Only six performances were staged till 1912.

It is interesting that it was produced with the musical ouverture called *Śakuntalā* written by Hungarian composer Karl (Károly) Goldmark. I have already mentioned how the adaptations in nineteenth century looked like. In the archives I have found the manuscript of translation into Croatian which shows that in Wolzogen's German translation there were only five acts left and almost not a word or scene corresponds to Sanskrit original. Only the frame of a love story between Śakuntalā and Duṣyanta is left. The translator of *Śakuntalā* from Sanskrit, Pero Budmani, ironically writes that it seems that public preferred the scenes which in original play were not present at all.[21]

Then for decades classical Indian theatrical world has not been present in Croatian National Theatre. There was a short interlude in 1915 when Tagore's *Chitra* was staged. Though

---

[21] Gönc Moačanin 1996: 81.

Tagore's dramas do not belong to *nāṭya*, they have all the elements that make it – text, music, dance, acting.

And then happened an unexpected encounter with real Indian *nāṭya* with Śūdraka's *Mṛcchakaṭika* thanks to great enthusiasm of a director Mladen Škiljan who in 1950s read its French translation and the play was so much on his mind and in his heart that at the end of 1970s he succeeded to stage it in the Croatian National Theatre. This was for the first time in Croatia that not an adaptation was staged but this *prakaraṇa* was fully performed with all its ten acts. I have made the translation of *Mṛcchakaṭika* into Croatian from Sanskrit in 1978. *The Clay Cart* (*Glinena kolica*) happened to be a great success, opening night was on 15 February 1979 and the performance was on the repertory till 1980. Unfortunately it has not been filmed, there is no video of it left, just some photographs. For famous Croatian actors their first encounter with such an unusual theatrical form and unknown world-view in the beginning seemed difficult. But at the dress rehearsal they entered the spirit of the play and acted with enjoyment through all the time the play was staged.

I shall now return back to reception of *nāṭya* in Europe, this time in twentieth century. Famous English director E.G. Craig was deeply interested in Indian theatrical tradition what can be seen from the introduction that A. Coomaraswamy wrote in his book *The Mirror of Gesture* (tr. of *Abhinayadarpaṇa*) published in 1917:

> Mr. Gordon Craig, who understands so well the noble artificiality of Indian dramatic technique, has frequently asked me for more detailed information than is yet available in this long neglected field . . . Craig's letter. . . . If there are books of technical instruction tell them to me I pray you. . . . I dread (seeing what it has already done in other arts here) the influence of finished article of the East; but

I crave the instruction of the instructors of the East.[22]

Of special interest is the reception of Indian theatre in the work of Western stage directors as well as the use of different techniques of Asian theatre. The introduction of the so-called Oriental techniques into the staging of some Indian theatrical works – techniques like the practice of *yoga*, methods of *kathakalī*, dance from Bali and Chinese acrobacy from Peking opera have nothing to do with the *prayoga* of the works of classical Indian theatre. These attempts were made by Polish director J. Grotowski and his Italian assistant E. Barba in sixties and seventies of the last century.

There were also attempts to stage some *nāṭya* pieces in a traditional way. *Mṛcchakaṭika* was staged in Poland in 1973 and translated from Sanskrit by Tadeusz Pobozniak. In Weimar in 1979 Viśākhadatta's *Mudrārākṣasa* was performed, also translated from Sanskrit by Wolfgang Morgenroth. Presently, I have no information about staging *nāṭya* in European countries in the last three decades.

There is a long list of theatrical works; translations of Indian dramas in different Western languages that started in the nineteenth century and last till now. In 1974 in Honolulu, University of Hawaii, an international conference on "Sanskrit Drama in Performance" was held with the performance of Bhāsa's *Svapnavāsadattā*. In America all three Kālidāsa's dramas were translated in the *Theater of Memory* edited by Barbara Stoller Miller. Recently Lyne Bansat-Boudon translated into French all Kālidāsa's dramas and edited a book entitled *L'thêâtre de l'Inde ancienne* (*Ancient Indian Theatre*). In Clay Library also all Kālidāsa's dramas are translated. In Germany there is a Bhāsa project The Würzburg Multimedia Databank on Sanskrit Drama and Theatre.

22 Coomaraswamy 1977: 1.

I have mostly concentrated on the question of the reception of the *nāṭya*'s *prayoga* and the subject of its reception in theoretical works, i.e. in books and articles could be a subject of new research.

Whether *nāṭya* can be faithfully transposed on modern stage in West or in East is questionable. In trying to reconstruct an art form which is for a long time a dead form because it was alive only while it presented the cultural world-view from which it arose, could only lead to failure. But to stage the works of *nāṭya*, taking into consideration of what is known till now about it, could be also a source of comparative theatrological insights as well as of emotional and spiritual inspirations, but the way which it leads to them is difficult because of different aesthetical world-views.

As can be seen, the interest in *nāṭya* and its reception in different forms is still present in the Western world.

References

Basham, A.L., 1959, *The Wonder that Was India*, New York: Grove Press.

Byrski, M.C., 1979, *Methodology of the Analysis of Sanskrit Drama*, Warszawa: Wydawnictva Universitetu Warszawskiego.

Coomaraswamy, A. and G.K. Duggirala, 1977, *The Mirror of Gesture*, New Delhi: Munshiram Manoharlal.

Gerow, E., 1978, *The Literatures of India*, Chicago: University of Chicago press.

Goethe, ed. 2007, Erich Trunz and Commentaries Herbert von Einem, München: Verlag C.H. Beck.

Gönc Moačanin, K., 2002, *Izvedbena obilježja klasičnih kazališnih oblika*, Zagreb: Hrvatsko filozofsko društvo.

———, 2014, *Nāṭya vs. Greek Tragedy*, in Radhavallabh Tripathi ed. *Nāṭyaśāstra in the Modern World,* pp. 63-76, New Delhi: Rashtriya Sanskrit Sansthan and D.K. Printworld.

——, 1996, *Sahṛdaya-književno putovanje sa srcem u Indiju*, Zagreb: Hrvatsko filozofsko društvo.

Kindermann, H., 1970, *Theatergeschichte Europas*, vol. 9, Salzburg: Otto Müller Verlag.

Sanskrit Drama in Performance, 1981, ed. Rachel van M. Baumer and James R. Brandon, Honolulu: The University Press of Hawaii.

Theatre of Memory: The Plays of Kālidāsa, ed. Barbara Stoler Miller, 1984, New York: Columbia University Press.

The Theatre of the Hindus, Delhi and Varanasi: Indological Book House (no year given in the book).

Wells, H.W., 1965, *The Classical Drama of the Orient*, Bombay: Asia Publishing House.

Winternitz, Moriz, 1968, *Geschichte der indischen Literatur*, vol. 3, Stuttgart: K.F. Koehler Verlag.

Contributors

Dr. Anindita Balslev is a philosopher based in India and Denmark. She serves on the boards of important international organizations/societies. Her educational, research and other professional experiences in India, Denmark, USA and France, have inspired her to create a forum entitled, 'Cross-Cultural Conversation' (CCC). Apart from many papers in professional journals, she is the author, editor and co-editor of several books. To mention a few: She is the author of *A Study of Time in Indian Philosophy* (3rd edn., 2009); *Cultural Otherness: Correspondence with Richard Rorty* (2000), *Indian Conceptual World* (2012) and *The Enigma of I-consciousness* (2013). She is the editor of *Cross Cultural Conversation* (1996), *On India: Self Image and Counter Image* (2013), and *On World Religions: Diversity, Not Dissension* (2014). [*address:* I-1667, 2nd Floor, Chittaranjan Park, NEW DELHI - 110 019, *e-mail:* <aninditabalslev@hotmail.com>].

Bettina Bäumer, born in Austria in 1940, completed her doctorate in Indology and philosophy at the University of Munich, Germany, in 1967, on the topic "Creation as Play: The Concept of Lila in Hinduism, its Philosophical and Theological Significance". Dr. Bäumer has been living in Varanasi since 1967. She has worked at Banaras Hindu University, as postdoctoral fellow and lecturer; as assistant and lecturer at the Institute of Indology, Vienna University during 1974-79 and as research director, Alice Boner Institute, Varanasi, during 1979–2000. She was Hon. Co-ordinator, Indira Gandhi National Centre for the Arts, Varanasi office 1986-95. She earned 'Habilitation' (qualification for professorship) in Religious Studies at the University of Vienna in 1997. She has been visiting professor (summer semester) at the universities of Berne, Vienna and Salzburg from 1995 to 2009, senior research fellow, Harvard University in 1994, fellow and visiting professor at the Indian Institute of Advanced Study, Shimla, from 2003-07. Bettina has done fieldwork in Orissa and in Kashmir, has organized seminars and workshops on non-dualist Kashmir Shaivism in India and Europe. She was awarded Indian citizenship in 2011. At present she is the director of Samvidalaya, Abhinavagupta Research Library, Varanasi. Her main fields of research and publication: non-dualistKashmir Shaivism; temple architecture, religious traditions and Śilpaśāstra of Orissa; Indian aesthetics; comparative mysticism. She has been editor of: *Kalātattvakośa: A Lexicon of Fundamental Concepts of the Indian Arts*, vols. I, II, III (1988-96), *Śilparatnakośa: A Glossary of Orissan Temple Architecture*, with R.P. Das as co-editor (1994). [*address*: Abhinavagupta Research Library, B-2/114, Bhadaini, 2nd Floor (Banaras Art Culture), VARANASI - 221 005, *e-mail*: <bettina.baeumer@utpaladeva.in>].

George Cardona, emeritus Professor in the University of Pennsylvania, is the author of several works on Indology, including *Pa ini, his work and its traditions*, the first volume of which has appeared. He also co-edited, with Dhanesh Jain, The Indo-Aryan Languages. [*address*: Postal: George Cardona, 72 Woodside Drive, Lumberton, NJ 08048 USA; *email*: <cardona@sas.upenn.edu>; <cardonagj@verizon.net>].

Hans Henrich Hock is Professor Emeritus of Linguistics and Sanskrit, University of Illinois. Major publications include *Studies in Sanskrit syntax* (ed., 1991), *An Early Upaniṣadic Reader* (2007), *Vedic Studies: Language, Texts, Culture, and Philosophy*: Proceedings of the Veda Section, 15th World Sanskrit Conference (ed., 2014). Honours include recognition as Vidyasagara by Mandakini, 10th World Sanskrit Conference, Bangalore (1997); award for

"Outstanding and Inspiring Leadership", Consulate General of India, Chicago (2003); election as Fellow of the Linguistic Society of America (Class of 2013). [*address*: Professor Emeritus, Department of Linguistics, University of Illinois, 4080 FLB, 707 S. Mathews, URBANA, IL 61801 (USA), *e-mail*: <hhhock@illinois. edu.].

John Brockington is Emeritus Professor of Sanskrit at the University of Edinburgh, UK, a Vice-President of the International Association of Sanskrit Studies, and the author or editor of several books and numerous articles, mainly on the Sanskrit epics and the history of Hinduism, and the translator with Mary Brockington of *Rāma the Steadfast: An Early Form of the Rāmāyaṇa* (2006). [*address*: 113 Rutten Lane, Yarnton, KIDLINGTON, OX5 1LT (UK), *e-mail*: <j.l.brockington@ed.ac.uk>].

Klara Gönc Moačanin, working mostly on Nāṭyaśāstra and *Mahābhārata*. Teaching Indian literature (Nāṭya, Śravya, Neo-Indo-Āryan and Draviḍian Literature, Indian Art, Indian History, Asian Theatre, Sanskrit Seminars (on *Mahābhārata*, Kālidāsa, Bhāsa, Nāṭyaśāstra, Śūdraka, etc.). Interested in comparative literature-published a book (in Croatian) *Theatrical Practice of Classical Theatrical Forms: Greek Tragedy-Indian Nāṭya-Japanese nõ*, and a number of articles in Croatian and English. Translated Śūdrakas's *Mṛcchakaṭika* for Croatian National Thetare that was performed in 1979-80. She has made translations from English, French, Hungarian and Sanskrit. [*address*: Senior Lecturer, Department of Indology and Far Eastern Studies, Faculty of Philosophy, I. Lucica 3,10000 ZAGREB, Croatia, *e-mail*: <29wisteria@gmail.com>].

Dr. Mahadevan is a Professor at the Indian Institute of Management Bangalore (IIMB) since 1992. He was also the Dean (Administration) of IIMB. Mahadevan has more than twenty years of wide-ranging experience in teaching, research, consulting and academic administration at IIMB, IIT Delhi and

XLRI, Jamshedpur. He obtained M.Tech and PhD from IIT Madras and B.E. from the College of Engineering, Guindy, Madras. He was conferred the ICFAI Best Teacher Award by the Association of Indian Management Schools in 2005. Professor Mahadevan's other interests include researching the possibility of using ancient Indian wisdom to address contemporary concerns. He was a member of the Central Sanskrit Board. [*address*: Indian Institute of Management Bangalore, Bannerghatta Road, BANGALORE - 560 076, *e-mail*: bmahadevan@iimb.ernet.in].

Mohan, S. Ram, is a multi-faceted scholar with postgraduate degrees in six subjects, in addition to a Master's degree in management and a PhD in strategic studies. Dr Ram Mohan is the editor of *Ramanodhayam*, a Tamil journal, and co-editor of *Mountain Path*, an English journal both dedicated to spiritual and cultural studies. He is the author of several books and has extensively toured and lectured in many countries of the world, including USA, Sweden, Singapore, Malaysia, Indonesia, Sri Lanka, etc. [*address*: 687, 46th Street 9th Sector, K.K. Nagar West, CHENNAI - 600 078 (T.N.), *e-mail*: <sethurammohan@yahoo.co.in>].

Pierre-Sylvain Filliozat, born in 1936 in France, is Professor of Sanskrit (Emeritus) and Member of the Academie des Inscriptions et Belles-lettres in Paris. He conducts research in several fields of Indology, Sanskrit grammar (Vyākaraṇa), poetry and poetics, Tantra, especially the Sanskrit literature of Śaiva Śiddhānta school, history of Indian architecture and temples. He has published books and articles in French, English and Sanskrit on Pāṇini's grammar, Patañjali's *Mahābhāṣya*, Śaivāgamas, temple architecture in Hampi, etc. [*address*: Prof. P.S. Filliozat 13, rue Rambuteau, 75004 PARIS (France), *e-mail*: <filliozat@dataone.in>; <filliozat@noos.fr>].

Prof. Radhavallabh Tripathi is one of the seniormost professors of Sanskrit in the country. He has served as Vice-Chancellor of Rashtriya Sanskrit Sansthan, Vice-Chancellor on additional charge at Shri Lal Bahadur Shasri Sanskrit Vidyapeeth and Vice-Chancellor in charge of Dr H.S. Gour University. He was visiting professor at Silpakorn University, Bangkok, for three years. Widely acclaimed for his original contributions to the study of Nāṭyaśāstra and Sāhityaśāstra, Prof. Tripathi has published 159 books, 216 research papers and critical essays as well as translations of more than thirty Sanskrit plays and some classics from Sanskrit into Hindi. He has received thirty-three national and international awards and honours for his literary contributions. He has been referred in various research journals on Indology. Research for PhD has been completed as well as is being carried on his creative writings in Sanskrit in a number of universities. Three journals brought out special numbers on his writings. Four books comprising studies on his creative and critical writings are also available. [*address*: M-83, 2nd floor, South City-I, Opp. Sector 40, Near HUDA Chowk, GURGAON (Haryana), *e-mail*: <radhavallabh2002@gmail.com>].

Prof. Satya Pal Narang (18.1.1942). M.A. PhD (Sastra-kavyas): University of Delhi. Worked: Lecturer, Reader, Professor: University of Delhi. Worked: Professor & HOD: Gurukul Kangri Vishvavidyalaya, Haridwar; Pondicherry Central University; University of Delhi; French Institute, Pondicherry. Shastracudamani: Rashtriya Sanskrit Sansthan, New Delhi. Working on the projects: A Pada-index of Classical Sanskrit Poems II; Kalidasa Bibliography-II. Pending: Kiratarjuniya; Mallinatha as a critic. Published about 175 papers and attended national and international conferences, seminars, etc. with papers. Field of Papers: Veda, Grammar, Linguistics and Lexicography, Dharmaśāstra, Classical Sanskrit Literature, Jainism, Sanskrit Poetics, Epigraphy, Purana, etc. [*address*: 31, Vidya Apartments, Opp. Jwalapuri - 5, Rohtak Road, DELHI - 110 087, *e-mail*: <spnarang@yahoo.com>].

Prof. T.S. Rukmani joined the department of religion, Concordia University, Montreal, Canada, as professor and chair for Hindu studies in 1996. She was the first chair for Hindu studies and Indian philosophy at the University of Durban Westville, Durban, South Africa before taking over her post in Canada. She held the post of principal of Miranda House, University of Delhi, for over ten years before she went to South Africa in 1993. She is the only academic in the Department of Sanskrit, University of Delhi, to have been honoured with the highest degree of D.Litt. She was awarded the Ida Smedley International Fellowship to work as a postdoctoral fellow on comparative philosophy, at Toronto University. She has been teaching and researching mainly in the areas of Hinduism, Advaita Vedānta and Sāṁkhya-Yoga. Amongst the many awards that Professor Rukmani has won are: DANAM/Taksha Institute Abhinavagupta Award for sustained achievement in Indic philosophy, 2009; Shivadasani Fellowship, Oxford Centre for Hindu Studies, Oxford University, UK, 2006; Sanskrit promotion in foreign lands by First Gita Global Conference, Bangalore, 2003; fellowship, Indian Institute of Advanced Study, Shimla, 2003 and 1989; The Delhi Sanskrit Academy award for Sanskrit scholarship, 1993.

Her four-volume work on Vijñānabhikṣu's *Yogavārttika* and her two-volume work on Śaṅkara's *Yogasūtrabhāṣyavivaraṇa* have been widely acclaimed in scholarly circles as significant contributions. She has also written and edited nine books dealing with different aspects of religion and philosophy, and has published many research papers in academic journals. Her latest book is: *Saṁnyāsin in the Hindu Tradition: Changing Perspectives* (2011). Professor Rukmani is a member on the advisory committee, *Oxford Journal of Hindu Studies*; and is a member in the consultative Committee, International Association for Sanskrit Studies. [*address:* Prof. T.S. Rukmani, 2 Earls Holme, KEMPSTON, mk42 8pG (UK), *e-mail:* <rukmani@alcor.concordia.ca>].

Vasundhara Filliozat, Daughter of Pandit Chennabasavappa Kavali, born in Haveri, Karnataka, south India, brought up in an environment soaked in Sanskrit and Kannada culture, is a historian of art and an epigraphist. She works alternatively in India to explore the archaeological and literary past of her country and in France to encourage knowledge and appreciation of the Indian civilization, still insufficiently known in the West. Her works on Hampi-Vijayanagara have been acknowledged in 2003, when she was honoured with the Award of the Government of Karnataka. She has been elected President of the 22nd Congress of the Karnataka History Academy. She has published about twenty books and numerous articles in Kannada, English and French. [*address*: Prof. Vasundhara Filliozat 13, rue Rambuteau, 75004 PARIS (France), *e-mail*: <filliozat@dataone.in>; <filliozat@noos.fr>].

Victoria Lysenko (D.Litt.), is the Head of Department of Oriental Philosophies, Institute of Philosophy, Russian Academy of Sciences and Professor at the Russian State University for Humanities (Moscow). Her researches focus on the history of Indian philosophy, and comparative philosophy. She translated from Sanskrit into Russian a number of philosophical texts, especially of the Vaiśeṣika and Buddhist schools. Recent books in English include *Classical Indian Philosophy Reinterpreted* (2007) and in Russian, *Immediate and Mediated Perception: Controversy Between Buddhist and Brahmanic Philosophers* (2011). Professor Lysenko has published about 200 papers in Russian, English and French on a wide range of themes including a body composition in Āyurveda and the philosophical schools of Vaiśeṣika and Sāṁkhya; Aristotle's Mean and the Buddha's Middle Path; Knowledge and faith in Early Buddhism; The mind-body problem in Early Buddhism; Śaṅkara's criticism of the Vaiśeṣika; Word and Being in the Teaching of Bhartṛhari on Action; Orientalism and the problem of the alien, etc. [*address*: Avtozavodskaya Street, 6, Ap. 183, 115280 - MOSCOW (Russia), *e-mail*: <vglyssenko@yandex.ru>].